West Virginia and Maryland

1 Harpers Ferry p. 28
2 Weverton Cliffs p. 34
3 White Rocks and Lambs Knoll p. 38
4 Washington Monument p. 43
5 Annapolis Rock p. 48
6 High Rock p. 53

Pennsylvania

7 Chimney Rocks p. 60
8 Hosack Run p. 65
9 Toms Run and Sunset Rocks p. 71
10 Pole Steeple p. 78
11 Center Point Knob p. 83
12 PA 850 to Tuscarora Trail p. 88
13 Cove Mountain South p. 93
14 Cove Mountain North p. 98
15 Clarks Ferry via Susquehanna Trail p. 104
16 Clarks Ferry and Peters Mountain p. 109
17 Table Rock p. 115
18 PA 325 to PA 443 p. 121
19 Cold Spring and Rausch Gap p. 128
20 Yellow Springs from PA 443 p. 133
21 Round Head and Shikellamy Overlook p. 140
22 Pulpit Rock and the Pinnacle p. 145
23 PA 309 to Bear Rocks p. 152
24 Mount Minsi p. 158

New Jersey

25 Sunfish Pond p. 166
26 Culvers Fire Tower Overlook p. 171
27 Lake Rutherford p. 176
28 New Jersey High Point p. 181
29 Wallkill River National Wildlife Refuge: Liberty Loop Trail p. 186
30 Pochuck Boardwalk p. 191
31 Wawayanda Mountain p. 196

New York

32 Eastern Pinnacles and Cat Rocks p. 204
33 Mombasha High Point p. 209
34 Island Pond and Fingerboard Mountain p. 214
35 Silver Mine Lake p. 220
36 West Mountain Loop p. 226
37 Bear Mountain Loop p. 231
38 Bear Mountain Zoo and Bridge p. 237
39 Anthonys Nose p. 242
40 Canopus Hill p. 247
41 Shenandoah Mountain p. 252
42 Nuclear Lake p. 257
43 Great Swamp and Dover Oak p. 262

BEST HIKES OF THE
APPALACHIAN
TRAIL

Mid-Atlantic

West Virginia · Maryland · Pennsylvania · New Jersey · New York

MATT WILLEN

MENASHA RIDGE PRESS
Your Guide to the Outdoors Since 1982

APPALACHIAN TRAIL
CONSERVANCY®

Best Hikes of the Appalachian Trail: Mid-Atlantic

Copyright © 2017 by Matt Willen
Copublished by Menasha Ridge Press and Appalachian Trail Conservancy
Distributed by Publishers Group West
Printed in the United States of America
First edition, first printing

Cover design by Scott McGrew
Text design by Annie Long
Cartography and elevation profiles by Scott McGrew
Cover and interior photographs by Matt Willen unless otherwise noted
Cover photos, clockwise from top: Cove Mountain South (see page 93), Bear
Mountain Loop (see page 231), Harpers Ferry (see page 28), and Mombasha High
Point (see page 209)
Frontispiece: The edge of Annapolis Rock with Greenbrier State Park in the
background (See Hike 5, page 48.)

Cataloging-in-Publication Data is on file with the Library of Congress.

MENASHA RIDGE PRESS
An imprint of AdventureKEEN
2204 First Ave. S., Suite 102
Birmingham, AL 35233

APPALACHIAN TRAIL CONSERVANCY
799 Washington St.
Harpers Ferry, WV 25425
appalachiantrail.org

Visit menasharidge.com for a complete listing of our books and for ordering
information. Contact us at our website, at facebook.com/menasharidge, or at twitter
.com/menasharidge with questions or comments. To find out more about who we are
and what we're doing, visit blog.menasharidge.com.

DISCLAIMER

This book is meant only as a guide to select routes along the Appalachian Trail.
This book does not guarantee hiker safety in any way—you hike at your own risk.
Neither Menasha Ridge Press nor Matt Willen is liable for property loss or damage,
personal injury, or death that result in any way from accessing or hiking the trails
described in the following pages. Please be especially cautious when walking in
potentially hazardous terrains with, for example, steep inclines or drop-offs. Do not
attempt to explore terrain that may be beyond your abilities. Please read carefully the
introduction to this book as well as further safety information from other sources.
Familiarize yourself with current weather reports and maps of the area you plan
to visit (in addition to the maps provided in this guidebook). Be cognizant of park
regulations and always follow them. Do not take chances.

Contents

OVERVIEW MAP   inside front cover

OVERVIEW MAP KEY   i

DEDICATION   vii

ACKNOWLEDGMENTS   viii

PREFACE   ix

HIKING RECOMMENDATIONS   xi

INTRODUCTION   1

West Virginia and Maryland   26

1 Harpers Ferry 28
2 Weverton Cliffs 34
3 White Rocks and Lambs Knoll 38
4 Washington Monument 43
5 Annapolis Rock 48
6 High Rock 53

Pennsylvania   58

7 Chimney Rocks 60
8 Hosack Run 65
9 Toms Run and Sunset Rocks 71
10 Pole Steeple 78
11 Center Point Knob 83
12 PA 850 to Tuscarora Trail 88
13 Cove Mountain South 93
14 Cove Mountain North 98
15 Clarks Ferry via Susquehanna Trail 104
16 Clarks Ferry and Peters Mountain 109
17 Table Rock 115
18 PA 325 to PA 443 121
19 Cold Spring and Rausch Gap 128
20 Yellow Springs from PA 443 133
21 Round Head and Shikellamy Overlook 140
22 Pulpit Rock and the Pinnacle 145
23 PA 309 to Bear Rocks 152
24 Mount Minsi 158

New Jersey 164

25 Sunfish Pond 166

26 Culvers Fire Tower Overlook 171

27 Lake Rutherford 176

28 New Jersey High Point 181

29 Wallkill River National Wildlife Refuge:
    Liberty Loop Trail 186

30 Pochuck Boardwalk 191

31 Wawayanda Mountain 196

New York 202

32 Eastern Pinnacles and Cat Rocks 204

33 Mombasha High Point 209

34 Island Pond and Fingerboard Mountain 214

35 Silver Mine Lake 220

36 West Mountain Loop 226

37 Bear Mountain Loop 231

38 Bear Mountain Zoo and Bridge 237

39 Anthonys Nose 242

40 Canopus Hill 247

41 Shenandoah Mountain 252

42 Nuclear Lake 257

43 Great Swamp and Dover Oak 262

APPENDIX A: Contact Information 269

APPENDIX B: Hiking Clubs and Organizations 271

APPENDIX C: Appalachian Trail Communities 272

INDEX. 273

ABOUT THE AUTHOR 281

ABOUT THE APPALACHIAN TRAIL CONSERVANCY 282

MAP LEGEND . . . . inside back cover

Dedication

This book is dedicated with much love and gratitude to my sons, Jackson and Ian, for helping me find The Way.

Acknowledgments

I AM INDEBTED TO MANY PEOPLE for their assistance in completing this project. I want to thank my good friend Jackson Galloway for his company and amusing commentary on many of the hikes in New York. The folks at the Appalachian Trail Conservancy and at the state parks and state forests that I visited provided me with much information that proved essential to what I have learned about the Appalachian Trail and the public lands that it passes through. I spoke with scores of thru- and day hikers along the trail, whom I probed with many questions and from whom I gained tons of information about where to go and what to avoid; thank you all.

I drew extensively on *Underfoot: A Geologic Guide to the Appalachian Trail* by V. Collins Chew (Appalachian Trail Conservancy, 2010) to help me understand the geology of the trail. I am very grateful for the availability of that resource.

Over the past year, I have worked with a bunch of great people at Menasha Ridge Press, and without their effort and dedication neither this book nor the others I have done would have been possible. They are Molly Merkle, Tim Jackson, Ritchey Halphen, Scott McGrew, Tanya Sylvan, Amber Kaye Henderson, and a host of others who have helped in large and small ways. Thank you very much.

Preface

SINCE MOVING TO CENTRAL PENNSYLVANIA IN 2001, I've done a lot of hiking along the Appalachian Trail corridor, and I have given loads of presentations on hiking at state parks, at public libraries, and to hiking clubs. Throughout this experience, I've encountered so many people who have expressed interest in the Appalachian Trail (A.T.). There are those who say, "I'd love to hike the whole trail someday." More often, though, I meet people who either don't have the desire to do the whole thing or just don't have the time to do so. Yet the A.T. holds an allure for them and for many others; it has a legendary status in American trail lore. Many people want to get some idea of what this whole Appalachian Trail thing is all about, and to get some sense of how it reflects our national heritage. This book is intended to help readers find out.

While the A.T. provides people with an opportunity to get outdoors and enjoy nature, perhaps the aspect of hiking the trail that stands out most to me is the experience of community associated with hiking it. Indeed, on some sections of trail that are easily accessible to metropolitan areas, you'll be walking among a steady stream of people, especially on weekends and holidays. Surprisingly, though, these are the sections where I intermingled least with people—most are traveling with friends and family with whom they interact. When I think of the sense of community that comes with hiking the trail, I think of those long stretches of trail where I would come across another lone hiker. Invariably, we'd stop, share stories, a snack or a cup of tea, smiles, and goodwill. One day while hiking up Wawayanda Mountain in New Jersey, I was feeling worn out from hiking every day and sleeping in my car at night. And then I met the nicest woman on the trail, who was running up and down the mountain. We stopped to talk for a few minutes. She told me that she came out almost every day for the past year. "I can do it

SOME TINY FALL WILDFLOWERS ALONG THE APPALACHIAN TRAIL NEAR PA 850
(See Hike 12, page 88.)

in half the time that it took me a year ago," she said excitedly. And she made sure that I knew where to go to get the view: "You don't want to go all the way to the top, now. There's a trail that leads out to the left. But you look like you know what you're doing." Then she set off for the parking lot. I felt so good after that few minutes of conversation that I started up with new lift in my stride. That kind of experience happens a lot on the trail. And it is the kind of experience that makes you feel that, even in your own solitude, you're participating in something bigger than yourself, and that, like you, there are others who go to the woods in search of things that other settings don't provide.

—*Matt Willen*

Hiking Recommendations

Best Hikes for Birding and Wildlife

20 Yellow Springs from PA 443 (p. 133)
29 Wallkill River National Wildlife Refuge:
    Liberty Loop Trail (p. 186)
30 Pochuck Boardwalk (p. 191)
38 Bear Mountain Zoo and Bridge (p. 237)
43 Great Swamp and Dover Oak (p. 262)

Best Hikes for Distinctive Natural Scenery

 9 Toms Run and Sunset Rocks (p. 71)
29 Wallkill River National Wildlife Refuge:
    Liberty Loop Trail (p. 186)
34 Island Pond and Fingerboard Mountain (p. 214)
42 Nuclear Lake (p. 257)
43 Great Swamp and Dover Oak (p. 262)

Best Hikes for Geological Formations

 2 Weverton Cliffs (p. 34)
 5 Annapolis Rock (p. 48)
10 Pole Steeple (p. 78)
22 Pulpit Rock and the Pinnacle (p. 145)
23 PA 309 to Bear Rocks (p. 152)
25 Sunfish Pond (p. 166)
32 Eastern Pinnacles and Cat Rocks (p. 204)
37 Bear Mountain Loop (p. 231)

Best Hikes for History

 1 Harpers Ferry (p. 28)
 4 Washington Monument (p. 43)
11 Center Point Knob (p. 83)
20 Yellow Springs from PA 443 (p. 133)
37 Bear Mountain Loop (p. 231)
40 Canopus Hill (p. 247)

Best Hikes for Kids

3   White Rocks and Lambs Knoll (p. 38)

10   Pole Steeple (p. 78)

11   Center Point Knob (p. 83)

17   Table Rock (p. 115)

30   Pochuck Boardwalk (p. 191)

38   Bear Mountain Zoo and Bridge (p. 237)

Best Hikes for Lakes, Streams, and Waterfalls

1   Harpers Ferry (p. 28)

19   Cold Spring and Rausch Gap (p. 128)

25   Sunfish Pond (p. 166)

27   Lake Rutherford (p. 176)

29   Wallkill River National Wildlife Refuge:
Liberty Loop Trail (p. 186)

33   Mombasha High Point (p. 209)

35   Silver Mine Lake (p. 220)

Best Hikes for Solitude

8   Hosack Run (p. 65)

14   Cove Mountain North (p. 98)

18   PA 325 to PA 443 (p. 121)

23   PA 309 to Bear Rocks (p. 152)

41   Shenandoah Mountain (p. 252)

Best Hikes for Views

6   High Rock (p. 53)

22   Pulpit Rock and the Pinnacle (p. 145)

24   Mount Minsi (p. 158)

26   Culvers Fire Tower Overlook (p. 171)

28   New Jersey High Point (p. 181)

31   Wawayanda Mountain (p. 196)

36   West Mountain Loop (p. 226)

39   Anthonys Nose (p. 242)

Introduction

About This Book

Best Hikes of the Appalachian Trail: Mid-Atlantic details 43 excellent day hikes along the approximately 440 miles of the Appalachian Trail (A.T.) that extend from the officially designated Appalachian Trail Community of Harpers Ferry, West Virginia; through Maryland, Pennsylvania, and New Jersey; to the New York and Connecticut state line. Making use of the many side trails that intersect with the A.T. corridor, the author and Menasha Ridge Press have worked in concert with the Appalachian Trail Conservancy to share some of the trail's extensive natural beauty and historical interest. The hikes presented in this book thus aim to provide readers with a diverse array of hiking experiences.

The section of the Appalachian Trail covered in this book passes through several distinct physiographic regions defined by geological characteristics common to each. The southernmost section of the trail covered here passes through the Blue Ridge Physiographic Province, which stretches from northern Georgia to south-central Pennsylvania east of the Great Appalachian Valley (or simply the Great Valley), a series of lowlands that extends from Alabama to Quebec. The geology of the trail in the Blue Ridge is underlain predominantly by Cambrian-era quartzite formed about 570 million years ago. Aside from a short stretch along the Potomac River outside of Harpers Ferry, West Virginia, the trail in this region generally follows the south-to-north-trending ridges of South Mountain, which rise to 1,000–2,000 feet in elevation. The first 11 hikes in this book are located along this approximately 100-mile-long stretch of trail between Harpers Ferry, West Virginia, and Boiling Springs, Pennsylvania, at the northern terminus of the Blue Ridge Physiographic Province. In addition to lovely wooded natural terrain, these first 11 hikes pass by areas rich in historic interest.

Harpers Ferry is notable for its role in the abolitionist movement, and Crampton's Gap in Maryland is the site of a memorial dedicated to war correspondents and is under National Park Service management. In southern Pennsylvania, the hikes take you by the sites of several iron furnaces. The hiking along South Mountain in the Blue Ridge Physiographic Province is quite pleasant, with mostly gently rolling terrain on a trail surface that is easy on the feet.

From Center Point Knob (hike 11), the original midpoint of the trail, the Appalachian Trail descends into the Cumberland Valley (a section of the Great Valley in Pennsylvania) at Boiling Springs, Pennsylvania, home of the Mid-Atlantic Regional Office of the Appalachian Trail Conservancy. The 17 miles of trail that pass through the Cumberland Valley—from Center Point Knob in the south to the junction of the A.T., Tuscarora Trail, and Darlington Trail on Blue Mountain in the north—is heavily populated and crossed by several major roads. I haven't included any hikes within this section.

North of the Cumberland Valley, the trail enters the Ridge and Valley Physiographic Province. Consisting of long, parallel ridges formed by broken folds of hard, erosion-resistant sandstone and quartzite, this physiographic province extends north from Alabama, makes a northeastern-trending arc through Pennsylvania, and comes to its northern terminus in southeastern New York. The A.T. enters this province at Blue Mountain, northwest of the Cumberland Valley in Pennsylvania, and follows it 203 miles east across the Susquehanna River and through the Delaware Water Gap to the New Jersey High Point. This section of trail has something of a notorious reputation for rough and rocky hiking: "the place where boots go to die," some have said. The reputation is somewhat well deserved. For most of the stretch, the trail sticks to the long ridges of Blue, Sharp, and Kittatinny Mountains, descending only to pass through wind or water gaps. The ridge walking is largely on level—though often rocky—ground, and the ascents and descents to them are typically steep and rugged, though not especially long. Though some of the roughest hiking on the mid-Atlantic A.T. can be found here, there are

HIKERS HAVE CREATED SOME UNUSUAL CAIRNS ALONG THE BANK OF SUNFISH POND. *(See Hike 25, page 166.)*

sections of pleasant hiking that lead to secluded and wild terrain and pass by old mining towns and historical resorts. Seventeen hikes in this book are located in this region.

The final 15 hikes in this book are located along the 100-plus miles of trail that stretch from the New Jersey High Point to the Connecticut state line. North of New Jersey High Point, the trail leaves Kittatinny Mountain and descends east into the Great Valley, where it passes through wetlands and low hills before ascending again into the Hudson Highlands. Through the Highlands, the trail passes among some of the oldest rocks on its length, coarse Precambrian gneiss dating back to an ancient mountain-building period more than 1 billion years ago. The terrain here is more varied, with flatland and rolling hills, than the extensive ridge walking characteristic to much of the mid-Atlantic region. These last hikes take you through the beautiful Wallkill River National Wildlife Refuge and the rolling terrain of New York's Bear Mountain and Harriman State Parks. East of Bear Mountain, the trail reaches its lowest point of elevation at the Hudson River crossing, passes what is reportedly the oldest tree along its 2,100-plus miles, and traverses a stunning mile-long boardwalk.

In choosing the hikes included in this book, I drew first on my knowledge from hiking the A.T. in the mid-Atlantic. To find out about the few places with which I was unfamiliar, I talked to people on the trail, asked loads of questions, and studied lots of maps. I have made use of the abundance of side and secondary trails that intersect the A.T. to create a variety of hikes that provides readers with a real sense of what the region has to offer and that provides some variation in the nature of the hikes other than out-and-back on the trail. I have also tried to accommodate differing tastes, interests, skill levels, and experience. So here you will find out-and-back hikes, loop hikes, long hikes, short hikes, easy and difficult hikes, hikes that are good for kids, and so forth. Indeed, the A.T. is a hiking trail, but it offers so much more than simply a walk in the woods. It is history and towns, crowds and solitude, dense forest and expansive views, rocks and dirt and pavement, birds and deer and salamanders, ponds and creeks and waterfalls and rivers, and more. There is even a trailside zoo! This book will help you to get a sense of the incredible diversity it has to offer.

I've provided ratings for several criteria to help give readers a sense of what to expect when planning their trip. Please see the information on "Star Ratings" on page 7. Readers will notice that none of the hikes receive 5 stars in each category. That is the nature of providing for variety. A hike such as the Bear Mountain Zoo and Bridge, which I included because you can't get a better hike for kids of all ages, is not going to merit 5 stars in either the difficulty or the solitude category. Nor should it. Readers might do better to consider the star ratings less a method of classifying quality than a method of providing a sense of character.

How to Use This Guidebook

The following sections will walk you through each of the organizational elements of the profiles as they're presented in this book. The goal is to make it as easy as possible for you to plan a hike you'll enjoy, a hike you'll remember, and a hike that matches whatever you're looking for on any given day.

Overview Map & Map Key

The overview map on the inside front cover shows the general location of each hike's primary trailhead. Each hike's number appears on the overview map, on the map key facing the overview map, and in the table of contents. Thus, if you know you will be traveling to a particular area, you can check that area on the overview map, find the appropriate hike numbers, and then flip through the book and easily find those hikes by looking up the hike numbers at the top of each profile page. Or if you find a specific hike on the overview map, you can locate the profile by following the number.

Trail Maps & Map Legend

In addition to the overview map, a detailed map of each hike's route appears with its profile. On each of these maps, symbols indicate the trailhead, the complete route, and topographic landmarks, such as creeks, overlooks, and peaks. A legend identifying the map symbols used throughout the book appears on the inside back cover.

To produce the highly accurate maps in this book, the author used a handheld GPS unit to gather data while hiking each route, and then sent that data to the publisher's expert cartographers. However, your GPS is never a substitute for sound, sensible navigation that takes into account the conditions that you observe while hiking. The GPS is a remarkable tool, but it can't replace knowing how to use a map and compass. If you're interested in learning more about using a GPS for navigation, check out *Outdoor Navigation with GPS*, third edition, by Stephen W. Hinch. Be sure to check out books and articles, or even take a class at your local outdoor store, on using a map and compass as well.

Further, despite the high quality of the maps in this guidebook, the publisher and author strongly recommend that every time you venture out into the woods, you always carry an additional, accurate, up-to-date map of the area in which you're hiking, such as the ones noted in each entry opener's listing for "Maps."

Elevation Profile (Diagram)

This diagram represents the rises and falls of the trail as viewed from the side over the complete distance (expressed in miles) for that trail. From this, you should be able to judge where the steep sections will come during the hike. Don't underestimate the intensity of a hike that may be associated with these diagrams.

On the diagram's vertical axis, or height scale, the number of feet indicated between each tick mark lets you visualize the climb. Use these side-view profiles, along with contour markings on the additional maps you will carry, to determine the relative intensity of the hike. To avoid making flat hikes look steep and steep hikes appear flat, varying height scales provide an accurate image of each hike's climbing challenge. For example, one hike's scale might rise to 3,000 feet, while others may reach only 600 feet.

The Hike Profile

Each hike profile opens with an information box that encapsulates all the details you'll need to know for that particular hike. The at-a-glance information includes the hike's star ratings (for scenery, trail condition, how appropriate the hike is for kids, hike difficulty, and solitude), GPS trailhead coordinates, the overall distance of the hike, trail configuration (out-and-back or loop), facilities, and contacts for local information. Each profile also includes a listing of the appropriate maps to have on hand for the hike (see "Trail Maps," page 5).

The text for each profile includes four sections: Overview, Route Details, Nearby Attractions, and Directions (for driving to the trailhead area). Here is an explanation of each of these elements.

★ **Overview** gives you a quick summary of what to expect on the trail.

★ **Route Details** takes you on a guided hike from start to finish, including landmarks, side trips, and possible alternate routes along the way.

★ **Nearby Attractions** mentions the nearest towns, as well as other trails or parks close by.

★ **Directions** will get you to the trailhead from a well-known road or highway.

Star Ratings

Here's a guide to interpreting the rating system of one to five stars in each of the five categories for each hike—scenery, trail condition, children, difficulty, and solitude.

SCENERY:

★★★★★	Unique, picturesque panoramas
★★★★	Diverse vistas
★★★	Pleasant views
★★	Unchanging landscape
★	Not selected for scenery

TRAIL CONDITION:

★★★★★	Consistently well maintained
★★★★	Stable, with no surprises
★★★	Average terrain to negotiate
★★	Inconsistent, with good and poor areas
★	Rocky, overgrown, or often muddy

CHILDREN:

★★★★★	Babes in strollers are welcome
★★★★	Fun for anyone past the toddler stage
★★★	Good for young hikers with proven stamina
★★	Not enjoyable for children
★	Not advisable for children

DIFFICULTY:

★★★★★	Grueling
★★★★	Strenuous
★★★	Moderate (won't beat you up—but you'll know you've been hiking
★★	Easy, with patches of moderate
★	Good for a relaxing stroll

SOLITUDE:

★ ★ ★ ★ ★   Positively tranquil

★ ★ ★ ★   Spurts of isolation

★ ★ ★   Moderately secluded

★ ★   Could be crowded on weekends and holidays

★   Steady stream of individuals/groups

GPS TRAILHEAD COORDINATES

As noted in the "Trail Maps" section on page 5, the author used a handheld GPS unit to obtain geographic data. In the opener for each hike profile, the coordinates—the intersection of the latitude (north) and longitude (west)—will orient you from the trailhead. Plug these into your own handheld GPS unit or your phone if you prefer to use that. And remember, a handheld GPS unit or GPS app in your phone does not replace having a map and compass and the knowledge to use them properly.

In some cases, you can park right at the trailhead. Other hiking routes require a short walk to the trailhead from a parking area.

You will also note that this guidebook uses the degree-decimal minute format for presenting the latitude and longitude GPS coordinates. The latitude and longitude grid system is likely quite familiar to you, but here is a refresher, pertinent to visualizing the GPS coordinates:

Imaginary lines of latitude—called parallels and approximately 69 miles apart from each other—run horizontally around the globe. The equator is established to be 0°, and each parallel is indicated by degrees from the equator: up to 90°N at the North Pole, and down to 90°S at the South Pole.

Imaginary lines of longitude—called meridians—run perpendicular to latitude lines. Longitude lines are likewise indicated by degrees. Starting from 0° at the Prime Meridian in Greenwich, England, they continue to the east and west until they meet 180° later at the International Date Line in the Pacific Ocean. At the equator, longitude lines also are approximately 69 miles apart, but that distance narrows as the meridians converge toward the North and South Poles.

The GPS coordinates map to latitude and longitude and are generated by a network of 24 geosynchronous satellites positioned such that they cover Earth's entire surface. A GPS unit locks onto at least three or four of those satellites to triangulate position. The system works well, but reception can be stymied by weather, dense forests, or deep canyons. To convert GPS coordinates given in degrees, minutes, and seconds to the format shown above in degrees–decimal minutes, the seconds are divided by 60. For more on GPS technology, visit usgs.gov.

DISTANCE & CONFIGURATION

The distance is the full, round-trip length of the hike from start to finish. If the hike description includes options for a shorter or longer hike, those round-trip distances will also be described here.

The configuration defines the trail as an out-and-back (taking you in and out via the same route, such as hiking to the summit of a mountain and then down the same way), loop, or some other configuration.

HIKING TIME

Hiking time varies in accordance with many different factors that include character of the trail surface, steepness of the trail, length of the hike, length of one's legs, one's mood and inclination for the day, how often one stops and for how long, how fast one likes to hike, and so forth. While I used my GPS unit to keep track of the length of time that I spent doing a particular route, I used 2 miles per hour as a general rule of thumb for the hiking times noted in this guidebook. For some hikes, that is pretty consistent with my pace, for others it is slower, and for others even a little faster. (I can dawdle with the best of them!) That pace typically allows time for taking photos, for admiring views, and for alternating stretches of hills and descents. When you're deciding whether or not to follow a particular trail described in this guidebook, be flexible. Consider your own pace, the weather, your general physical condition, and your energy level on that day.

HIGHLIGHTS

Many of these hikes take you past spectacular highlights, which will be noted here. These may include waterfalls, historic sites, or other features that draw hikers to this trail.

ELEVATION

In each hike's key information, you will see the elevation at the trailhead and another figure for the peak height on that route. The full hike profile also includes a complete elevation profile (see "Elevation Profile" on page 6).

ACCESS

No fees are required for any of these hikes. However, trailhead parking fees will sometimes be noted here. If there are any restrictions on hours to access the trail (such as sunrise–sunset), that will also be mentioned here.

MAPS

Maps of your hiking route and the surrounding area are essential. Resources for maps, in addition to those in this guidebook, are listed here. (As previously noted, the publisher and the author recommend that you carry more than one map—and that you consult those maps before heading out on the trail to resolve any confusion or discrepancy.) I typically relied on the official trail maps published by the Appalachian Trail Conservancy in concert with the regional trail associations: the Potomac Appalachian Trail Club in West Virginia and Maryland, the Keystone Trails Association in Pennsylvania, and the New York–New Jersey Trail Conference. Maps can be purchased from the Appalachian Trail Conservancy at atctrailstore.org.

I am a big fan of U.S. Geological Survey topo maps for helping me to identify features on the landscape and have provided the name of the 7.5-minute quadrant(s) relevant for each hike. Many state parks through which the trail passes provide excellent maps that detail side trails that aren't on other maps. Many of those maps are available on the PDF Maps app that can be loaded onto an iPad or a smartphone. It is available from Avenza Systems Inc. (avenza.com).

FACILITIES

This information includes restrooms, water, picnic areas, campgrounds, and other basics at or near the trailhead.

CONTACT

Listed here are phone numbers and websites for checking trail conditions and gleaning other day-to-day information.

COMMENTS

In the Comments section of each chapter, I have included information that seemed to me important to point out ahead of time about the individual hike. In some cases, for example, the comments address the availability of local attractions or amenities; in other cases they address matters of convenience pertaining to parking or fees; and sometimes they will let you know if a hike strikes me as especially good for the family, offers something really interesting, or just really impressed me.

Weather

With some exception, the Appalachian Trail in the mid-Atlantic region is a four-season trail, and each season offers a different kind of experience for hikers. The summer months provide the benefits of warm days and long nights. While hiking during any of the summer months can be excellent for allowing you to knock about in shorts and a T-shirt with a light pack, as the summer progresses into July, August, and September, the days can become quite warm and humid. Temperatures in the 80s and even 90s are not uncommon. You would do well in these months to do your hiking early in the morning while the air is still cool from the evening before. By late September, cooler temperatures and drier air make for days as crisp as the changing leaves, which can be spectacular throughout the entire region. The days are shorter, the bugs are gone, and the nights and mornings have a little bit of a chill to them. But you do want to be prepared for cold wind and rain, which are not uncommon.

In recent years, I have discovered that winter can be a great time to be out on the trails. The days are indeed short; the paths can get very icy, treacherously so, in places; and foul weather can turn dangerous quickly. You need to consider all of these when planning your hike. Do shorter hikes. Carry appropriate clothes, food, and extra gear—an extra pair of thermal pants and top, a thermos of hot tea, and cleats for my boots are among the additions to my winter day pack. But during the winter, you encounter fewer people and no bugs, the views are more abundant on account of the absence of leaves, and the stark winter light increases the sense of solitude and seclusion. Sections of the trail are even suitable for snowshoeing (I highly recommend Clarence Fahnestock Memorial State Park in New York for this activity) when conditions allow. Though cold, if you are prepared, winter hiking offers a vision of the forest that is truly distinctive.

Come March and April, the A.T. begins to see a lot more activity. Thru- and section hikers start out on their long trips. Day hikers are more abundant. Flowers bloom, then the trees, and suddenly it seems like every cave and crack and crevice has some critter or another ducking in and out of it. If you want to see wildlife, spring is the time to do it. This can be a great season for hiking, with daytime temperatures reaching into the 50s and 60s. March and April can be damp, though, with regular rain and cool days. Hypothermia is a real risk—be prepared! During the spring, the trail and forest floor can also get quite muddy. Grease up those boots, wear your gaiters, and use extra caution on wet, rocky overlooks.

The following table lists average temperatures and precipitation by month for the mid-Atlantic region. For each month, "Hi Temp" is the average daytime high, "Lo Temp" is the average nighttime low, and "Rain or Snow" is the average precipitation.

MONTH	HI TEMP	LO TEMP	RAIN OR SNOW
January	38° F	23° F	3.19"
February	41° F	25° F	2.87"
March	51° F	33° F	3.58"

MONTH	HI TEMP	LO TEMP	RAIN OR SNOW
April	63° F	42° F	3.31"
May	73° F	51° F	4.61"
June	81° F	61° F	3.98"
July	86° F	66° F	3.23"
August	84° F	64° F	3.23"
September	76° F	57° F	3.66"
October	64° F	45° F	3.07"
November	53° F	36° F	3.54"
December	42° F	28° F	3.23"

For the best weather prediction for your chosen Appalachian Trail hike, visit weather.gov, the National Weather Service website. Enter the nearest town to your hike. Note that the temperatures given here are from stations in cities and towns; for higher elevations, subtract 3.5°F per 1,000 feet of elevation from the nearest recording station to get a better idea of the temperature.

In addition to predictions for that town, you will see a scrollable map. Scroll the map for your exact trailhead position, and then click on the trailhead position for a pinpoint forecast. Then you will be prepared for the ensuing weather on your Appalachian Trail hike. For more detailed weather forecasting and historical data, check out the following sites:

★ noaa.gov   ★ usclimatedata.com   ★ weatherbase.com

Water

How much is enough? Well, one simple physiological fact should convince you to err on the side of excess when deciding how much water to pack: a hiker walking steadily in 90°F heat needs approximately 10 quarts of fluid per day. That's 2.5 gallons. A good rule of thumb is to hydrate prior to your hike, carry (and drink) 6 ounces of water for every mile you plan to hike, and hydrate again after the hike. For most people, the pleasures of hiking make carrying water a relatively minor price to pay to remain safe and healthy. So pack more water than you anticipate needing even for short hikes.

If you are tempted to drink "found" water, do so with extreme caution. Many ponds and lakes encountered by hikers are fairly stagnant and the water tastes terrible. Drinking such water presents inherent risks for thirsty trekkers. Giardia parasites contaminate many water sources and cause the dreaded intestinal giardiasis that can last for weeks after ingestion. For information, visit the Centers for Disease Control and Prevention website at cdc.gov/parasites/giardia.

In any case, effective treatment is essential before using any water source found along the trail. Boiling water for 2–3 minutes is always a safe measure for camping, but day hikers can consider iodine tablets, approved chemical mixes, filtration units rated for giardia, and UV filtration. Some of these methods (for example, filtration with an added carbon filter) remove bad tastes typical in stagnant water, while others add their own taste. As a precaution, carry a means of water purification to help in a pinch and if you realize you have underestimated your consumption needs.

Clothing

Weather, unexpected trail conditions, fatigue, extended hiking duration, and wrong turns can individually or collectively turn a great outing into a very uncomfortable one at best—and a life-threatening one at worst. Thus, proper attire plays a key role in staying comfortable and, sometimes, in staying alive. Here are some helpful guidelines:

★ *Choose silk, wool, or synthetics for maximum comfort* in all of your hiking attire—from hats to socks and in between. Cotton is fine if the weather remains dry and stable, but you won't be happy if that material gets wet.

★ *Always wear a hat, or at least tuck one into your day pack* or hitch it to your belt. Hats offer all-weather sun and wind protection as well as warmth if it turns cold.

★ *Be ready to layer up or down* as the day progresses and the mercury rises or falls. Today's outdoor wear makes layering easy, with such designs as jackets that convert to vests and zip-off or button-up legs.

★ *Wear hiking boots or sturdy hiking sandals with toe protection.* Flip-flopping along a paved urban greenway is one thing, but never hike a trail in open sandals or casual sneakers. Your bones and arches need support, and your skin needs protection.

★ *Pair that footwear with good socks!* If you prefer not to sheathe your feet when wearing hiking sandals, tuck the socks into your day pack; you may need them if the weather plummets or if you hit rocky turf and pebbles begin to irritate your feet. And, in an emergency, if you have lost your gloves, you can use the socks as mittens.

★ *Don't leave rainwear behind,* even if the day dawns clear and sunny. Tuck into your day pack, or tie around your waist, a jacket that is breathable and either water-resistant or waterproof. Investigate different choices at your local outdoors retailer. If you are a frequent hiker, ideally you'll have more than one rainwear weight, material, and style in your closet to protect you in all seasons in your regional climate and hiking microclimates.

Essential Gear

Today you can buy outdoor vests that have up to 20 pockets shaped and sized to carry everything from toothpicks to binoculars. Or, if you don't aspire to feel like a burro, you can neatly stow all of these items in your day pack or backpack. The following list showcases never-hike-without-them items, in alphabetical order, as all are important:

★ *Extra clothes* (raingear, warm hat, gloves, and change of socks and shirt)

★ *Extra food* (trail mix, granola bars, or other high-energy foods)

★ *Flashlight or headlamp* with extra bulb and batteries

★ *Insect repellent* (For some areas and seasons, this is extremely vital.)

★ *Maps and a high-quality compass* (Even if you know the terrain from previous hikes, don't leave home without these tools. And, as previously noted, bring maps in addition to those in this guidebook, and consult your maps prior to the hike. If you are versed in GPS usage, bring that device, too; but don't rely on it as your sole navigational tool, as battery life can dwindle or die, and be sure to compare its guidance with that of your maps.)

★ *Pocketknife* and/or multitool

★ *Sun protection,* including sunglasses, lip balm, and sunscreen (Note the expiration date on the tube or bottle.)

★ *Water* (Bring more than you think you will drink. Depending on your destination, you may want to bring a container and iodine or a filter for purifying water in case you run out.)

★ *Whistle* (This little gadget will be your best friend in an emergency.)

★ *Windproof matches and/or a lighter,* as well as a fire starter

First Aid Kit

In addition to the items above, those below may appear overwhelming for a day hike. But any paramedic will tell you that the products listed here, in alphabetical order, are just the basics. The reality of hiking is that you can be out for a week of backpacking and acquire only a mosquito bite. Or you can hike for an hour, slip, and suffer a bleeding abrasion or broken bone. Fortunately, these listed items will collapse into a very small space. You also can purchase convenient, prepackaged kits at your pharmacy or online.

★ Adhesive bandages

★ Antibiotic ointment (Neosporin or the generic equivalent)

★ Athletic tape

★ Benadryl or the generic equivalent, diphenhydramine (in case of allergic reactions)

★ Blister kit (such as moleskin/Spenco 2nd Skin)

★ Butterfly-closure bandages

★ Elastic bandages or joint wraps

★ Epinephrine in a prefilled syringe (typically by prescription only, and for people known to have severe allergic reactions to hiking occurrences such as bee stings)

★ Gauze (one roll and a half dozen 4-by-4-inch pads)

★ Hydrogen peroxide or iodine

★ Ibuprofen or acetaminophen

Pack the items in a waterproof bag, such as a zip-top bag. Note: Consider your intended terrain and the number of hikers in your party before you exclude any article cited above. A gentle stroll may not inspire you to carry a complete kit, but anything beyond that warrants precaution. When hiking alone, you should always be prepared for a medical need. And if you are a twosome or with a group, one or more people in your party should be equipped with first aid material.

General Safety

The following tips may have the familiar ring of a parent's voice as you take note of them.

★ *Always let someone know where you will be hiking* and how long you expect to be gone. It's a good idea to give that person a copy of your route, particularly if you are headed into any isolated area. Let them know when you return.

★ *Always sign in and out of any trail registers provided.* Don't hesitate to comment on the trail condition if space is provided; that's your opportunity to alert others to any problems you encounter.

★ *Do not count on a cell phone for your safety.* Reception may be spotty or nonexistent on the trail, even on an urban walk—especially if it is embraced by towering trees.

★ *Always carry food and water,* even for a short hike. And bring more water than you think you will need. (That cannot be said often enough!)

★ *Stay on designated trails.* Even on the most clearly marked trails, there is usually a point where you have to stop and consider in which direction to head. If you become disoriented, don't panic. As soon as you think you may be off track, stop, assess your current direction, and then retrace your steps to the point where you went astray. Using a map, a compass, and this book, and keeping in mind what you have passed thus far, reorient yourself, and trust your judgment on which way to continue. If you become absolutely unsure of how to continue, return to your vehicle the way you came in. Should you become completely lost and have no idea how to find the trailhead, remaining in place along the trail and waiting for help is most often the best option for adults and always the best option for children.

★ *Always carry a whistle,* another precaution that cannot be overemphasized. It may be a lifesaver if you do become lost or sustain an injury.

★ *Be especially careful when crossing streams.* Whether you are fording the stream or crossing it on a log, make every step count. If you have any doubt about maintaining your balance on a log, ford the stream instead: use a trekking pole or stout stick for balance *and face upstream as you cross.* If a stream seems too deep to ford, turn back. Whatever is on the other side is not worth risking your life.

★ *Be careful at overlooks.* While these areas may provide spectacular views, they are potentially hazardous. Stay back from the edge of outcrops, and make absolutely sure of your footing; a misstep can mean a nasty and possibly fatal fall.

★ *Standing dead trees and storm-damaged living trees pose a significant hazard to hikers.* These trees may have loose or broken limbs that could fall at any time. While walking beneath trees, and when choosing a spot to rest or enjoy your snack, look up!

★ *Know the symptoms of subnormal body temperature known as hypothermia.* Shivering and forgetfulness are the two most common indicators of this stealthy killer. Hypothermia can occur at any elevation, even in the summer, especially when the hiker is wearing lightweight cotton clothing. If symptoms present themselves, get to shelter, hot liquids, and dry clothes ASAP.

★ *Know the symptoms of heat exhaustion (hyperthermia).* Lightheadedness and loss of energy are the first two indicators. If you feel these symptoms, find some shade, drink your water, remove as many layers of clothing as practical, and stay put until you cool down. Marching through heat exhaustion leads to heatstroke—which can be fatal. If you should be sweating and you're not, that's the signature warning sign. Your hike is over at that point—heatstroke is a life-threatening condition that can cause seizures, convulsions, and eventually death. If you or a companion reaches that point, do whatever can be done to cool the victim down and seek medical attention immediately.

★ *Ask questions.* State forest and park employees are there to help. It's a lot easier to solicit advice before a problem occurs, and it will help you avoid a mishap away from civilization when it's too late to amend an error.

★ *Most important of all, take along your brain.* A cool, calculating mind is the single most important asset on the trail. It allows you to think before you act.

★ *In summary:* Plan ahead. Watch your step. Avoid accidents before they happen. Enjoy a rewarding and relaxing hike.

Animal, Insect, and Plant Hazards

Hikers should remain aware of the following concerns regarding plant and wildlife, described in alphabetical order.

BLACK BEARS

Though encountering a black bear is conceivable along any stretch of the trail in the mid-Atlantic region, you are most likely to encounter them in eastern Pennsylvania and along Kittatinny Mountain between the Delaware Water Gap and New Jersey High Point. Though attacks by black bears are uncommon, the sight or approach of a bear can give anyone a start. If you encounter a bear while hiking, remain calm and avoid running in any direction. Make loud noises to scare off the bear and back away slowly. If you feel the need to carry something to deter an approaching bear, a small fog horn is lightweight, inexpensive, and quite effective. In primitive and remote areas, assume bears are present; in more developed sites, check on the current bear situation prior to hiking. Most encounters are food related, as bears have an exceptional sense of smell and not particularly discriminating tastes. While this is of greater concern to backpackers and campers, on a day hike, you may plan a lunchtime picnic or munch on an energy bar or other snack from time to time. So remain aware and alert.

MOSQUITOES

Ward off these pests with repellent and/or repellent-impregnated clothing. Insect repellents with DEET are very effective. In some areas, mosquitoes are known to carry the West Nile virus, so all due caution should be taken to avoid their bites. Mosquito season in the mid-Atlantic tends to come with the warm weather, beginning in June and lasting through the summer and into early September. Areas with vernal pools and standing water tend to be worse than on the ridges.

POISON IVY, OAK, AND SUMAC

Recognizing and avoiding poison ivy, oak, and sumac are the most effective ways to prevent the painful, itchy rashes associated with these plants. Poison ivy occurs as a vine or ground cover, 3 leaflets to a leaf; poison oak occurs as either a vine or shrub, also with 3 leaflets; and poison sumac flourishes in swampland, each leaf having 7–13 leaflets. Urushiol, the oil in the sap of these plants, is responsible for the rash. Within 14 hours of exposure, raised lines and/or blisters will appear on the affected area, accompanied by a terrible itch. Refrain from scratching, because bacteria under your fingernails can cause an infection. Wash and dry the affected area thoroughly, applying a calamine lotion to help dry out the rash. If itching or blistering is severe, seek medical attention. If you do come into contact with one of these plants, remember that oil-contaminated clothes, hiking gear, and pets can easily cause an irritating rash on you or someone else, so wash not only any exposed parts of your body but also any exposed clothes, gear, and pets.

SNAKES

Rattlesnakes, cottonmouths, copperheads, and corals are among the most common venomous snakes in the United States, and hibernation season is typically October–April. Rattlesnakes like to bask in the sun and won't bite unless threatened.

In the region described in this book, you will possibly encounter timber rattlesnakes or copperhead snakes. In several mid-Atlantic states, timber rattlesnakes are a protected species; killing them is illegal. However, the snakes you most likely will see while hiking will be nonvenomous species and subspecies. The best rule is to leave all snakes alone, give them a wide berth as you hike past, and make sure any hiking companions (including dogs) do the same.

When hiking, stick to well-used trails, and wear over-the-ankle boots and loose-fitting, long pants. Do not step or put your hands beyond your range of detailed visibility, and avoid wandering around in the dark. Use extra caution when scrambling among the rocky ridgecrests and viewpoints common to this region; these are prime terrain for timber rattlesnakes, which are more common in Pennsylvania than people are aware. Step *onto* logs and rocks, never *over* them, and be especially careful when climbing rocks. Always avoid walking through dense brush or willow thickets.

TICKS

Ticks are often found on brush and tall grass, where they seem to be waiting to hitch a ride on a warm-blooded passerby. In recent years, they have become abundantly common throughout the mid-Atlantic region. Adult ticks are most active April–May and again October–November. Among the varieties of ticks, the black-legged tick, commonly called the deer tick, is the primary carrier of Lyme disease. Lyme disease is a potentially serious and difficult-to-treat illness. A bull's-eye rash around the site of the bite is the classic sign of bite from a Lyme-infected tick, though it does not always appear. Other symptoms tend to be flulike, and consequently Lyme is often misdiagnosed.

The best treatment for Lyme disease is prevention. Wear light-colored clothing, making it easier for you to spot ticks before they migrate to your skin. At the end of the hike, visually check your hair, back of neck, armpits, and socks. During your posthike shower, take a moment to do a more complete body check. For ticks that are already embedded, removal with tweezers is best. Grasp the tick close to your skin, and remove it by pulling straight out firmly. Do your best to remove the head, but do not twist. Use disinfectant solution on the wound. If you remove an embedded tick, watch for signs of a developing rash around the site where the tick was embedded. If no rash develops but you begin to feel ill during the next 10 days (though longer is not uncommon), inform your doctor that you removed a tick. You can save a removed tick in a bag and speak to your physician about having it tested. I have done this; the tick tested positive for Lyme, and my physician decided that treating me was a better course of action than waiting for symptoms to appear.

Hunting

Separate rules, regulations, and licenses govern the various hunting types and related seasons. Though there are generally no problems along the A.T., hikers may wish to forgo their trips during the big-game seasons, when the woods suddenly seem filled with orange and camouflage. November and December are the big hunting months in the mid-Atlantic region. Hikers should wear at least 250 square inches of blaze orange during these months. That amounts to at least a vest and a hat. Blaze orange is intentionally a color that is hard on the eyes, and I have discovered that the secret to making it desirable to wear is to get clothing that serves a purpose. For about $20, I picked up a nice nylon blaze orange vest with a bunch of large pockets into which I can fit camera accessories, granola bars, a voice recorder, maps, and all sorts of little things that I no longer have to remove my pack to access. I wear it all the time. I also have a nice orange sweatshirt made out of fleece that is always with me October–January.

Regulations

Though this book is geared toward the day hiker, some of the hikes included are suitable for overnight or weekend trips. Certain regulations do apply when using the trail for overnight trips. In Pennsylvania, especially east of the Susquehanna River, much of the trail passes through state game lands. Camping on state game lands is prohibited except for A.T. thru-hikers entering and leaving the game lands at separate locations. Similarly, camping along the trail in most state parks is prohibited except in designated areas, which means trail shelters and the surrounding area. Some state parks also regulate that these be used for thru-hikers only. If you are planning an overnight trip, be sure to check with the agency where you are traveling for its regulations. See Appendix A for contact information. If you are out for a weekend trip, as a courtesy to long-distance thru-hikers who are doing day after day on the trail, I recommend carrying a tent and using it rather than shelter space. Nearly all of the shelters have places to pitch a tent nearby.

Though there are no permits or fees required to do any of the hikes in this book, be aware that you may in places have to pay for parking and that parking regulations vary from place to place. I have provided instructions for where to park for each of the hikes and have noted if there are any fees or regulations of which you need to be aware. State parks tend to be open sunrise–sunset, and that means that you should plan to complete hikes within state parks during daylight hours.

Trail Etiquette

Always treat the trail, wildlife, and fellow hikers with respect. Here are some reminders.

★ Plan ahead in order to be self-sufficient at all times. For example, carry necessary supplies for changes in weather or other conditions. A well-planned trip brings satisfaction to you and to others.

★ Hike on open trails only.

★ Respect trail and road closures (ask if not sure), avoid possible trespassing on private land, and obtain all permits and authorization as required. Also, leave gates as you found them or as marked.

★ Be courteous to other hikers, bikers, equestrians, and others you encounter on the trails.

★ Never spook wild animals or pets. An unannounced approach, a sudden movement, or a loud noise startles most critters, and a surprised animal can be dangerous to you, to others, and to itself. Give animals plenty of space.

★ Observe the yield signs around the region's trailheads and backcountry. Typically, they advise hikers to yield to horses, and bikers yield to both horses and hikers. By common courtesy, on hills, hikers and bikers yield to any uphill traffic. When encountering mounted riders or horse packers, hikers can courteously step off the trail, on the downhill side if possible. So the horse can see and hear you, calmly greet the riders before they reach you and do not dart behind trees. Also resist the urge to pet horses unless you are invited to do so. In this region, equestrians and bikers are only allowed on the Appalachian Trail on the section that follows the C&O Canal Towpath.

★ Leave only footprints. Be sensitive to the ground beneath you. This also means staying on the existing trail and not blazing any new trails.

★ Be sure to pack out what you pack in. No one likes to see the trash someone else has left behind.

Tips on Enjoying Hiking in the Mid-Atlantic

One of the distinguishing features about the Appalachian Trail in the mid-Atlantic region is that it passes so close to many of the region's major metropolitan areas. It is only 35 miles from New York City, where it crosses the Palisades Parkway. While this situation provides easy access to the trail for many people, it also means that the trail can get busy in certain areas and especially on weekends. In the profiles for each hike, I have noted when that is the case. If you are interested in solitude, you would do well to plan your hike for during the week. The difference in experience of hiking on a Monday as compared to a Saturday or Sunday can be remarkable.

The proximity to large population centers can also inspire carelessness. Widespread cell phone coverage and close proximity to roads and towns can lead to complacency, and complacency to poor decision making. I was surprised how unreliable cell phones can be while working on this book, even using a major service provider. Whether you are just planning for a short trip of a couple of miles or something more challenging, be sure to bring adequate gear in the event of an emergency and to let someone know where you are going and when you plan to return.

Another effect of being in such close proximity to large population centers is that around the trail you'll often find some interesting local culture. I've provided information with each chapter on things nearby the trailheads when I've found something worth noting. But I recommend getting out and exploring on your own to see what is around. Some of the little towns in the most distant reaches of the trail can have the best places for breakfast or supper. While working on this book, I have discovered that hiking for 5 or 6 hours followed by poking around a little town afterward can make for an enjoyable and sometimes surprising day.

NEW JERSEY HIGH POINT MONUMENT *(See Hike 28, page 181.)*

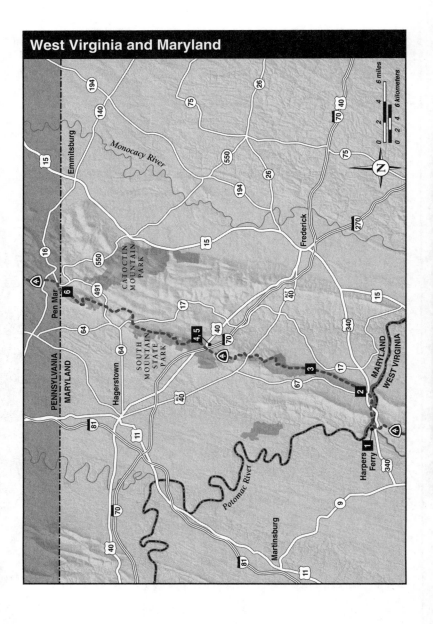

West Virginia and Maryland

THE VIEW TO MARYLAND'S GREENBRIER STATE PARK FROM ANNAPOLIS ROCK
(See Hike 5, page 48.)

1 HARPERS FERRY p. 28

2 WEVERTON CLIFFS p. 34

3 WHITE ROCKS AND LAMBS KNOLL p. 38

4 WASHINGTON MONUMENT p. 43

5 ANNAPOLIS ROCK p. 48

6 HIGH ROCK p. 53

Harpers Ferry

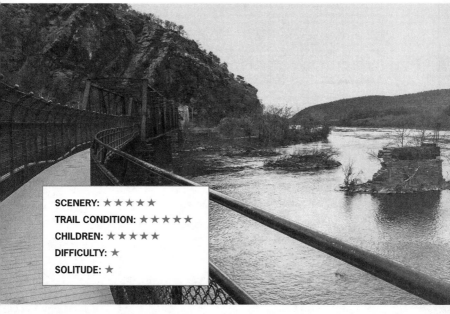

SCENERY: ★ ★ ★ ★ ★
TRAIL CONDITION: ★ ★ ★ ★ ★
CHILDREN: ★ ★ ★ ★ ★
DIFFICULTY: ★
SOLITUDE: ★

THE VIEW DOWNSTREAM FROM THE CONFLUENCE OF THE POTOMAC AND SHENANDOAH RIVERS

GPS TRAILHEAD COORDINATES: N39° 19.523' W77° 44.431'

DISTANCE & CONFIGURATION: 2.1-mile loop

HIKING TIME: 1 hour to all day

HIGHLIGHTS: Historic Harpers Ferry, Jefferson Rock, confluence of Shenandoah and Potomac Rivers

ELEVATION: 527' at the Appalachian Trail Conservancy office; 245' at the Potomac River

ACCESS: Open 24/7; no fees or permits required. Parking is very limited in Harpers Ferry; the A.T.C. recommends parking on Washington Street downhill from its office.

MAPS: National Park Service *Harpers Ferry National Historical Park;* town map available at Appalachian Trail Conservancy office in Harpers Ferry; USGS *Harpers Ferry*

FACILITIES: Restrooms, food and drink available at the numerous museums and establishments in town

CONTACT: Appalachian Trail Conservancy, 304-535-6331, appalachiantrail.org

COMMENTS: This is a great hike for the whole family. Plan on spending a fair amount of time visiting the Lower Town.

Overview

Beginning at the Appalachian Trail Conservancy (A.T.C.) Visitor Center, this hike makes a loop through the historic Lower Town of Harpers Ferry, which encompasses the point of land at the confluence of the Potomac and Shenandoah Rivers. The whole town is in effect a museum, with many of the buildings containing exhibits.

Route Details

Harpers Ferry is best known as the site of John Brown's Raid in 1859. Along with 21 armed men, John Brown led a revolt intended to initiate a rebellion against slavery. The men captured and occupied the federal armory's fire engine and guard house, now referred to as John Brown's Fort, near the confluence of the Potomac and Shenandoah Rivers. Ultimately, they were captured by a group of marines led by Colonel Robert E. Lee, and Brown was hanged. The event, however, was prescient in that it in many respects foretold the Civil War, which began two years later.

Begin this hike at the A.T.C. Visitor Center at the corner of Washington Street and Storer College Place in Harpers Ferry. From the visitor center, follow blue blazes southbound along Storer College Place. The road ends at Fillmore Street. Make a left onto Fillmore Street and then a quick right onto the footpath through the Storer College campus. The path is blazed as it passes through the campus. Storer College, a historically black college, began as a school for freed slaves. Now the buildings are used by the National Park Service. The large building on the right as you enter the campus is the Stephen T. Mather Training Center for the National Park Service.

Continue across the campus following the blue blazes, down a set of steps, and through a small parking lot, where the path exits from the southwest corner and becomes a dirt track in woods. Just below the parking area, the path joins the Appalachian Trail (A.T.), and onto it you will turn left (northbound), heading east above the Shenandoah River. The first point of interest along the trail is

Harpers Ferry

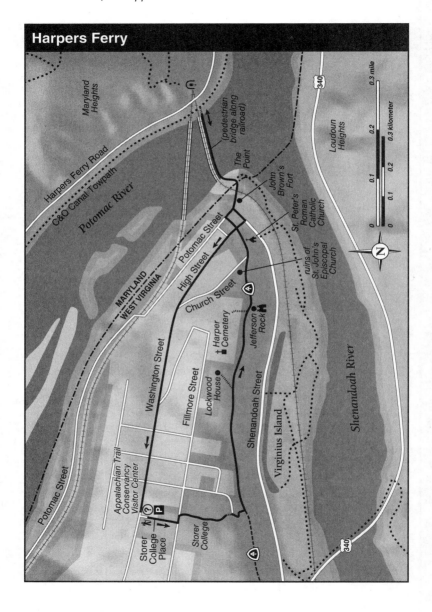

Jefferson Rock, about 0.5 mile from gaining the Appalachian Trail. Along the way, the trail hugs the cliffs and passes through the woods high above the river. Some old stone walls indicate that you are entering the historic section of town, and a set of steps leads up to the Lockwood House.

Beyond these steps, the trail begins a steady descent and soon comes out to Jefferson Rock on the right (0.7 mile). The view from the large slab of rock is outstanding. Thomas Jefferson, for whom the rock is named, declared the view from here to be one of "the most stupendous scenes in Nature." To your right you get a view up the Shenandoah River Valley to the south and west, and to the left, you can look downstream past a church steeple and over Harpers Ferry to the confluence of the Potomac and Shenandoah Rivers and the Potomac River Valley beyond.

From Jefferson Rock, the path is paved. It descends a little more steeply toward the old town of Harpers Ferry. Shortly beyond the rock, the A.T. passes the ruins of St. John's Episcopal Church on the left. The A.T. continues down steps to Church Street and past St. Peter's Roman Catholic Church on the right, the steeple of which dominates the view from Jefferson Rock. Continue down Church Street to its end at High Street. At this point, the A.T. crosses High Street and passes through a small courtyard. Instead of following it,

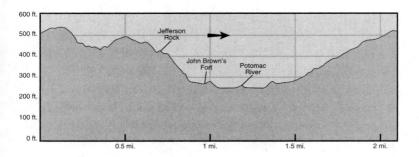

turn right and follow High Street to its end at Shenandoah Street. Directly across from High Street on Shenandoah is the foundation of one of the old arsenals that dates back to the days of John Brown.

To the right (west) along Shenandoah Street, you'll find the information center for the Harpers Ferry National Historical Park and several museums. To your left, you will be looking at John Brown's Fort, the small stone building where John Brown was captured. The John Brown Museum is on the north side of Shenandoah Street next to Stephenson's Hotel.

Continue along Shenandoah Street to the east, and pick up the A.T. again at its end. Turn right and walk past John Brown's Fort and beneath the railroad tracks. Once beyond the tracks, the A.T. bends to the left and follows the footpath alongside the train tracks over the Potomac at the confluence with the Shenandoah River. The railroad

WHITE HALL TAVERN IS LOCATED JUST ACROSS THE STREET FROM THE FAMOUS FORT AT HARPERS FERRY.

section of the bridge is a bit of an eyesore, but the scenery includes items of both natural and historical interest and is still quite lovely in this area. From the A.T.C. Visitor Center to the east side of the bridge is about 1.1 miles. Here the railroad enters a tunnel below Maryland Heights, and the A.T. descends a set of steps to the C&O Canal Towpath. You can hike to the top of Maryland Heights via a side trail gained from the canal path upstream along the Potomac River. A map detailing the route is available at the A.T.C. Visitor Center.

After returning to town, follow the A.T. blazes a short distance along Potomac Street, and then to the left through the little courtyard across to High Street. Once on High Street, turn right. High Street eventually becomes Washington Street, at the corner of Church Street, and in 0.75 mile it returns to the A.T.C. Initially, along High Street in downtown, you'll walk past several shops and a couple of restaurants, all in old historical buildings.

Nearby Attractions

Really, the whole town is full of nearby attractions. The main visitor center for Harpers Ferry National Historical Park (nps.gov/hafe) is located about 2 miles from downtown following Shenandoah Street. Shuttle buses run between the visitor center and downtown. If you would like to grab a bite to eat along the hike, I recommend Bistro 840 (304-535-1860; bistro1840.com) on the west side of High Street, about two blocks uphill from downtown, or the Potomac Grille (304-535-1900) directly across the street from it.

Directions

From US 340 in Harpers Ferry, West Virginia, an officially designated Appalachian Trail Community, head north onto Union Street. Follow Union Street 0.4 mile to Washington Street. Turn right onto Washington Street and follow it 0.2 mile to Storer College Place. The Appalachian Trail Conservancy Visitor Center is on the southeast corner at 799 Washington St.

Weverton Cliffs

SOME OLD INITIALS CARVED INTO WEVERTON ROCKS PROVIDE THE FOREGROUND FOR THIS VIEW OF THE POTOMAC RIVER.

SCENERY: ★ ★ ★ ★ ★
TRAIL CONDITION: ★ ★ ★ ★
CHILDREN: ★ ★
DIFFICULTY: ★ ★ ★
SOLITUDE: ★ ★

GPS TRAILHEAD COORDINATES: N39° 19.980' W77° 40.988'

DISTANCE & CONFIGURATION: 2.0-mile out-and-back

HIKING TIME: 1.5 hours

HIGHLIGHTS: Excellent view of the Potomac River

ELEVATION: 382' at trailhead; 845' on the trail just above cliffs

ACCESS: Open 24/7; no fees or permits required

MAPS: Potomac Appalachian Trail Club *Appalachian Trail Across Maryland, Sections 1 to 7;* USGS *Harpers Ferry*

FACILITIES: None

CONTACT: South Mountain State Park, 301-791-4767, tinyurl.com/southmtnsp

COMMENTS: This short but popular hike is a somewhat less crowded alternative to the Maryland Heights hike just outside of Harpers Ferry, which can get very busy on weekends.

Overview

It's pretty straightforward: follow the Appalachian Trail (A.T.) from the parking lot for a mile to the overlook at Weverton Cliffs.

Route Details

Though not an especially long hike, the trip up to Weverton Cliffs will provide you with a bit of an aerobic workout as well as a great view. It's a good hike with the kids, though they do need to be prepared for walking uphill for a mile.

Begin the hike at the parking area near the south end of Weverton Cliffs Road. The small town of Weverton dates back to the 1820s, and during the Civil War, many troops passed through the area on their way to major battles to the north. The A.T. passes right beneath the lot to the south, and the best way to get on it is to walk east along the shoulder of Weverton Cliffs Road for about 200 feet. Weverton Road makes a sharp left and heads north; the A.T. crosses at the bend. Follow the trail into the woods and begin the mile-long ascent to the cliffs. Though the trail surface is dirt and pleasant walking for the entire hike, the surface of the forest is rather rocky and gets even more so the higher you get.

Along the way, the terrain gets gradually steeper as you progress farther east. Ultimately you'll haul yourself up several switchbacks, and they get tighter together the farther up the hillside you progress. At about 0.6 mile, the trail passes beneath the west-facing Weverton Cliffs in the area of a switchback. At 0.85 mile, you gain the ridge and the terrain flattens out. A blue-blazed trail out to the cliffs departs to the right (south). Follow the trail 0.15 mile to the overlook at the cliffs. While the overlook has several pine trees scattered about it that partially obstruct the view, what you get is quite amazing. Below you, the Potomac River has cut its way through the ridge, and the landscape takes in the river channel from east to west. Many rapids, rocks, and islands are visible in both directions.

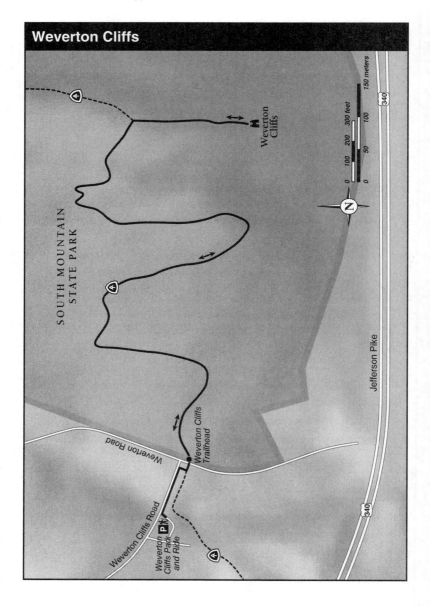

These west-facing cliffs, like those you will encounter farther north at Annapolis Rock (see page 48), were formed by an upslope of rock from the east. The ledges of quartzite that form the cliffs mark the edge of the folded shelf. Weverton Cliffs and the water gap through which the Potomac River flows mark the southern end of South Mountain in Maryland. Virginia is directly across the river, and West Virginia is to the west. From this point, the Appalachian Trail stays to the ridge of South Mountain all the way to Pennsylvania, 40 miles to the north. South Mountain State Park extends for nearly the entire length, and several other state parks share the ridgeline as well.

Nearby Attractions

If you haven't already made it to Harpers Ferry (see page 28), that would be the place to head after doing this hike.

Directions

From Harpers Ferry, West Virginia, follow US 340 north 3.3 miles. Take the exit for MD 67 north toward Boonsboro, Maryland. Follow MD 67 0.25 mile, and turn right onto Weverton Road. The large park-and-ride lot will be on the right.

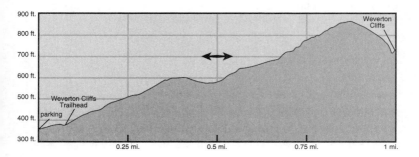

White Rocks and Lambs Knoll

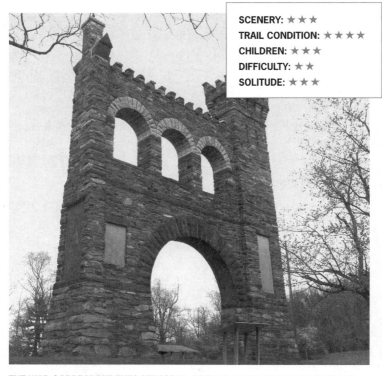

SCENERY: ★ ★ ★
TRAIL CONDITION: ★ ★ ★ ★
CHILDREN: ★ ★ ★
DIFFICULTY: ★ ★
SOLITUDE: ★ ★ ★

THE WAR CORRESPONDENTS MEMORIAL ARCH IS AN UNUSUAL BUT STRIKING BIT OF ARCHITECTURE IN MARYLAND'S GATHLAND STATE PARK.

GPS TRAILHEAD COORDINATES: N39° 24.357' W77° 38.362'

DISTANCE & CONFIGURATION: 9.2-mile balloon

HIKING TIME: 3 hours

HIGHLIGHTS: View from White Rocks, attractive forested ridge

ELEVATION: 915' at trailhead; 1,765' at Lambs Knoll

ACCESS: Open 24/7; no fees or permits required

MAPS: Potomac Appalachian Trail Club *Appalachian Trail Across Maryland, Sections 1 to 7;* USGS *Keedysville* and USGS *Middletown*

FACILITIES: Restrooms at Gathland State Park

CONTACT: Gathland State Park, 301-791-4767, tinyurl.com/gathlandsp

Overview

This hike follows the Appalachian Trail (A.T.) north along South Mountain to the White Rocks overlook. From there, you can make a loop over Lambs Knoll. Though the views on the knoll are obstructed, the hike is pleasant and fairly secluded.

Route Details

This hike begins at Gathland State Park on Gapland Road in Crampton's Gap at the crest of South Mountain. In addition to a very nice picnic area, Gathland State Park has a very obvious and unusual memorial, the War Correspondents Memorial Arch, dedicated to war correspondents who died in war. Constructed in 1896, the large, ornate stone arch was constructed here because the land was once the mountain home of Civil War correspondent George Alfred Townsend (whose pen name was Gath, hence the name of the park). It is now a National Historic Monument superintended by the National Park Service.

From the parking lot at Gathland State Park, follow the A.T. northbound past the ruins of an old stone building. It is interesting to note that the ridge of South Mountain, now traversed by the Appalachian Trail, was the route of the Underground Railroad during the 19th century, which fleeing slaves followed north to freedom in Pennsylvania. The trail climbs steeply for the first 0.3 mile, but then it levels out. The next 2.5 miles consist of very pleasant hiking in the woods. The trail surface is mostly soft dirt and is easy on the feet. The path follows the crest of the ridge at about 1,420 feet in elevation that varies little for the duration of the hike. At 2.9 miles, the trail meets the head of the blue-blazed access trail to the Bear Spring Cabin that drops off to the east. The cabin is owned and managed by the Potomac Appalachian Trail Club; reservations can be made via patc.net.

From the side trail, the A.T. makes a sharp turn to the west (left) and ascends a short distance before curving back around to the east. At 3.5 miles, it reaches the small clearing atop White Rocks, a small blocky outcrop of quartzite on the east side of the ridge. This is a nice place to

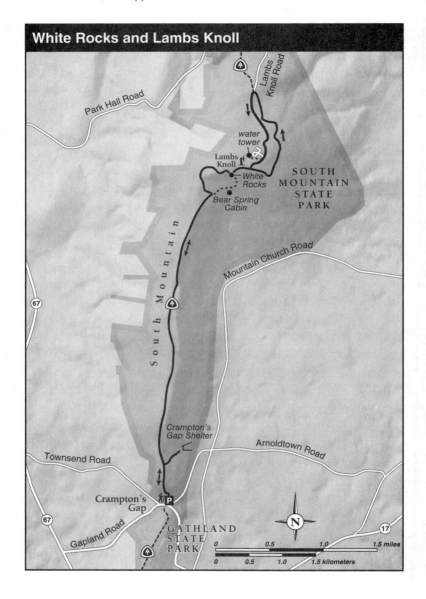

White Rocks and Lambs Knoll

Park Hall Road

Lambs Knoll Road

water tower

Lambs Knoll

White Rocks

Bear Spring Cabin

SOUTH MOUNTAIN STATE PARK

South Mountain

Mountain Church Road

67

Crampton's Gap Shelter

Arnoldtown Road

Townsend Road

Crampton's Gap

67

Gapland Road

GATHLAND STATE PARK

N

| 0 | 0.5 | 1.0 | 1.5 miles |

| 0 | 0.5 | 1.0 | 1.5 kilometers |

17

sit and take a break. Unlike all of the west-facing overlooks on the hikes in Maryland described in this book, White Rocks offers a view to the southeast. The terrain is a little more rolling in this direction, as you are now looking out toward the southernmost reach of the Catoctin Mountains. From the overlook, a blue-blazed trail drops to the east. This is the north end of the Bear Spring Cabin access trail, the southern end of which you passed 0.5 mile back.

Most people who are out for a day hike usually turn back at White Rocks. I was intrigued by Lambs Knoll, which lay just 0.25 mile farther north along the trail. In my mind, I had pastoral visions of broad, grassy meadows, populated by herds of mutton on the hoof. In fact, as I found out, Lambs Knoll is tree covered, and its summit is home to several communication towers. Nonetheless, if you feel like you could use a little more of a hike, you can make a pleasant loop of about 2.3 additional miles around and over the top. You won't get any view to speak of, but it is a pleasant walk. At 1,758 feet, Lambs Knoll is the second-highest point in South Mountain State Park next to Quirauk Mountain (see the map for High Rock, page 54).

From White Rocks, continue northbound along the trail. After 0.2 mile, you'll pass the end of the loop. The spot is easy enough to notice: a distinct trail heads off to the left. To be sure, however, that you have the right spot, it is best to complete the loop in a

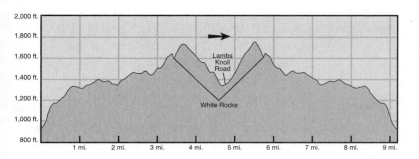

counterclockwise direction, returning to the A.T. at this spot. To do so, continue northbound on the A.T., traversing below the highest part of Lambs Knoll to the east through more open forest. The trail becomes a bit rocky through this section, but it stays mostly level. After about 0.9 mile, it begins to descend, and after it levels out again, it continues another 0.2 mile out to Lambs Knoll Road, which is paved and only one lane with pullouts every 0.1 mile or so. Turn left onto Lambs Knoll Road and follow it uphill 0.75 mile.

When you near the top of Lambs Knoll, the road forks. The right fork leads out to what appears to be a water tower. The left fork leads up to some communication towers past a gate. Take the left road, walk past the gate, past a field on the left, and up to the fenced-in tower area. Follow a distinct footpath south, along the east side of the fence to its end, and then to the right around the back of the fence. The path enters the woods and descends a short distance (150 feet) back to the Appalachian Trail. Turn right and return to White Rocks and then on to Gathland State Park.

Nearby Attractions

While you are here, Gathland State Park (see page 38) is worth a visit. Gapland Lodge, south of Gapland Road, has an exhibit on the Civil War battle at Crampton's Gap, one of several battles that took place along South Mountain. Dan's Restaurant and Tap House in nearby Boonsboro, Maryland (3 N. Main St.; 301-432-5224; drnth.com), at the corner of MD 34 and US 40 Alternate, has excellent food, cool photographs from the Prohibition area, and a very nice waitstaff.

Directions

From Boonsboro, Maryland, follow US 40 Alternate south 0.5 mile. Turn right onto MD 67 and follow it south about 7.75 miles to Gapland Road. Turn left onto Gapland Road and follow it 1.0 mile east to the obvious memorial on top of South Mountain. Parking is on the north side of the road.

Washington Monument

SCENERY: ★ ★ ★ ★
TRAIL CONDITION: ★ ★ ★ ★
CHILDREN: ★ ★ ★
DIFFICULTY: ★ ★
SOLITUDE: ★ ★ ★ ★

RESIDENTS OF NEARBY BOONSBORO, MARYLAND, CELEBRATED INDEPENDENCE
DAY IN 1827 BY BUILDING AND DEDICATING THE FIRST INCARNATION OF THIS
MONUMENT TO GEORGE WASHINGTON.

GPS TRAILHEAD COORDINATES: N39° 32.133' W77° 36.241'

DISTANCE & CONFIGURATION: 6.4-mile out-and-back

HIKING TIME: 3.5 hours

HIGHLIGHTS: Washington Monument, excellent views from the power line crossings

ELEVATION: 1,232' at trailhead; 1,525' at monument

ACCESS: Open 24/7; no fees or permits required

MAPS: Potomac Appalachian Trail Club *Appalachian Trail Across Maryland, Sections 1 to 7;*
USGS *Myersville*

FACILITIES: Restrooms and picnic facilities at Washington Monument State Park

CONTACT: South Mountain State Park, 301-791-4767, tinyurl.com/southmtnsp

COMMENTS: Though close to the populated area of Frederick, Maryland, this hike can
provide a bit more solitude than you'll get heading north to Annapolis Rock.

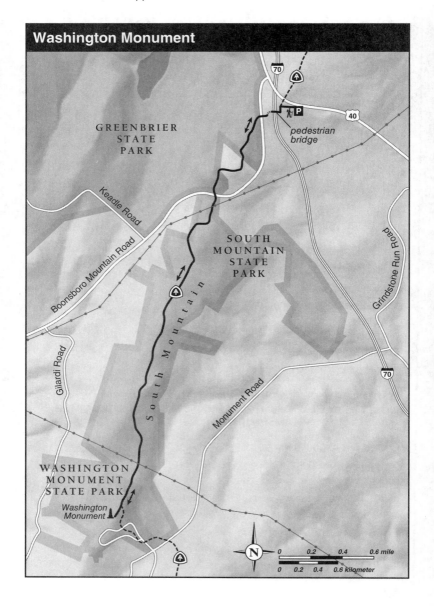

Washington Monument

GREENBRIER STATE PARK

pedestrian bridge

Keadle Road

Boonsboro Mountain Road

SOUTH MOUNTAIN STATE PARK

Grindstone Run Road

South Mountain

Gilardi Road

Monument Road

WASHINGTON MONUMENT STATE PARK

Washington Monument

0   0.2   0.4   0.6 mile
0   0.2   0.4   0.6 kilometer

Overview

This hike follows the Appalachian Trail (A.T.) from the parking lot on US 40 southbound along South Mountain to Washington Monument State Park. The clearing at the monument provides an excellent view to the northwest. Picnic facilities are available at the park south of the monument.

Route Details

Begin at the large A.T. parking area on the south side of US 40 just east of the bridge over I-70. Walk out of the parking lot to the west to the end of the old US 40 pavement. Turn left and follow the path downhill toward the footbridge over I-70. Follow the A.T. southbound over the footbridge. At the south end of the bridge, climb a few steps and follow the trail about 75 yards as it passes through private property and across Boonsboro Mountain Road. Enter the woods and begin climbing. Initially the trail is a bit rocky.

At 0.9 mile, the A.T. crosses Boonsboro Mountain Road again. Not far beyond the road, the trail crosses a significant power line cut that offers a nice view off to the west. The Appalachian Trail ascends a hill south of the power line and traverses the west side of a knoll through a pretty stand of mountain laurel. I passed through this area

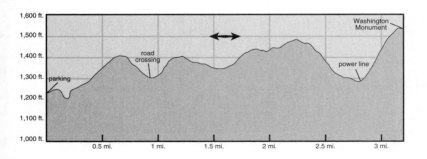

the morning after a night of heavy winds, and I was quite surprised by how many downed tree limbs and trees were scattered about the woods and across the trail. Even more surprising were the fresh piles of bark that obviously had been loosened from the dead trees by the action of the wind causing them to bend. Seeing all this served as a good reminder that when walking through or camping in the forest during heavy wind, you need to be alert to the possibility of branches or standing dead trees falling on you.

At 2.8 miles, the A.T. crosses another power line clearing. This one, in fact, is quite wide. As you look up at it from the lowlands in the west, it appears as if someone took a set of hair clippers and cut a neat, wide swath through the woods over the top of South Mountain. Beyond the power lines, the trail climbs more steeply for 0.3 mile and then soon enters Washington Monument State Park. Upon entering the park, you'll first come to an access road entering from the east. The A.T. does not actually go up to the monument but follows the access road out to the main parking area for the park south of the monument. So leave the A.T. and walk the last hundred yards or so along the road up to the monument.

Not to be confused with the giant obelisk of the same name in Washington, D.C., this Washington Monument is a 32-foot-tall round tower made from local quartzite. The tower was originally, though not completely, built on July 4, 1827, by the residents of nearby Boonsboro to commemorate George Washington. At the end of the day, it stood 15 feet high and 54 feet around. It was extended to 30 feet high later in the year. The original tower eventually fell into disrepair and was reconstructed by the Civilian Conservation Corps in the mid-1930s. It was added to the National Register of Historic Places in 1972. It is an impressive and solid-looking monument that takes in an equally impressive view to the Great Valley in the west over a boulder field. In the clearing next to the tower, you will also find a memorial to a fallen police officer inscribed with words from General Thomas "Stonewall" Jackson: "Let us cross over the river, and rest under the shade of the trees."

A TRAIL SIGN POINTS THE WAY NORTH WITH THE WASHINGTON MONUMENT IN THE BACKGROUND.

Nearby Attractions

A visitor center at Washington Monument State Park has exhibits on the natural and cultural history of the area and a picnic area. Nearby Greenbrier State Park has a beautiful lake and an excellent campground. The entrance to Greenbrier is only a mile west of the parking lot on US 40.

Directions

From Frederick, Maryland, follow US 40 west 11 miles. The large A.T. parking lot is on the south side of the road at the top of South Mountain. If you cross over I-70, you have gone too far.

5 # Annapolis Rock

SCENERY: ★ ★ ★ ★
TRAIL CONDITION: ★ ★ ★ ★ ★
CHILDREN: ★ ★ ★
DIFFICULTY: ★ ★ ★
SOLITUDE: ★ ★

LOOKING WEST OVER ANNAPOLIS ROCK TOWARD THE GREAT VALLEY IN MARYLAND

GPS TRAILHEAD COORDINATES: N39° 32.133' W77° 36.241'

DISTANCE & CONFIGURATION: 5.2-mile out-and-back

HIKING TIME: 3 hours

HIGHLIGHTS: Excellent view from Annapolis Rock

ELEVATION: 1,232' at trailhead; 1,708' on the trail above rocks

ACCESS: Open 24/7; no fees or permits required

MAPS: Potomac Appalachian Trail Club *Appalachian Trail Across Maryland, Sections 1 to 7;* USGS *Myersville*

FACILITIES: Privy and a spring at Annapolis Rock campground

CONTACT: South Mountain State Park, 301-791-4767, tinyurl.com/southmtnsp

COMMENTS: The campground at Annapolis Rock is restricted to tents only, and no campfires are allowed.

Overview

This popular hike follows the Appalachian Trail (A.T.) northbound from US 40 along South Mountain to Annapolis Rock, accessed by a side trail heading west. A longer variation of this hike can be made by continuing along the A.T. for another mile to the side trail to Black Rock, which is also on the west side of the ridge.

Route Details

The Annapolis Rock hike is very popular for several reasons: It is close to Frederick, Maryland; the hiking is pleasant and mostly easy going; there is a campground near the rocks so it sees its share of backpackers; and the view from Annapolis Rock is superb. Its hard, fractured cliffs of quartzite that drop abruptly to the west are also popular with area rock climbers.

Begin hiking at the large A.T. parking area on the south side of US 40 just east of the bridge over I-70. Walk out of the parking lot to the west to the end of the old US 40 pavement. Turn left and follow the path downhill toward the footbridge over I-70. A sign at the bridge says that the distance to Annapolis Rock is 2.2 miles. Turn right onto the A.T. northbound and continue underneath US 40. After getting away from the noise of the highways, the trail climbs on to a ridge, and the hiking becomes very pleasant. The trail is mostly dirt. The grade is moderate at its steepest point, but it is generally flat most of the way. You are walking through a lovely oak–hickory forest along a broad flat ridge.

Around 0.5 mile, you'll pass beneath some power lines, and shortly thereafter, the blue-blazed trail to the Pine Knob Shelter departs to the left. Continue along the A.T., climbing to a crest in the ridge. At the top of the ridge, a grassy path departs to the right, to the top of Pine Knob. The view from the knob is mostly obstructed, but it is a nice spot to visit. From the crest, the path descends a short distance and then traverses across the head of an east-draining hollow. Afterward, it passes below a knob to the west and into a saddle

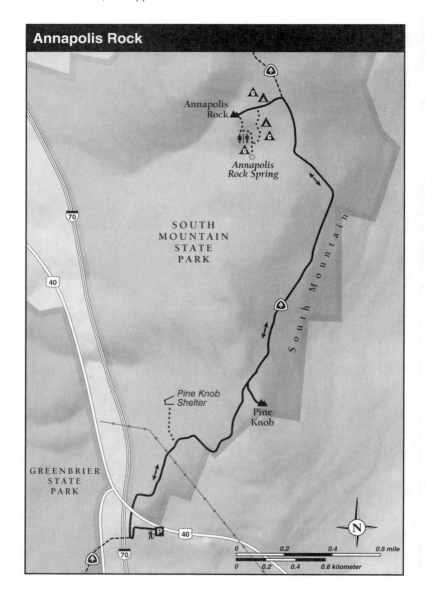

Annapolis Rock

Annapolis Rock

Annapolis Rock Spring

SOUTH MOUNTAIN STATE PARK

South Mountain

Pine Knob Shelter

Pine Knob

GREENBRIER STATE PARK

P

N

| 0 | 0.2 | 0.4 | 0.6 mile |

| 0 | 0.2 | 0.4 | 0.6 kilometer |

on the north side of it. A short and gentle ascent takes you to the top of another small knob and the blue-blazed side trail on the left to Annapolis Rock and Annapolis Springs.

Follow the blue-blazed trail downhill and out to the rocks (0.3 mile). You'll immediately notice just how heavily used this area is. A campground is located to the south of the trail, and a tent for a care-taker is on the north side of the trail across from it. The campground is restricted to tents only. There is no fee for camping here, but the sites are first come, first served. Beyond the campground, you'll reach Annapolis Rock, which offers a spectacular 180-degree panorama to the west. To the southwest, you can see the lake at Greenbrier State Park. To the west-northwest, you can see a drag strip in the bottom of the Great Valley (I mention that because I couldn't figure out what it was and so drove around looking for it). And to the north, you can see how far Annapolis Rock extends in a kind of cove along the ridge.

If you should find Annapolis Rock to be crowded when you get there and are up for a couple more miles of hiking, I recommend heading over to Black Rock. Walk back out to the A.T., turn left, and continue northbound an additional mile. You'll find another blue-blazed side trail on the left that takes you out to Black Rock in about 100 yards. It is almost equally impressive as Annapolis Rock, but the extra 2-mile round-trip tends to keep the crowds at bay.

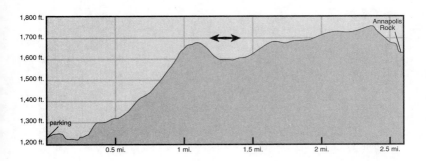

Nearby Attractions

A visitor center at nearby Washington Monument State Park has exhibits on the natural and cultural history of the area and a picnic area. Nearby Greenbrier State Park has a beautiful lake and an excellent campground. The entrance to Greenbrier is only a mile west of the parking lot on US 40.

Directions

From Frederick, Maryland, follow US 40 west 11 miles. The large A.T. parking lot is on the south side of the road at the top of South Mountain. If you cross over I-70, you have gone too far.

A LITTLE BIT OF SPRINGTIME SHOWS ITSELF ON THE FIRST DAY OF APRIL.

High Rock

SCENERY: ★ ★ ★ ★
TRAIL CONDITION: ★ ★
CHILDREN: ★ ★
DIFFICULTY: ★ ★ ★
SOLITUDE: ★

A FAIR AMOUNT OF GRAFFITI GRACES HIGH ROCK IN MARYLAND, BUT IT DOESN'T DISSUADE PEOPLE FROM COMING TO ENJOY THE VIEW.

GPS TRAILHEAD COORDINATES: N39° 42.966' W77° 30.425'

DISTANCE & CONFIGURATION: 5.0-mile loop

HIKING TIME: 4 hours

HIGHLIGHTS: Excellent view at High Rock, Pen Mar County Park

ELEVATION: 1,326' at trailhead; 1,840' at High Rock

ACCESS: Trail: open 24/7. Pen Mar County Park: Monday–Friday, 11 a.m.–sunset; Saturday–Sunday, 9 a.m.–sunset. Parking is in the lot at Pen Mar County Park. If parking overnight for hiking on the trail, you will need to get a parking placard from Washington County Parks & Facilities.

MAPS: Potomac Appalachian Trail Club *Appalachian Trail Across Maryland, Sections 1 to 7;* USGS *Smithsburg*

FACILITIES: Restroom and pavilions at Pen Mar County Park

CONTACT: Washington County Parks & Facilities, 240-313-2700, washco-md.net/parks _facilities/p-PenMarPark.shtm

COMMENTS: Exercise great caution at High Rock when wet.

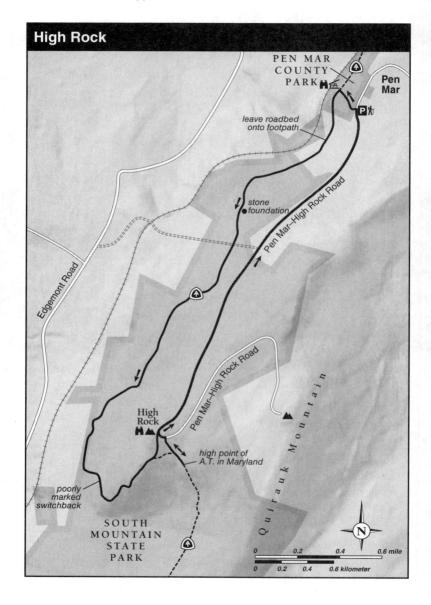

High Rock

PEN MAR COUNTY PARK

Pen Mar

leave roadbed onto footpath

Pen Mar–High Rock Road

stone foundation

Edgemont Road

High Rock

Pen Mar–High Rock Road

high point of A.T. in Maryland

Quirauk Mountain

poorly marked switchback

SOUTH MOUNTAIN STATE PARK

N

| 0 | | 0.2 | | 0.4 | | 0.6 mile |

| 0 | 0.2 | 0.4 | | 0.6 kilometer |

Overview

This northernmost hike in Maryland follows the Appalachian Trail (A.T.) southbound along the west flank of South Mountain and then up to the excellent overlook at High Rock. To make a loop, the hike follows Pen Mar High Rock Road back to the parking area.

Route Details

Begin at Pen Mar County Park in Washington County, Maryland, just south of the state line with Pennsylvania. In the late 19th century, Pen Mar Park was the site of a resort that was extremely popular with visitors from nearby (70 miles away) Baltimore, Maryland. In its heyday, the park sported an amusement park, with a movie theater, dance pavilion, and playground, among other conveniences. The popularity of the park declined by the 1930s, and it ultimately fell into disuse. Now it is operated as a county park by Washington County in Maryland. Pick up the A.T. and follow it southbound from near the pavilion and overlook. The trail begins by following an old road cut from the park for 0.5 mile. Then the A.T. departs the roadbed as a wide soft footpath to the left, with dirt and very few rocks.

At 1 mile, you'll pass an old circular stone foundation on the left about 80 feet across. You can walk up on top of it and look

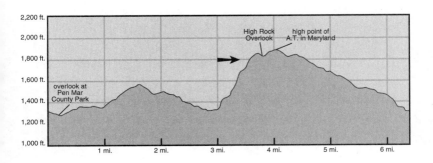

down into it; a fire ring is located at the bottom. I have been unable to determine what this feature is, but I suspect that it dates back to the Civil War. Afterward, the trail joins an old logging grade, and after a short climb in the vicinity of a private residence, it passes through a gas pipeline cut and across an old forest road.

Two miles into the hike, the trail gets very rocky and passes through an unusual stand of oak trees with twisted and gnarled top branches. After 0.5 mile of difficult walking, the trail bends to the east and begins to climb. You'll encounter a couple of switchbacks in this area, one of which is not especially well blazed, and it is apparent that people have walked right past it. The ascent of the hillside makes for pretty tough going, but it doesn't last very long, and soon the terrain levels out and becomes much more pleasant. At 3.1 miles, you'll reach a junction with a blue-blazed side trail with a sign that says HIGH ROCK OVERLOOK, AT SOUTH. Essentially, the blue-blazed trail provides access to High Rock, which the A.T. bypasses, and will eventually rejoin the A.T. about 0.25 mile farther along, where you will find a sign that reads HIGH ROCK OVERLOOK, AT NORTH. I doubt anyone actually skips going out to High Rock, but if you stick to the A.T., you will miss it.

Turn left and follow the blue-blazed trail over to High Rock, which is 0.25 mile farther (3.25 miles total). High Rock Overlook is an interesting phenomenon for more than just geological reasons. The overlook is a large, and quite tall, outcrop of hard quartzite, the top of which is at the level of the road and the parking lot. It drops off to the west a good 75 feet or more, providing an excellent view of the Great Valley. In spite of several signs admonishing people not to do so, the entire thing has been spray-painted with graffiti in quite an elaborate array of colors. In fact, there were people spray-painting it as I stood on top. In spite of the defacement of the natural wonder, all of the painting seemed to me to be rather compelling from a sort of Pop Art aesthetic. The top of the overlook slopes gently to its precipitous western edge, and you should exercise great caution in the rain, as the surface gets very slippery. The situation is exacerbated by the abundance of spray paint. The interest of the view to the west is second only to the intrigue of the graffiti.

From High Rock, you can make an easy loop out of the hike by following Pen Mar–High Rock Road back to the parking area. The hike along the road is just shy of 2 miles long and takes about 40 minutes. The road is busy on weekends, enough so that you might be best doing the hike as an out-and-back trip. But it is not so busy during the week. For those who might be interested, according to the official Potomac Appalachian Trail Club map, the highest point of the A.T. in Maryland is located along the first mile of trail south of High Rock. The location is not identified by any landmark, but I investigated and it seems to be just beyond a short, steep, rocky rise not far south of the junction with the blue-blazed High Rock Trail. There is no marker.

Nearby Attractions

Monterey Pass Pub & Eatery (717-387-5418; montereypasspub.com) is located at the corner of Pen Mar Road and Old PA 16. It opens at 4 p.m. and serves dinner beginning at 5 p.m. Directly behind it is Blondies (717-762-9030; blondies-pa.com), which is also a pub that shares the same building but is a different establishment. It has good burgers and sandwiches and opens for lunch at 11 a.m.

Directions

From the officially designated Appalachian Trail Community of Waynesboro, Pennsylvania, follow PA 16 east 8 miles to Pen Mar Road. Turn right onto Pen Mar Road and follow it 1.0 mile to Pen Mar County Park. Parking is on the left side of the road across from the park.

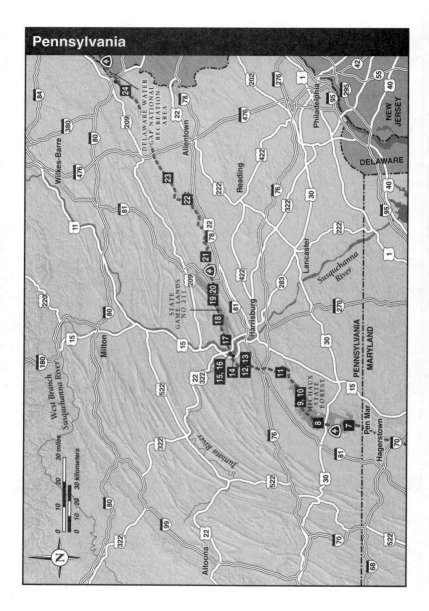

Pennsylvania

THINGS CAN GET PRETTY BUSY ON A WEEKEND ON TOP OF POLE STEEPLE, WHICH IS UNDERSTANDABLE GIVEN THE BREATHTAKING SETTING AND BEAUTIFUL VIEW. *(See Hike 10, page 78.)*

7   CHIMNEY ROCKS p. 60

8   HOSACK RUN p. 65

9   TOMS RUN AND SUNSET ROCKS p. 71

10   POLE STEEPLE p. 78

11   CENTER POINT KNOB p. 83

12   PA 850 TO TUSCARORA TRAIL p. 88

13   COVE MOUNTAIN SOUTH p. 93

14   COVE MOUNTAIN NORTH p. 98

15   CLARKS FERRY VIA SUSQUEHANNA TRAIL p. 104

16   CLARKS FERRY AND PETERS MOUNTAIN p. 109

17   TABLE ROCK p. 115

18   PA 325 TO PA 443 p. 121

19   COLD SPRING AND RAUSCH GAP p. 128

20   YELLOW SPRINGS FROM PA 443 p. 133

21   ROUND HEAD AND SHIKELLAMY OVERLOOK p. 140

22   PULPIT ROCK AND THE PINNACLE p. 145

23   PA 309 TO BEAR ROCKS p. 152

24   MOUNT MINSI p. 158

Chimney Rocks

SCENERY: ★ ★ ★ ★
TRAIL CONDITION: ★ ★ ★
CHILDREN: ★ ★ ★
DIFFICULTY: ★ ★ ★
SOLITUDE: ★ ★ ★ ★

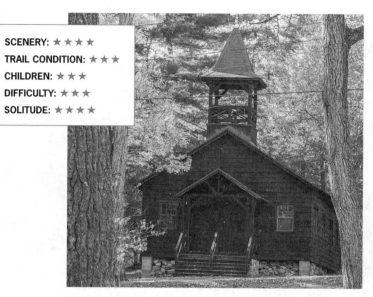

THE OLD CHURCH ACROSS THE ROAD FROM THE OLD FORGE PICNIC AREA

GPS TRAILHEAD COORDINATES:
Old Forge Picnic Area trailhead: N39° 47.729' W77° 28.972'
Alternate trailhead on Old Forge Road: N39° 48.090' W77° 28.630'

DISTANCE & CONFIGURATION: 5.1-mile balloon (3.7 miles if you park at the A.T. crossing on Old Forge Road)

HIKING TIME: 3–4 hours

HIGHLIGHTS: Nice view from Chimney Rocks

ELEVATION: 900' at trailhead at picnic area; 990' at trailhead on Old Forge Road; 1,960' at Chimney Rocks

ACCESS: Open 24/7; no fees or permits required

MAPS: Keystone Trails Association *Map 4, Appalachian Trail, US Route 30 to PA–MD State Line;* USGS *Fairfield* and USGS *Iron Springs*

FACILITIES: Toilet, picnic facilities, and water at Old Forge Picnic Area; privy at Tumbling Run Shelters

CONTACT: Michaux State Forest, 717-352-2211, tinyurl.com/michauxsf

COMMENTS: Parking is limited on Old Forge Road. There is one spot south of the creek with space for two cars and another north of the creek with space for three.

Overview

This excursion offers a pretty good workout, as it ascends nearly 1,000 feet in 1.5 miles. But the view from the rocks over the Waynesboro Reservoir and the surrounding valley is worth the effort; be sure to bring along a camera and plenty of water. I've laid out the loop section of this trip in a counterclockwise direction (up the Appalachian Trail and down an unnamed blue-blazed side trail) so that the steepest bit of the trail is completed on the ascent (for the sake of those of us with creaky knees). If you decide to do the reverse, my impression is that the unnamed blue-blazed side trail might be more difficult to follow hiking up it than going down it.

Route Details

Begin the hike from the Old Forge Picnic Area, which has plenty of parking, water at a building next to the trailhead, and several places to picnic in a serene setting underneath some expansive shade trees. From the parking lot, pick up the Appalachian Trail (A.T.) northbound at the southeast corner of the grassy area, directly behind the small pump house. The trail enters the woods heading east and meanders through some moist woodland over some old puncheons and steps for 0.3 mile to Rattlesnake Run Road, which it crosses, and then continues through much of the same for another 0.4 mile to Old Forge Road, where the trail and the road cross Tumbling Run. Alternately one can begin the hike here, which will knock 1.5 miles off of the total trip and make for a balloon hike with a very short string. Parking at Old Forge Road, however, is limited to two cars south of the bridge over Tumbling Run, and three cars north. Parking along the road is not permitted.

Upon reaching Old Forge Road, follow the A.T. along the shoulder over the creek and then north (left) back into the woods. After 0.25 mile of flat walking, you'll come to a fork in the trail. An unnamed blue-blazed trail turns left, and the A.T. (and this hike) heads to the right. The Tumbling Run Shelters and several camping

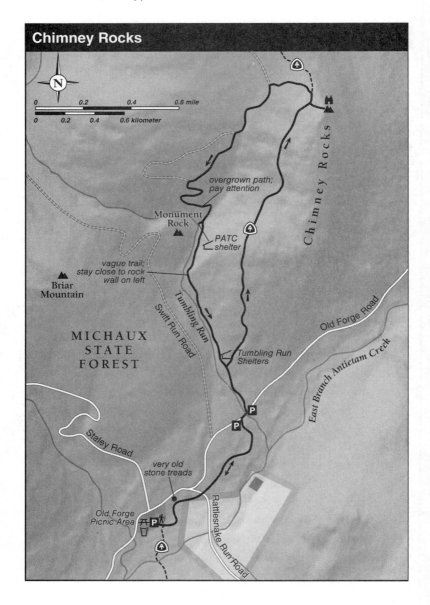

Chimney Rocks

N

| 0 | 0.2 | 0.4 | 0.6 mile |
| 0 | 0.2 | 0.4 | 0.6 kilometer |

overgrown path; pay attention

Monument Rock

PATC shelter

Chimney Rocks

vague trail; stay close to rock wall on left

Briar Mountain

Swift Run Road

Tumbling Run

MICHAUX STATE FOREST

Old Forge Road

Tumbling Run Shelters

East Branch Antietam Creek

Staley Road

very old stone treads

Old Forge Picnic Area

Rattlesnake Run Road

spots are located between the two trails just beyond the fork. As I passed the shelters, I spoke with a couple of hikers who were from Israel and were hiking the trail from the Hudson River to Harpers Ferry. I dropped my pack and chatted for a while, inquiring about sections they would recommend in New Jersey and New York. They gave me plenty of information, and soon I was back on my way.

From the shelters, the A.T. climbs for the next 1.1 miles. Though it never gets really steep, the grade is consistent, and by the time you reach the ridgetop, you'll have worked up a good sweat. Upon reaching the ridge, you'll see a sign marking the blue-blazed trail toward Chimney Rocks, located 0.25 mile to the south (right) along the ridge. A few minutes of walking along that trail will take you to the top of a large, blocky outcrop at the ridge, looking out over an excellent view of the Waynesboro Reservoir. This is a great place to hang out and take a nice, long break. Beware, however, that the rocks are prime timber rattlesnake habitat. They aren't abundant, but this would be a good place to run across one.

To make the loop back to the shelters, hike back to the junction with the Appalachian Trail. Continue on the A.T. northbound 100 feet or so, and then pick up a blue-blazed footpath north and west (turn left off the A.T.). Follow it to an old forest road in 0.25 mile at a flat area where there is a sign for Chimney Rocks. The path follows blue blazes down the forest road for 0.25 mile to a fork. It continues

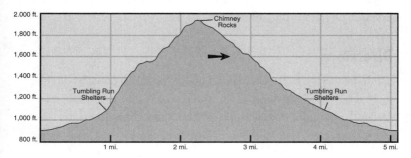

from the fork downhill to the left and shortly thereafter arrives at a series of switchbacks. While the route is fairly obvious all along, at the fourth switchback (1.0 mile from the A.T.; you will be turning to the south, or right), the path was overgrown enough that wandering off into the woods didn't seem inconceivable. It bears paying a little extra attention.

Just beyond that last switchback, the trail forks again at a very large pine tree. To the right at the fork, the trail crosses over Tumbling Run via a couple of planks and ascends to the Hermitage Cabin, one of the Potomac Appalachian Trail Club cabins (reservations required). Staying left at the big tree, the trail follows the east side of the creek, which has obviously flooded recently. In the area of a long rock outcrop on the left, the path is a little difficult to follow. Following the outcrop to its end, along the easiest course within 10 feet or so of it, the trail soon reappears and veers a little more eastward just beyond the cliff. Another 0.5 mile and you are back at the junction with the A.T. near the shelters, the end of the loop. From here, the parking area is another 1.7 miles along the A.T. southbound.

Nearby Attractions

The Old Forge Picnic Area at the trailhead is a nice place to relax. Caledonia State Park, which has picnicking, camping, and swimming facilities, is located to the north at the intersection of US 30 and PA 233 (see directions for Hosack Run on page 70).

Directions

From the intersection of US 30 and PA 233 near Caledonia State Park in Fayetteville, Pennsylvania, continue on PA 233 south 6.0 miles to South Mountain Road. Head east on South Mountain Road 1.8 miles. Turn right onto Old Forge Road and follow it south 4.0 miles. Parking and the picnic area will be on the left side of the road across from a prominent old church.

Hosack Run

SCENERY: ★ ★ ★ ★ ★
TRAIL CONDITION: ★ ★ ★
CHILDREN: ★ ★ ★
DIFFICULTY: ★ ★ ★
SOLITUDE: ★ ★ ★ ★ ★

WITH ITS HANGING PLANTS, CLEAN SLEEPING QUARTERS, AND METAL ROOF, THE QUARRY GAP SHELTER IS EXTRAORDINARILY WELL MAINTAINED.

GPS TRAILHEAD COORDINATES: N39° 54.612' W77° 29.187'

DISTANCE & CONFIGURATION: 6.0-mile balloon

HIKING TIME: 3.5–4 hours

HIGHLIGHTS: Spectacular rhododendron forest, the wild and secluded Hosack Run

ELEVATION: 957' at trailhead; 1,816' at top of Hosack Run

ACCESS: Open 24/7. If parking at Caledonia State Park overnight, you must register at the park office.

MAPS: Keystone Trails Association *Map 2–3, Appalachian Trail, PA Route 94 to US Route 30*; USGS *Caledonia Park*

FACILITIES: Restrooms, water, picnic facilities, swimming pool, and camping at Caledonia State Park

CONTACT: Caledonia State Park, 717-352-2161, dcnr.state.pa.us/stateparks/findapark /caledonia

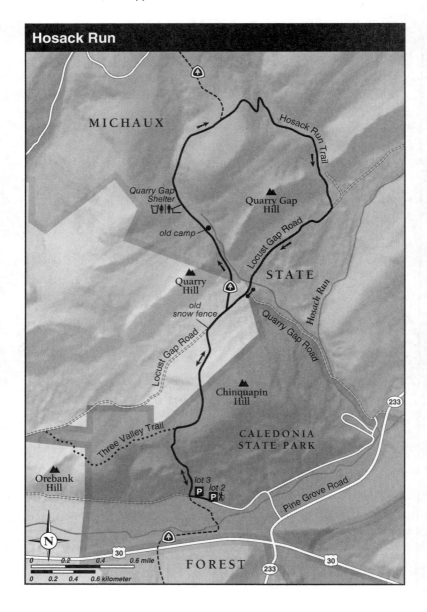

Hosack Run

MICHAUX

Hosack Run Trail

Quarry Gap Shelter

old camp

Quarry Gap Hill

Locust Gap Road

STATE

Hosack Run

Quarry Hill

old snow fence

Quarry Gap Road

Locust Gap Road

Chinquapin Hill

CALEDONIA STATE PARK

233

Three Valley Trail

Orebank Hill

lot 3

lot 2

P P

Pine Grove Road

N

0   0.2   0.4   0.6 mile

0   0.2   0.4   0.6 kilometer

30

30

233

FOREST

233

Overview

A fine loop hike with a section of out-and-back to begin and end, this excursion traces the entire length of the wild and secluded Hosack Run, a short, steep-sided, and rhododendron-filled valley. Of particular interest will be the rhododendron forest along the Appalachian Trail (A.T.), which at times is so thick that it is like walking through a tunnel. This hike is exceptionally beautiful in late spring when the flora is in bloom.

Route Details

I've done a loop over Hosack Run via the A.T. several times from the Long Pine Run Reservoir trailhead to the north and have always loved it. This variation of the loop, which provides more A.T. miles, begins to the south at Caledonia State Park. Start hiking from parking lot 2 at the day-use area of the state park, following the service road that runs along the north side of the parking lots to the west. The A.T. crosses the service road about 100 yards beyond lot 3, and at the crossing, the hike picks up the trail northbound (turn right). The first 0.5 mile or so of the A.T. offers hiking that is, shall we say, a little bit stiff. It initially climbs some steep, rocky steps from the service road and then continues meandering up a steep hollow at a

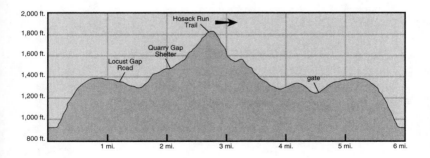

pretty good grade for 0.6 mile. Approaching the top of the hollow, the trail makes a single, small switchback, which serves as a good marker that the grind is almost over. Soon, the trail tops out on a ridge at the junction with the Three Valley Trail on the left.

From the trail junction, follow the A.T. north (right) and traverse along the western slope of Chinquapin Hill another 0.6 mile until you reach Locust Gap Road, bordered on either side by the remains of an old snow fence. The A.T. turns right here (northeast) and in a short distance (0.15 mile), it bears left (north) up into the steep-sided Quarry Gap. The rhododendron forest along this section of trail is remarkable. The trees are so dense in places that the feeling is of walking through a tunnel. A couple of tenths of a mile along they open up in the area of an old camp on the right, and then they get dense again as the trail climbs several stone steps into the heart of Quarry Gap.

At 2 miles, the trail reaches a small clearing at the Quarry Gap Shelter, about as nice a place to spend the night on the A.T. as any I could imagine. The shelter is clean and well kept and is divided into two sides that will sleep four to six people each. It has a sheltered

PUNCHEONS ACROSS THE CREEK NORTH OF THE QUARRY GAP SHELTER

eating area and is almost always adorned with fresh hanging plants placed there by JIM STAUCH "INNKEEPER," as a sign on the shelter reads. There are also tent platforms, a privy, and water. After a rest and a drink, follow the A.T. farther into the gap. Initially, the trail beyond the shelter provides for level but fairly rocky and awkward walking. Then it crosses the creek, becoming less awkward but considerably more steep.

The steep walking continues for 0.75 mile. Then the trail levels out and the Hosack Run Trail enters from the northeast (right) at a well-marked junction (2.7 miles). Turn right onto the Hosack Run Trail and follow blue blazes through oak and hickory trees over the ridge and via switchbacks that descend the steep hillside into Hosack Run, which is in effect a short, steep-sided hollow. The descent is not very long, less than 0.5 mile, and the bottom of the valley is an area about as remote and secluded as one can imagine. The forest floor is thick with rhododendrons. When I was last through here, just as I was saying to myself, "If I were some kind of reclusive animal [which at times I am], this is where I would want to be," I heard something crashing off into the woods on the far side of the creek. I never could ascertain what it was, other than big, but it got my blood running.

The Hosack Run Trail now continues along the west side of the hollow above the creek and the most dense underbrush for 0.3 mile, at which point it descends and crosses to the east side of the small creek and soon thereafter back to the west. The hiking throughout the hollow is somewhat slowgoing on account of many roots growing up through the trail, but it is quite beautiful. The east side of the hollow, which is covered with talus and rock outcrops, is especially impressive.

Soon enough, Hosack Run widens, and the trail meets Locust Gap Road, marked with a sign at a clearing. Continuing now to the southwest (turn right) along Locust Gap Road, the hiking is level and easy and passes by some clearings, which provide nice, sunny places to rest. At 4.7 miles, Locust Gap Road crosses the end of Quarry Gap Road at a gate and then ascends back to the junction with the A.T. in 0.1 mile, completing the loop section of the hike. From the junction with the A.T., about 1.2 miles of hiking, mostly downhill, remain back to the parking area.

Nearby Attractions

Caledonia State Park has several excellent campgrounds, picnic facilities, and two pavilions, as well as a swimming area. Pine Grove Furnace State Park is located 15 miles north on PA 233. The Appalachian Trail Museum is located there and is well worth visiting. Visit atmuseum.org for information and hours.

Directions

This hike begins and ends in Caledonia State Park, located on US 30 at the junction with PA 233 east of Chambersburg, Pennsylvania. From I-81, take Exit 16, and head east on US 30 8.6 miles. Turn left onto PA 233, and go 0.2 mile to the park entrance on the left. Drive past the park office and visitor center, and follow the park road around toward the day-use area. Park in lot 2 or 3. The A.T. crosses the service road that passes the parking areas on the north side about 100 yards west of lot 3.

9 # Toms Run and Sunset Rocks

THE OLD FURNACE STACK AT PINE GROVE FURNACE STATE PARK STANDS RIGHT NEXT TO THE APPALACHIAN TRAIL.

SCENERY: ★ ★ ★ ★
TRAIL CONDITION: ★ ★
CHILDREN: ★
DIFFICULTY: ★ ★ ★
SOLITUDE: ★ ★ ★

GPS TRAILHEAD COORDINATES: N40° 1.900' W77° 18.312'

DISTANCE & CONFIGURATION: 7.9-mile balloon

HIKING TIME: 4–5 hours

HIGHLIGHTS: Camp Michaux, the Sunset Rocks ridge, the center point of the A.T. as of 2016

ELEVATION: 858' at the trailhead; 1,460' atop Sunset Rocks

ACCESS: Open 24/7. If parking overnight at Pine Grove Furnace State Park, you must register at the park office.

MAPS: Keystone Trails Association Map 2–3, Appalachian Trail, PA Route 94 to US Route 30; USGS Dickinson

FACILITIES: Restrooms, general store, picnic facilities, and campground at Pine Grove Furnace State Park

CONTACT: Pine Grove Furnace State Park, 717-486-7174, tinyurl.com/pinegrovefurnacesp

COMMENTS: Though none of the hiking on this excursion is especially steep or difficult, the Sunset Rocks ridge does require some scrambling over rock outcrops and a little bit of route finding. It is worth noting that the rocks along the ridge provide excellent habitat for timber rattlesnakes.

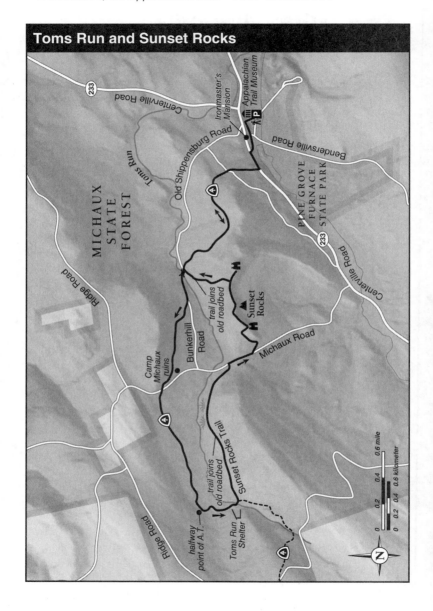

Toms Run and Sunset Rocks

Overview

My favorite hike in the Michaux State Forest area, this hike follows the Appalachian Trail (A.T.) from Pine Grove Furnace State Park for roughly 4 miles to the Toms Run Shelter where it picks up the Sunset Rocks Trail. The 0.5-mile hike through and over and around the rocks along the ridge is great fun, and the overlook at the end can't be beat for the view and for the big, flat sitting rock (a nice place for an afternoon siesta).

Route Details

Begin this hike at the Furnace Stack parking area at Pine Grove Furnace State Park, following the A.T. southbound in front of the Appalachian Trail Museum. The museum has several exhibits on the history of the trail and is well worth visiting. From the museum, the trail heads south (left), passes in front of the park's general store, and then follows Bendersville Road past the Ironmaster's Mansion hostel for a short distance to PA 233. Turn south (left) on PA 233, and walk along the east verge of the road to the second power line pole, where the A.T. crosses the road and enters the woods along a private drive heading north (0.4 mile).

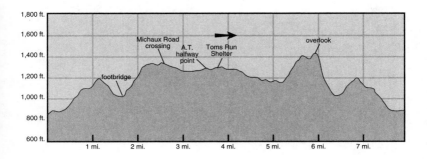

Follow the trail for a little over a mile until you reach Toms Run, where a footbridge crosses the small creek and the Sunset Rocks Trail departs to the left. The loop section of the hike begins and ends here. I was once tempted to do the loop clockwise from this location and set off up to Sunset Rocks. The trail is a steep grind of about 0.6 mile to the ridge. After I got there, I didn't feel like going any farther, and I just came back down. The loop offers a much more pleasant hike when done counterclockwise; all of the climbing is gradual, and Sunset Rocks provides an excellent climax near the end of the trip.

TOMS RUN DOESN'T GET MUCH BIGGER THAN THIS BEFORE IT FLOWS INTO MOUNTAIN CREEK.

After crossing Toms Run, continue southbound along the A.T. up a short hill to a gated road. This is Bunkerhill Road. If you are interested in visiting the Camp Michaux ruins, which I recommend, the best course of action is to follow Bunkerhill Road out to Michaux Road, turn right, and walk up to the parking area for the ruins. Camp Michaux has had several previous lives before its current status as a historical site. It served as a Civilian Conservation Corps camp during the Great Depression, a prisoner of war camp during World War II, and a church camp after the war. From the ruins, you can regain the A.T. by walking up Michaux Road a couple of hundred yards farther to where the A.T. crosses the road. If you are not interested in visiting Camp Michaux, cross Bunkerhill Road and follow the A.T. uphill through some tall brush and woods 0.8 mile to where it crosses Michaux Road and reenters the woods at a gated forest road.

From Michaux Road, the trail follows an old forest road west 1.1 miles to the Toms Run Shelter. A level, dirt path that is easy on the feet, it passes through a forest that, in the summer, has a dense understory of rich green ferns. About 0.25 mile shy of the shelter resides the current midpoint of the A.T., which changes every few years as sections are rerouted and the trail gets longer or shorter. A regal post and sign identify its location. The Toms Run Shelter is located at the site of an old logging settlement, and the remains of a chimney stack still stand in the vicinity of the shelter.

From the shelter, continue along the A.T. a short distance, crossing Toms Run, to the southern terminus of the blue-blazed Sunset Rocks Trail on the left (4.0 miles). Rather rough on the ankles for a distance, this trail proceeds east for a level but rocky mile until it too reaches Michaux Road, which the trail follows south (right). The trail reenters the woods on the left after 0.25 mile at a private driveway. Follow the blazes around the perimeter of the property and then up to a nice viewpoint on the west end of Little Rocky Ridge. This is a good spot to stow any gear you might be carrying in your hands (such as a camera or hiking poles) because you will need both of them for traversing the ridge.

Beyond the viewpoint on the ridge, the hike takes on a different character. For the next 0.5 mile, the trail weaves along a dramatic rocky ridge that requires some scrambling as well as a bit of route finding and decision making. Though blue blazes continue along the ridge, at several points the trail splits, with one direction offering an awkward walk-around and the other direction offering a more exposed climb over. None of the route is any more difficult than scrambling at times, though a misstep in places could have unpleasant consequences. Bear in mind that the rocks are prime habitat for timber rattlesnakes, of which a good population exists in this part of the state. I've never seen one, but I always exercise caution and look before sticking my hands and feet into cracks and crevices.

The difficulties are over with when the trail arrives at a dirt saddle on the ridge and descends precipitously to the north. Resist the temptation to descend immediately, for the best is yet to come. Continuing along the ridge to the east from the saddle, an indistinct trail winds uphill through the pine trees 0.15 mile to an outstanding and very secluded overlook—Sunset Rocks proper. Plan on spending quite a bit of time here. The rocks are called Sunset Rocks for good reason, and if you choose to watch the sun set, bear in mind that an additional 2.0 miles of hiking remain between the ridge and the trailhead.

From the overlook, return to the saddle and follow the trail off the ridge to the north. Though the descent is not long, it is steep. Descending to the A.T. at Toms Run takes about 20 minutes, and walking back to the parking area takes another 40 minutes.

Nearby Attractions

Aside from Pine Grove Furnace State Park, which has lakes for swimming and canoeing as well as a nice campground, the Appalachian Trail Museum is located right next to the parking area. The museum is a must-visit for any A.T. hiker worth his or her salt, as well as for anyone who is simply interested in the trail's history. It is a small museum, but it packs a lot of information, with exhibits on the

THE PRESENT (2016) MIDPOINT OF THE APPALACHIAN TRAIL IS A COUPLE OF HUNDRED YARDS NORTH OF THE TOMS RUN SHELTER. UNTIL A FEW YEARS AGO IT WAS NEAR POLE STEEPLE, SEVERAL MILES TO THE NORTH. *(See Hike 10, page 78.)*

history of the trail, some of its early hikers, and all kinds of trail trivia. My favorite exhibit describes the construction and replacement of trail signs, which includes an early endpoint sign from the summit of Mount Katahdin (I swear it is the same one from when I first climbed Katahdin in 1973). The museum includes a small shop, staffed by volunteers, that has books, maps, mugs, and other A.T. paraphernalia. Visit atmuseum.org for hours.

Directions

From I-81, near Newville, Pennsylvania, take Exit 37, and head 8.1 miles south on PA 233. Turn left onto Bendersville Road to enter the park. The trailhead and parking area are located around the corner from the Pine Grove Furnace State Park office near the general store. Park in the A.T. section of the Furnace Stack parking lot. The A.T. skirts the parking lot to the north and west.

Pole Steeple

SCENERY: ★ ★ ★ ★
TRAIL CONDITION: ★ ★
CHILDREN: ★ ★ ★ ★
DIFFICULTY: ★ ★
SOLITUDE: ★

THE APPALACHIAN TRAIL MUSEUM IN THE BACKGROUND IS LOCATED NEXT TO THE PARKING LOT FOR THE A.T. IN PINE GROVE FURNACE STATE PARK.

GPS TRAILHEAD COORDINATES: N40° 1.898' W77° 18.314'

DISTANCE & CONFIGURATION: 5.8-mile out-and-back or balloon variation

HIKING TIME: 3–4 hours

HIGHLIGHTS: Overlook atop Pole Steeple

ELEVATION: 850' at trailhead; 1,312' at Pole Steeple

ACCESS: Open daily, sunrise–sunset; no fees or permits required

MAPS: Keystone Trails Association *Map 2–3, Appalachian Trail, PA Route 94 to US Route 30;* USGS *Dickinson*

FACILITIES: Restrooms, general store, picnic facilities, and campground at Pine Grove Furnace State Park

CONTACT: Pine Grove Furnace State Park, 717-486-7174, tinyurl.com/pinegrovefurnacesp

COMMENTS: This hike can be very busy on weekends.

Overview

Pole Steeple could very well be the most visited backcountry overlook that I have been to in Pennsylvania. Expect crowds on nice weather weekends. But the view and the setting are about as good as it gets in southern Pennsylvania, with the tall cliffs and forest canopy spread out beneath you. This excursion avoids much of the traffic on the Pole Steeple Trail from the main trailhead and parking area near Laurel Lake by following the Appalachian Trail (A.T.) from the Pine Grove Furnace Stack to the Pole Steeple Trail on top of Piney Mountain and out to the overlook.

Route Details

Pole Steeple is likely the most popular hike in Pine Grove Furnace State Park and probably all of Michaux State Forest for good reason: it is easily accessible and the overlook is quite dramatic with excellent views to the west. But the popularity comes with a price: both the overlook and the main access trail can be quite crowded. When I did the hike on a pleasant Saturday in October, the overlook was verging on mayhem—kids, dogs, families, and people shouting and singing songs. But much of the crowding depends on timing; I have also been there when not a soul was around. Plus, the overlook is spacious and people come and go, so visiting it is definitely worth the effort.

This hike to Pole Steeple follows the A.T. northbound from the Furnace Stack parking area in Pine Grove Furnace State Park to the upper junction with the Pole Steeple Trail. It consequently has the advantage of being less traveled than the main route from Mountain Road. From the parking area, follow the A.T. due east (northbound on the trail). For the first 0.5 mile, it follows a service road and paved footpath through a day-use area, past a concession, and ultimately across Mountain Creek out to the scenic Fuller Lake. Upon reaching the lake, the A.T. turns left (still east) onto another service road that is shared with bicyclists for 0.5 mile along Mountain Creek to a gate. The creek along the path for the final 0.25

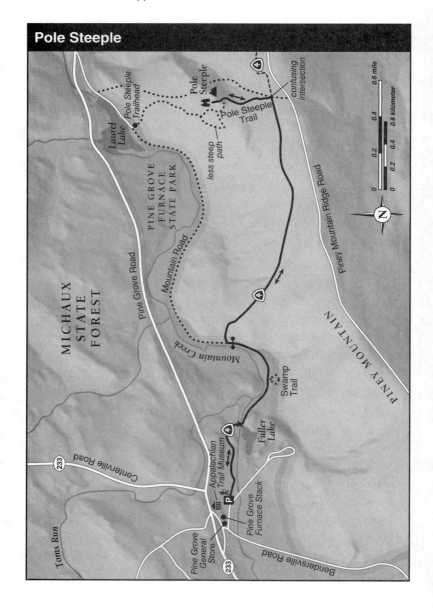

Pole Steeple

Pole Steeple

confusing intersection

Pole Steeple Trailhead

Pole Steeple Trail

less steep path

Laurel Lake

PINE GROVE FURNACE STATE PARK

Mountain Road

Pine Grove Road

MICHAUX STATE FOREST

Mountain Creek

Swamp Trail

Fuller Lake

Appalachian Trail Museum

Piney Mountain Ridge Road

PINEY MOUNTAIN

Toms Run

Centerville Road

233

Pine Grove General Store

Pine Grove Furnace Stack

Bendersville Road

233

N

0   0.2   0.4   0.6 mile

0   0.2   0.4   0.6 kilometer

mile is quite lovely, especially when the leaves are changing color. Beyond the gate, the road (now Mountain Road) heads north and east. It is paved and open to vehicular traffic, which is very light.

At the gate, the A.T. heads east (right) onto an old forest road and climbs for the next mile onto Piney Mountain. At the time of this writing, the A.T. along this section was rutted and washed out on account of recent heavy rains. So the walking was a bit rough in places and the trail moderately steep. But I would still recommend the hike for children age 10 or older as it is never really unpleasant or difficult. The forest is quite pretty along the ascent as well, especially off to the north where it consists of large hickory and oak trees. Approaching the ridge, the A.T. levels off and is less rugged, and the hiking becomes quite pleasant. At 2.4 miles, the A.T. comes to a broad saddle on the ridge and a confusing junction of several trails going off in five directions, including the path just completed. Two paths leave the A.T. to the north. The Pole Steeple Trail, identified by an old sign and blue blazes, makes the sharpest left of the two and heads directly north. I have run into people who have inadvertently taken the wrong path, which can make for a long expedition to places other than Pole Steeple. Be sure that you are following blue blazes and on the correct path before venturing too far afield.

Once on the Pole Steeple Trail, follow the blazes 0.3 mile toward the overlook. Just before reaching the overlook, the trail

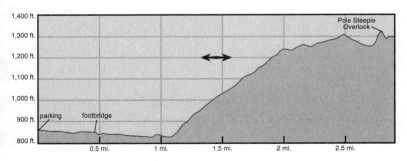

passes the descent path to the main trailhead on the left, and then climbs a series of stone steps to the overlook. Please exercise caution here. The cliffs are 50 feet or so tall, and there is some loose rock.

To make this an out-and-back hike, retrace the route back to the A.T. and follow it southbound. To make a balloon configuration, follow the signs and blazes for the Pole Steeple Trail down to the main trailhead and parking area on Mountain Road (0.75 mile). From the trailhead, head west (left) and follow Mountain Road back to the A.T. at the aforementioned gate. From the gate, it is 1.0 mile back to the parking area.

Nearby Attractions

Aside from Pine Grove Furnace State Park, which has lakes for swimming and canoeing as well as a nice campground, the Appalachian Trail museum is located right next to the parking area. The museum is a must-visit for any A.T. hiker worth his or her salt, as well as for anyone who is simply interested in the trail's history. It is a small museum, but it packs a lot of information, with exhibits on the history of the trail, some of its early hikers, and all kinds of trail trivia. My favorite exhibit describes the construction and replacement of trail signs, which includes an early endpoint sign from the summit of Mount Katahdin (I swear it was the one from when I first climbed Katahdin in 1973). The museum includes a small shop, staffed by volunteers, that has books, maps, mugs, and other A.T. paraphernalia. Visit atmuseum.org for hours.

Directions

From I-81, near Newville, Pennsylvania, take Exit 37, and head 8.1 miles south on PA 233. Turn left onto Bendersville Road to enter the park. The trailhead and parking area are located around the corner from the Pine Grove Furnace State Park office near the general store. Park in the A.T. section of the Furnace Stack parking lot. The A.T. skirts the parking lot to the north and west.

Center Point Knob

THE OLD CARLISLE IRON WORKS FURNACE AT THE BOILING SPRINGS TRAILHEAD FOR CENTER POINT KNOB

GPS TRAILHEAD COORDINATES: N40° 8.877' W77° 7.419'

DISTANCE & CONFIGURATION: 5.4-mile out-and-back

HIKING TIME: 3 hours

HIGHLIGHTS: Carlisle Furnace, Center Point Knob, pretty walk through open fields

ELEVATION: 471' at trailhead; 1,100' at Center Point Knob

ACCESS: Open 24/7; no fees or permits required

MAPS: Keystone Trails Association *Map 2–3, Appalachian Trail, PA Route 94 to US Route 30;* USGS *Mechanicsburg* and *Dillsburg*

FACILITIES: Restroom and picnic tables at Carlisle Iron Works Furnace

CONTACT: Appalachian Trail Conservancy, Mid-Atlantic Regional Office, 717-258-5771, appalachiantrail.org; Cumberland Valley Appalachian Trail Club, cvatclub.org

COMMENTS: The first (and last) mile or so of this hike follows the A.T. right-of-way through private farmland. Please be sure to stay on the trail and obey posted signs.

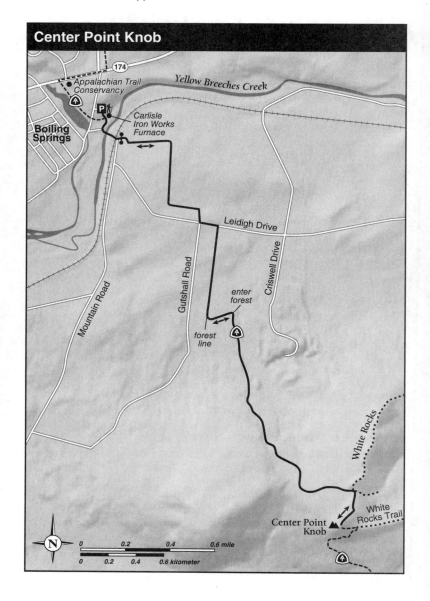

Center Point Knob

174

Yellow Breeches Creek

Appalachian Trail
Conservancy

P

Carlisle
Iron Works
Furnace

Boiling
Springs

Leidigh Drive

Mountain Road

Gutshall Road

Criswell Drive

enter
forest

forest
line

White Rocks

Center Point
Knob

White
Rocks Trail

N

| 0 | 0.2 | 0.4 | 0.6 mile |
| 0 | 0.2 | 0.4 | 0.6 kilometer |

Overview

So named because it once was the center point of the Appalachian Trail (A.T.), Center Point Knob is a pretty little hill just a couple of miles south of Boiling Springs, Pennsylvania, the home of the mid-Atlantic office of the Appalachian Trail Conservancy (A.T.C.) and an officially designated Appalachian Trail Community. Though the knob is tree covered, you can still obtain a nice view from the top, which is an excellent place to picnic. It's a good family outing.

Route Details

Though Center Point Knob is kind of an insignificant little bump of a hill with a semiobstructed view, the hike to it makes for a very pleasant couple of hours along the trail. Plus, the top of the knob is a very serene place to spend some time. The hike begins at the Carlisle Iron Works Furnace parking area in Boiling Springs. Dating back to 1760, the blast furnace structure is an impressive monument to the industrial history of the region. From the parking lot, follow the A.T. southbound across the footbridge over a tributary of Yellow Breeches Creek and to the right. The A.T. heads west along this little penin-sula and ultimately continues to Mountain Road, which it follows over Yellow Breeches Creek proper. Mountain Road is a fairly busy thoroughfare and the stone bridge over the creek is narrow, so use

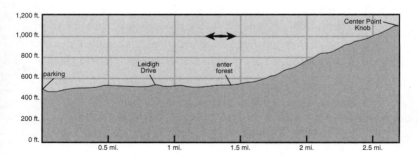

caution while crossing. Once over the creek, the trail leaves the main road to the left at a gate onto a service road, which it follows east through some trees to the edge of a large field where a sign indicates that the A.T. turns right; a campground for A.T. hikers lies straight ahead. Follow the A.T. to the south (right), staying in the forest for a short distance, and then follow it east (left) out into the field.

For the next 0.5 mile, the A.T. makes its way east and south across cornfields and meadows, and the hiking couldn't be more pleasant. The path is easy to follow, level and smooth; posts with white blazes are placed every hundred yards or so along the trail; the hills that form the north edge of South Mountain spread out to the south; and the fields provide habitat for all sorts of songbirds and hawks, such that carrying binoculars is not a bad idea. Follow the trail posts through the fields and out to Leidigh Drive. Cross the road and follow the shoulder east (left) for a hundred yards or so. The A.T. turns south (right) from the road and follows the edge of a cornfield directly to the forest. Upon reaching the forest, the A.T. heads east (left) once more and follows the edge of the woods for a short distance before heading south (right) and entering the woods. All of the turns are well marked.

Once in the woods, the trail begins the ascent to Center Point Knob, following a small drainage to the east. The climb begins very gently at first and gets gradually steeper farther up the hillside. It climbs only about 400 feet over the course of a mile, so it is never especially steep. At 2.5 miles, the trail reaches a saddle on the ridge, a point where some confusion can occur, especially during the fall when leaves are covering the ground. The ubiquitous white A.T. blazes are, surprisingly, not so ubiquitous in this area. A faint trail continues straight over the ridge; that is the *incorrect* path. The correct path along the A.T. turns right and continues to the south along the ridge. Another trail to the north (left) heads to White Rocks, which may be of interest to some hikers. The White Rocks Ridge is, in effect, a stretch of tall, east-facing cliffs popular with local rock climbers. The trail follows the cliff band on its west side, and there are several places where one can scramble on top to take in a view.

From the saddle, follow the A.T. south along the ridge to the summit of Center Point Knob, identified by a large stone block with a plaque depicting a hiker. Center Point Knob at one time marked the center point of the A.T., now located about 18 miles south near the Toms Run Shelter (see page 71). From Center Point Knob, heading north back toward Boiling Springs, the A.T. descends into the Cumberland Valley, where it remains for 17 miles until it climbs Blue Mountain, atop of which it meets the Darlington and Tuscarora Trails (see page 88). Though the top of Center Point Knob is covered with pine trees, a view can be had toward the northwest to another hill (identified incorrectly as Center Point Knob on some maps) and over the Cumberland Valley. To complete the hike, retrace the route back to Boiling Springs.

Nearby Attractions

The mid-Atlantic Appalachian Trail Conservancy regional office is located on the trail in Boiling Springs. You can stop here for information and to chat with thru-hikers. The office has a small shop, which sells a selection of maps and guidebooks and a small selection of A.T. paraphernalia (such as shirts and hats).

Directions

You'll need to get to the trailhead in Boiling Springs, Pennsylvania, which can be no small matter. The easiest, though not the shortest, way to get there is to pick up PA 74 in Carlisle, Pennsylvania, and follow it south about 5 miles to PA 174. Turn right onto PA 174 and follow it 1.9 miles to Boiling Springs. As you approach town, turn left onto Bucher Hill Road. Follow this road 0.25 mile to the parking area for the Carlisle Iron Works Furnace on the left. If you pass Bucher Hill Road, you will come to the A.T.C. office on the left next to the pond in the center of town in about 0.25 mile, and you can stop there and turn around (Bucher Hill Road would be the first significant right coming from the A.T.C. office).

PA 850 to Tuscarora Trail

SCENERY: ★ ★ ★
TRAIL CONDITION: ★ ★ ★
CHILDREN: ★ ★ ★
DIFFICULTY: ★ ★
SOLITUDE: ★ ★ ★ ★ ★

SOME OF THE PRETTY MEADOWS THE TRAIL PASSES THROUGH BEFORE ASCENDING TO THE DARLINGTON AND TUSCARORA TRAILS

GPS TRAILHEAD COORDINATES: N40° 19.311' W77° 4.686'

DISTANCE & CONFIGURATION: 5.2-mile out-and-back

HIKING TIME: 3.5 hours

HIGHLIGHTS: Lots of quiet and solitude; meeting point of Tuscarora, Darlington, and Appalachian Trails; Darlington Shelter

ELEVATION: 669' at trailhead; 1,202' at Tuscarora Trail

ACCESS: Daily, sunrise–sunset; no fees or permits required

MAPS: Keystone Trails Association *Map 1, Appalachian Trail, Susquehanna River to PA Route 94;* USGS *Wertzville*

FACILITIES: Privy at Darlington Shelter

CONTACT: Pennsylvania Game Commission, 717-787-4250, tinyurl.com/pagamelands; Susquehanna Appalachian Trail Club, satc-hike.org

Overview

While this hike offers little in the way of panoramic views, it follows an especially secluded section of the Appalachian Trail (A.T.) up to the crest of Blue Mountain, where the Tuscarora Trail meets the Darlington Trail.

Route Details

The beginning of this hike is distinctive. From the parking area, the A.T. southbound proceeds south across a broad rolling meadow, then to the west across Millers Gap Road and through another rolling meadow bounded to the north by farmland. To the north, Cove Mountain defines the horizon; to the south, you can view Blue Mountain and the series of rises and ridges that ascend to it. Such open, rolling terrain without an abundance of development is uncommon for the A.T. in Pennsylvania, where the trail typically passes through forest and along (and over) ridges.

After 0.5 mile of walking through this terrain, make an abrupt turn to the south (left) and enter a wooded hollow that divides two meadows rising to the east and west. The last time I passed through here, I spooked a dozen turkeys drinking from the little creek in the hollow. Continue into the hollow, and soon you'll reach a concrete water tank located on the side of the trail, filled with clear water. After another 0.25 mile, the A.T. emerges from the end of the hollow and crosses a gravel road that doesn't appear on any of my maps. It looks recently constructed, and looking as far as I could down it, I spied a gate, which suggests that it may be a private drive. From that road, follow the trail as it climbs gently to the south through a forest of oak and hickory trees to an old logging road where it veers to the east (left). Follow that over and around the crest of a low ridge, Little Mountain, heading to the west after crossing the ridge. As the trail descends the south side of the ridge into a small valley, the atmosphere of the hike changes dramatically. The forest is considerably more densely treed than the other side of the ridge, creating a

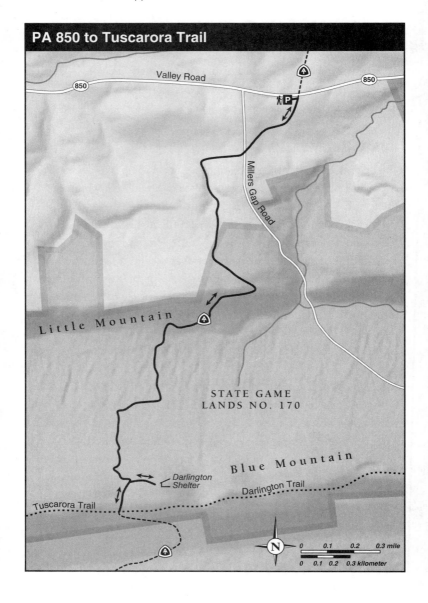

PA 850 to Tuscarora Trail

landscape of tall vertical shafts in the low morning sun. After a short descent, the trail reaches the valley floor, wooded, broad, and flat; a more secluded spot I could hardly imagine. The only sounds you are likely to hear are the occasional call of a crow or rattle of woodpecker atop the whisper of leaves shaking in the breeze.

From the low point of the valley, at 1.5 miles, the trail climbs quite gently for 0.3 mile before becoming considerably steeper for the next 0.5 mile. While it never gets unpleasantly precipitous, you'll likely break a sweat even on a cool fall morning. Just as it begins to level out and traverse the hillside, you may spy a double blaze on a tree, indicating that the trail should turn directly uphill, though the path appears to continue straight (east) across the hillside. Stick to the well-worn path, which makes a switchback to the west after 0.1 mile from the double blaze, and just beyond that, you reach the blue-blazed side trail to the Darlington Shelter.

Save a trip to the shelter for the return, and continue along the A.T. to the ridgetop, 0.2 mile distant, which is reached easily in another 5 minutes. While there is no view to be had from the ridge, a very comfortable log is located at the junction of the Darlington, Tuscarora, and Appalachian Trails. From here, the Darlington Trail extends east 7.7 miles along Blue Mountain. The Tuscarora Trail extends 110 miles southbound to the Maryland and West Virginia state line. The Tuscarora Trail—along with the Big Blue Trail, which extends an additional

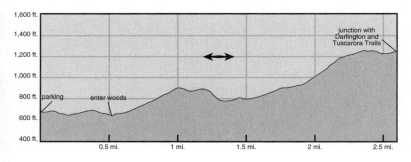

142 miles south from the Tuscarora to the A.T. in Virginia—was constructed as an alternate route to the A.T.

On the descent, you can make a stop at the shelter, where you are likely to run into other people. From the shelter, it is about 1–1.5 hours walking back to the car.

Nearby Attractions

Blue Mountain Outfitters (717-957-2413; bluemountainoutfitters .net) is located in Marysville, Pennsylvania, on US 11 about 0.5 mile south of PA 850 on the east side of the road. Though it specializes in paddling gear, it carries an assortment of outdoor gear, as well as a nice selection of outdoor-related books.

Directions

From I-81, near Harrisburg, Pennsylvania, take Exit 65 for US 11/US 15 and Marysville (this is the first exit after crossing the Susquehanna River heading south and the last exit before crossing the Susquehanna heading north). Follow US 11 north 2.0 miles to Marysville. Head west (left) on PA 850 (there is a traffic light at the intersection). Follow PA 850 7.8 miles to where the A.T. crosses the highway (signed). A small trailhead parking area is just beyond on the south (left) side of the road. If this lot is full, a state game lands parking area is located a mile east on the south side of the road.

Cove Mountain South

SCENERY: ★ ★ ★ ★
TRAIL CONDITION: ★ ★ ★ ★
CHILDREN: ★ ★ ★
DIFFICULTY: ★ ★ ★
SOLITUDE: ★ ★ ★ ★

THE VIEW SOUTH TOWARD THE SUSQUEHANNA RIVER FROM COVE MOUNTAIN

GPS TRAILHEAD COORDINATES: N40° 19.311' W77° 4.686'

DISTANCE & CONFIGURATION: 5.2-mile out-and-back

HIKING TIME: 3.5 hours

HIGHLIGHTS: Excellent view from the pipeline clearing on Cove Mountain

ELEVATION: 669' at trailhead; 1,300' at top of Cove Mountain

ACCESS: Daily, sunrise–sunset; no fees or permits required

MAPS: Keystone Trails Association *Map 1, Appalachian Trail, Susquehanna River to PA Route 94;* USGS *Wertzville*

FACILITIES: None

CONTACT: Pennsylvania Game Commission, 717-787-4250, tinyurl.com/pagamelands; Susquehanna Appalachian Trail Club, satc-hike.org

COMMENTS: This hike passes through Pennsylvania state game lands, and hikers should follow regulations for wearing blaze orange during hunting seasons (see page 22).

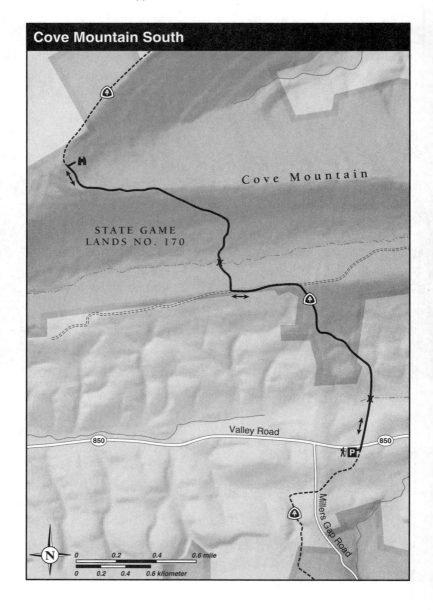

Cove Mountain South

Cove Mountain

STATE GAME
LANDS NO. 170

Valley Road

850

850

Miller's Gap Road

N

| 0 | 0.2 | 0.4 | 0.6 mile |

| 0 | 0.2 | 0.4 | 0.6 kilometer |

Overview

This hike provides the shortest and easiest access to the top of Cove Mountain. Though the final ascent is steep, it is not very long, and the view from the top is spectacular. Plan to have lunch on top or to take a long break.

Route Details

Cove Mountain is distinct among the Ridge and Valley Physiographic Province in central Pennsylvania. While nearly all of the ridges and valleys are linear, running parallel to one another along the geological fold that formed the Appalachians, the ridge that forms Cove Mountain actually curves around, forming a 15-mile-long V-shaped ridge that begins and ends as water gaps on the Susquehanna River separated by only 5 miles. The effect is the creation of a large cove bounded by the ridge on the west side of the river. The phenomenon is easily observed from US 22/US 322 north of Harrisburg. On the east side of the river, the northern ridge of Cove Mountain continues as Peters Mountain, the southern ridge as Second Mountain.

This southern approach to Cove Mountain begins at the parking area on PA 850 like the previous hike. (You could do that hike and this in a long day, totaling about 10.5 miles with nearly 2,000 feet

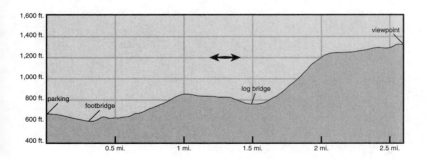

of elevation gain.) Follow the Appalachian Trail (A.T.) northbound across PA 850 and into an open meadow for 0.3 mile. At the end of the meadow, the trail crosses a small creek and muddy area via a bridge and some treads. The path then enters the woods, where it stays for the next 2.3 miles.

At about a mile, the trail joins a logging road, onto which it heads west (left). The A.T. leaves the road to the north (right) at 1.3 miles into the hike, at a well-placed (by the volunteers of the Susquehanna Appalachian Trail Club, which maintains this section of trail) log across the road. If it were not there, hikers would inherently wander past the turn in the A.T. onto private property. After turning, the trail descends into a lovely hollow filled with young pine trees that look as soft as they are to touch. At the bottom of the hollow, cross a small creek via a footbridge made of two logs. On the tree at the north end of the bridge, a sign intended for southbound hikers recommends collecting water from this creek because the water supply at the Darlington Shelter is unreliable.

From the creek, you'll begin to climb the south flank of Cove Mountain. At first, the ascent is quite gentle. After 0.25 mile, the

A BIT OF FERN READY TO DROP BEFORE WINTER SETS IN

trail veers to the west (left) along an old skidway, and it gets steep. Chug away up the hill for about 20 minutes. Right before gaining the ridge, the trail gets rocky, and then it levels out. For the remaining 0.5 mile, the terrain is generally flat. Soon the trail veers to the north and emerges from the woods at a little wooden sign in the shape of an arrow pointing east and understatedly inscribed with the word VIEW.

About 200 feet to the east of the sign, you'll find a fire ring and a clearing and, oh yes, a spectacular view of the Susquehanna River and its islands to the southeast. When I arrived here in the fall, I walked over to where the A.T. reenters the woods to the north, just to see what the view was like to the west. Rolling ridges and a few farms define the landscape on that side of the ridge. Interestingly, the foliage in that direction was much more advanced than to the east, and the forest below with all its colors reminded me of a bowl of Trix cereal, with all of its multicolored balls of flavor, that I used to eat when I was a kid.

Nearby Attractions

Blue Mountain Outfitters (717-957-2413; bluemountainoutfitters .net) is located in Marysville, Pennsylvania, on US 11 about 0.5 mile south of PA 850 on the east side of the road. Though it specializes in paddling gear, it carries an assortment of outdoor gear, as well as a nice selection of outdoor-related books.

Directions

From I-81, near Harrisburg, Pennsylvania, take Exit 65 for US 11/US 15 and Marysville (this is the first exit after crossing the Susquehanna River heading south and the last exit before crossing the Susquehanna heading north). Follow US 11 north 2.0 miles to Marysville. Head west (left) on PA 850 (there is a traffic light at the intersection). Follow PA 850 7.8 miles to where the A.T. crosses the highway (signed). A small trailhead parking area is just beyond on the south (left) side of the road. If this lot is full, a state game lands parking area is located a mile east on the south side of the road.

Cove Mountain North

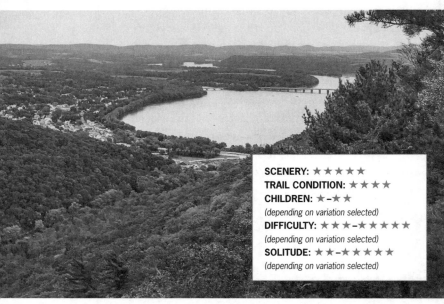

SCENERY: ★ ★ ★ ★ ★
TRAIL CONDITION: ★ ★ ★ ★
CHILDREN: ★ – ★ ★
(depending on variation selected)
DIFFICULTY: ★ ★ ★ – ★ ★ ★ ★ ★
(depending on variation selected)
SOLITUDE: ★ ★ – ★ ★ ★ ★ ★
(depending on variation selected)

THE VIEW NORTH AND EAST OVER SHERMAN CREEK AND THE SUSQUEHANNA RIVER FROM HAWK ROCK

GPS TRAILHEAD COORDINATES: N40° 22.982' W77° 1.979'

DISTANCE & CONFIGURATION: 11.3-mile balloon, with several shorter variations

HIKING TIME: 7–8 hours for the entire route

HIGHLIGHTS: Outstanding views from Hawk Rock and the pipeline clearing atop Cove Mountain, lots of solitude

ELEVATION: 365' at trailhead; 1,331' near high point of Cove Mountain

ACCESS: Daily, sunrise–sunset; no fees or permits required

MAPS: Keystone Trails Association *Map 1, Appalachian Trail, Susquehanna River to PA Route 94;* USGS *Wertzville* and *Duncannon*

FACILITIES: Privy at Cove Mountain Shelter

CONTACT: Pennsylvania Game Commission, 717-787-4250, tinyurl.com/pagamelands;

Susquehanna Appalachian Trail Club, satc-hike.org

COMMENTS: While the hike to Hawk Rock is less than a mile in length, the trail gains nearly 800 feet in elevation. You should consider this before hiking the route with children. The A.T. passes through Pennsylvania state game lands near the pipeline clearing, and hikers should follow regulations for wearing blaze orange during hunting season (see page 22).

Overview

This hike offers several variations that are suitable for trips of a couple of hours, a full day, or even overnight, making use of the Cove Mountain Shelter. The view from Hawk Rock is spectacular and panoramic. The pipeline clearing far out on the ridge offers great views to the southeast and west.

Route Details

Cove Mountain from the north offers myriad possibilities for excellent trips along the Appalachian Trail (A.T.), which include an out-and-back hike to Hawk Rock (about 2 miles round-trip); an out-and-back hike to the pipeline cut on Cove Mountain (about 11 miles round-trip); adding the remote blue-blazed side trail in the valley to the north of Cove Mountain, making a loop with a section of out-and-back to the pipeline (11.3 miles); or running a shuttle to the parking area on PA 850 and making a trip on the A.T. over Cove Mountain for a total of about 8 miles (see the previous hike on page 93 for a description of the trail between the pipeline and PA 850).

Follow the signed trail to Hawk Rock from the southwest corner of the parking area at the Duncannon recycling center. At 0.2 mile, the trail joins the A.T. southbound (turn right) and proceeds uphill 0.6 mile to a switchback and then another 0.1 mile up to Hawk Rock. Though the hike up to Hawk Rock is not especially long at less than a mile in length, it does provide a stiff hill climb. I typically allow 30 minutes from the parking lot to the overlook. Forty-five minutes to an hour is more realistic, especially if you take your time to enjoy the scenery and the nice stone bench alongside the trail about halfway up. Geologically, the hike to Hawk Rock is very interesting because the trail passes through a slide of car-size quartzite boulders. Such slides are uncommon in this part of Pennsylvania, and this one is a testament to the steepness of the mountainside and the effects of freeze–thaw erosion working on the hard geology over millions of years.

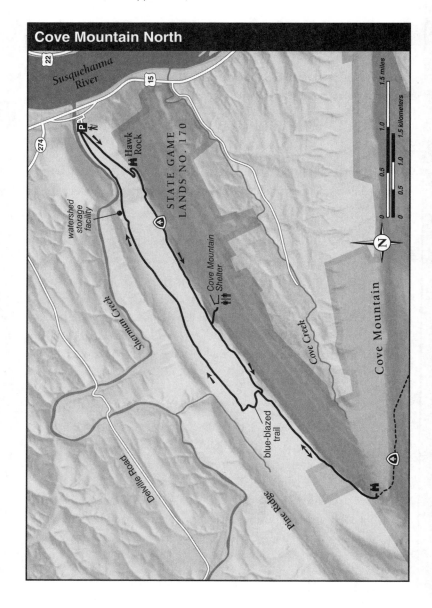

Cove Mountain North

The view from the overlook extends 180 degrees, from Peters Mountain and the meandering Susquehanna River Valley to the east, over Sherman Creek toward Newport in the north, and out toward Bunker Hill and Perry County in the west.

From Hawk Rock, continue southbound on the A.T., following the north ridge of Cove Mountain to the west. At 2.7 miles, blue blazes and a sign mark the side trail to the Cove Mountain Shelter. The shelter has a privy and is located 0.25 mile downhill from the trail. The shelter is unusual because it has no steps up into it from the ground. That is because its "maintainers are trying to convince local porcupines to party in the woods, not the shelter," as a sign explains. Beyond the shelter trail, the A.T. follows the ridge west another 3.0 miles out to the pipeline clearing, which offers impressive views to the Susquehanna River to the southeast and toward Perry County to the west. The hiking is quite secluded and generally flat for the entire distance. If you are planning to do the entire loop with the out-and-back section to the pipeline, you'll need to locate the unnamed blue-blazed side trail that departs from the A.T. to the north, which can be a bit difficult to find. The trail is located midway between the Cove Mountain Shelter trail and the pipeline. The best way to gauge its location walking southbound on the A.T. is either by GPS or by noting the appearance of a broad, wooded hollow to the north

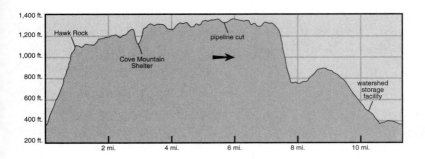

WHITE BANEBERRY IS ALSO KNOWN AS DOLLS EYES FOR GOOD REASON.

(right) of the trail. The junction is just beyond that on the right (N40° 21.439' W77° 05.005'). It is easier to locate returning from the pipeline because the blue blazes face west, and a prominent double blaze indicates its location.

Follow the side trail and descend to the north. Here the character of the hike changes dramatically. The trail is initially not very steep, but it is rather rocky. It obviously follows the path of an old logging skidway. About 0.25 mile down the trail, it bends to the east on a broader old track for 0.1 mile and then makes a precipitous descent straight downhill to the north. The trail is well blazed for its entire length, and it ends at an old forest road where several trees have been painted with big splotches of blue.

The blazes end at the road, but the route finding couldn't be easier. Turn right and follow the road east back to the car. I have always had the feeling when I left the A.T. on the ridge that the hike would be downhill all the way back to the car. Not so. Initially the road ascends to the head of a small valley and passes over a saddle before it begins the descent into the Sherman Creek valley. During the summer and early fall, the road can be a bit overgrown with grasses for about 0.5 mile. But the overgrowth is not a hindrance to hiking, and before long, the grass gives way to dirt. During spring, the forest and meadows along the road are home to a large variety of wildflowers. And some open fields on the left make good habitat for hawks.

Nearby Attractions

The Doyle Hotel (717-834-6789) at 9 N. Market St. in Duncannon, Pennsylvania, an officially designated Appalachian Trail Community, is a popular layover for thru-hikers. It is a good place to stop for a meal or refreshments and to hear stories about people's experiences and encounters on the trail.

Directions

From the intersection of US 22 and US 322 in Harrisburg, Pennsylvania, go 17 miles on US 22 West. Take the exit for PA 849 south to Duncannon. After crossing over the Juniata River, PA 849 turns right onto Newport Road, but you should continue straight into and through Duncannon on North Market Street for 1.3 miles. At the south end of town, follow signs for US 11, turning left onto South Main Street just after passing beneath US 11. Do not get on the highway. Follow South Main Street (which turns into Inn Road) 0.4 mile over Sherman Creek, and turn right onto Little Boston Road. Make the next right onto Watershed Road, which takes you to the town's recycling center. Park at the recycling center, being careful not to park in areas that are posted NO PARKING. The Hawk Rock trailhead is at the southwest corner of the parking area.

15 Clarks Ferry via Susquehanna Trail

SCENERY: ★ ★ ★ ★
TRAIL CONDITION: ★ ★ ★ ★
CHILDREN: ★ ★ ★ ★
DIFFICULTY: ★ ★ ★
SOLITUDE: ★ ★

ONE OF MANY HORNETS' NESTS I ENCOUNTERED

GPS TRAILHEAD COORDINATES: N40° 23.742' W77° 0.535'

DISTANCE & CONFIGURATION: 3.9-mile balloon

HIKING TIME: 2 hours

HIGHLIGHTS: Beautiful views of the Susquehanna River Valley

ELEVATION: 345' at trailhead; 1,257' on Peters Mountain

ACCESS: Open 24/7; no fees or permits required

MAPS: Keystone Trails Association *Appalachian Trail in Pennsylvania, Sections 7 & 8: Susquehanna River to Swatara Gap;* USGS *Duncannon* and USGS *Halifax*

FACILITIES: Privy at Clarks Ferry Shelter

CONTACT: Susquehanna Appalachian Trail Club, satc-hike.org

COMMENTS: The rocks at the overlook provide habitat for timber rattlesnakes, so exercise caution before placing your hands or feet into cracks and crevices.

Overview

This hike provides a nice, slightly longer, and more secluded variation to one of the more popular Appalachian Trail (A.T.) hikes in the Harrisburg area by following the Susquehanna Trail up to the A.T. on Peters Mountain. As a result, the hike provides a few more viewpoints and a nice walk along the ridge. Hikers can also easily access the Clarks Ferry Shelter from the junction of the Susquehanna and Appalachian Trails.

Route Details

Located just a few miles north of the Harrisburg metropolitan area, the hike up to the crest of Peters Mountain overlooking the Susquehanna River at Clarks Ferry is one of the more popular A.T. hikes in central Pennsylvania. The rewards for the mile-long uphill climb are great views up and down the Susquehanna River Valley from the rock outcrops that form the crest of the mountain. Personally, I have always preferred the hike described here, which makes a loop along the crest of Peters Mountain via the Susquehanna Trail and the A.T., to the out-and-back hike to the ridge via the A.T. The variation provides access to plenty of views along the ridge, many of which are less obstructed by trees than the more popular spot at the end of the ridge above the river.

From the car, head north about 50 yards to the obvious A.T. sign indicating the place to cross the railroad tracks east of the river and River Road. Cross the tracks and begin hiking uphill along the trail northbound, first via a set of steps and then along a couple of switchbacks. After the switchbacks, the trail traverses the hillside through tall oak and hickory trees heading southwest about 0.5 mile to the junction with the Susquehanna Trail. Head east (left) onto the Susquehanna Trail (well marked with blue blazes). The Susquehanna Trail rejoins the A.T. a mile from this spot atop Peters Mountain. Follow this level track 0.4 mile to where it crosses the old logging road. Taking the logging road to the east will start you down the long and

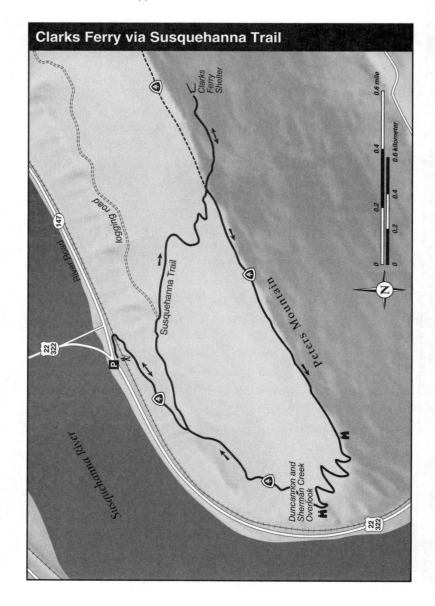

Clarks Ferry via Susquehanna Trail

difficult trek described in the next hike profile. For this hike, though, continue across the logging road and follow the Susquehanna Trail as it makes a meandering, and sometimes a little steep, ascent of Peters Mountain. After 0.6 mile of climbing, the Susquehanna Trail tops out on the ridge, where it meets the A.T. If you have an inclination, or are out for the night, turn left and follow the A.T. northbound to the east, and in 0.25 mile, you'll reach the side trail to the Clarks Ferry Shelter. The shelter has space for six to eight people to sleep, and some tenting is available in the woods nearby.

If you don't have an interest in visiting the shelter, follow the A.T. southbound, heading west along the ridge, which at times requires you to do a little scrambling over and around some rock outcrops. One outcrop, at 2.2 miles, offers a fine view to the south, and shortly thereafter the trail passes over to the north side of the ridge and past numerous outcrops that you can scramble on top of, find a space you can call your own, and take a nice break. The largest outcrops are at the end of the ridge above the Susquehanna River, but these also tend to be the most popular places for people to congregate; if you want solitude, look for a place to rest before crossing over to the north side of the ridge. Bear in mind that this is prime habitat for timber rattlesnakes, and they are often seen in the area. (Note that they are endangered, and it's illegal to kill them in Pennsylvania.)

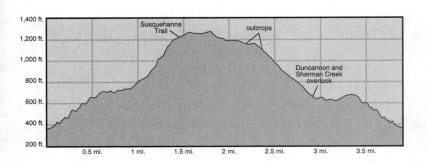

107

From the ridgecrest, descend through a series of switchbacks, and at the bottom of them, you'll find the last scenic viewpoint—an opening through the trees toward Sherman Creek and the town of Duncannon (3 miles). From here, it is another 0.5 mile to the lower junction with the Susquehanna Trail, and then 0.4 mile to the parking area.

Nearby Attractions

The Doyle Hotel (717-834-6789) at 9 N. Market St. in Duncannon, Pennsylvania, an officially designated Appalachian Trail Community, is a popular layover for thru-hikers. It is a good place to stop for a meal or refreshments and to hear stories about people's experiences and encounters on the trail.

Directions

From I-81 north of Harrisburg, Pennsylvania, follow US 22/US 322 north 11.8 miles to the PA 147/Halifax exit. The parking area is on the left at the end of the exit ramp. If this area is full, overflow parking is available on the left side about 50 yards farther. The trailhead is at the obvious A.T. sign just beyond the stop sign looking north.

THIS PAINTED TURTLE WAS KIND ENOUGH TO POSE FOR A PHOTOGRAPH, BRIEFLY.

Clarks Ferry and Peters Mountain

SCENERY: ★ ★ ★ ★
TRAIL CONDITION: ★ ★ ★
CHILDREN: ★
DIFFICULTY: ★ ★ ★ ★
SOLITUDE: ★ ★ ★ ★

VIEW TO THE NORTH FROM THE POWER LINES ATOP PETERS MOUNTAIN

GPS TRAILHEAD COORDINATES: N40° 23.742' W77° 0.535'

DISTANCE & CONFIGURATION: 10.6-mile balloon

HIKING TIME: 6–7 hours

HIGHLIGHTS: Beautiful views of the Susquehanna River Valley

ELEVATION: 345' at the trailhead; 1,360' on Peters Mountain

ACCESS: Open 24/7; no fees or permits required

MAPS: Keystone Trails Association *Appalachian Trail in Pennsylvania, Sections 7 & 8: Susquehanna River to Swatara Gap;* USGS *Duncannon* and USGS *Halifax*

FACILITIES: Privy at Clarks Ferry Shelter

CONTACT: Susquehanna Appalachian Trail Club, satc-hike.org

COMMENTS: Winter and spring are the best seasons for this hike due to a lack of travel on the lower part of the route. Wear blaze orange during hunting season (see page 22).

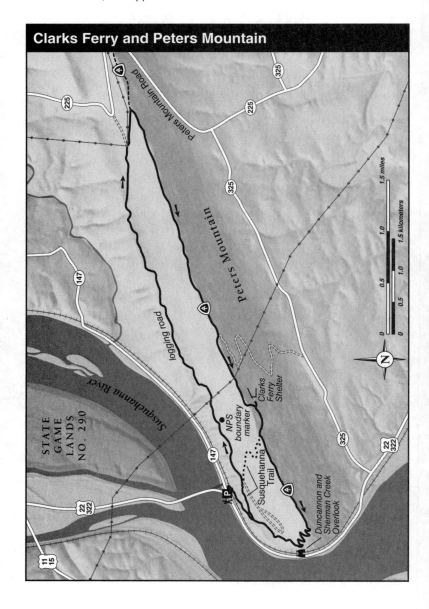

Clarks Ferry and Peters Mountain

Peters Mountain Road

Peters Mountain

logging road

Susquehanna River

STATE GAME LANDS NO. 290

Clarks Ferry Shelter

NPS boundary marker

Susquehanna Trail

Duncannon and Sherman Creek Overlook

1.5 miles

1.5 kilometers

Overview

This hike provides a long, secluded day trip along an old logging road near the base of Peters Mountain. Halfway through the trip, the hike ascends to the crest of the mountain, where it joins the Appalachian Trail (A.T.). It follows the A.T. 6 miles back to the trailhead, passing some excellent views of the Susquehanna River Valley to the north and south.

Route Details

I have long looked at the logging road that is depicted on maps as running east and west below the ridge of Peters Mountain, eventually joining the A.T. about 5 miles from Clarks Ferry, and wondered about the possibility of a long loop hike heading out on that and back on the A.T. On a Saturday late in September, I could no longer curtail my curiosity, and I grabbed my pack and set off to check it out.

From the car, head north about 50 yards to the obvious A.T. sign indicating the place to cross the railroad tracks east of the river and River Road. Cross the tracks and begin hiking uphill along the trail, first via a set of steps and then along a couple of switchbacks. After the switchbacks, the trail traverses the hillside through tall oak and hickory trees, heading southwest about 0.5 mile to the junction

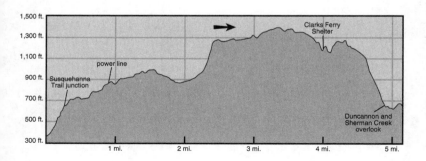

with the Susquehanna Trail. Head east (left) onto the Susquehanna Trail (well marked with blue blazes) and continue along this level track an additional 0.4 mile to where it crosses the old logging road.

At the logging road, I stopped and had a look down it as far I could see. It was covered with tall grasses and weeds, through which not a single boot appeared to have traveled. A hundred yards along there was a tree lying across the trail, and I half suspected that I might run into many such obstacles along its length. I headed east along the logging road, leaving the security of the Susquehanna Trail behind. Though the road is rather thick with tall grass and weeds, the walking is level and not at all difficult to follow. Over the first 0.5 mile, I encountered two trees across the path, neither of which created too difficult an obstacle to negotiate.

A THRU-HIKER TAKES A BREAK AT THE CLARKS FERRY SHELTER.

At 1.5 miles into the hike (0.6 mile along the logging road) a white National Park Service boundary marker with an A.T. symbol is nailed to a tree to the right of the logging road. At 1.9 miles, the road passes beneath a significant power line clearing, complete with tall steel towers and an excellent view to the north. From this point, the logging road is more heavily traveled, displaying evidence of both foot and all-terrain vehicle traffic. Nonetheless, the setting feels quite secluded, having left the din of traffic speeding along US 22/US 322 long behind, and the forest is quite beautiful—it would be a great place to hike in late October when the leaves are changing. Along the next mile, I encountered two black racer snakes coiled on the side of the trail, both of which were quite camera shy, and a small box turtle about 6 inches long.

At 2.8 miles, the road is joined from the northwest (downhill) by another logging road. At 4.4 miles, some power lines enter the road cut from the north and split, with one set of wires heading east along the road and the other back into the woods to the southwest. This is the one part of the trip that involves making a critical route-finding decision. If you continue straight along the road to the east, you'll end up at Peters Mountain Road (PA 225) in 0.5 mile and have to backtrack to this spot. Instead, head southwest (right) and follow the power line uphill. The decision doesn't seem obvious until you reach the first pole above the road, and then you see the power line cut and the trail heading east and uphill to the crest of Peters Mountain. Due to foreshortening, the trail looks much steeper than it is. Though the power line cut looks overgrown, there is a good path along it slightly right of center. After 10 or 15 minutes of climbing, just below the ridge (4.8 miles), the power line cut is crossed by a track that looks as if it has been trammeled by a million Vibram soles. It has. This is the A.T., and onto it you will turn right and head west along the crest of Peters Mountain.

After joining the A.T., the hiking is generally level for the next 3.0 miles. At times the trail is a bit rocky, as the ridgetops in Pennsylvania tend to be, and at times it is nice, smooth dirt. All along the ridge are rock outcrops that offer places to rest and soak up the views. At 7.0 miles, the A.T. joins an old logging path that descends from the ridge to the south. Be sure to stay to the right and on top of the ridge. At 7.5 miles, pass through the upper end of that large power line cut that you passed several hours ago. Not far beyond, the ridge and the trail descend a couple of hundred feet and meet with the blue-blazed side trail that descends to the Clarks Ferry Shelter, about 500 feet to the southeast.

From the shelter path, the ridge climbs again before leveling off at the upper junction with the Susquehanna Trail. Continue along the ridge, following the A.T., which at times requires a little scrambling over and around some rock outcrops. At 9.1 miles, the A.T. comes to the end of the ridge above the Susquehanna River at some of the largest rock outcrops. Descend the ridge through a series of switchbacks, at the bottom of which is the last scenic viewpoint—an opening through the trees toward Sherman Creek and the town of Duncannon (9.7 miles). From here, it is another 0.5 mile to the lower junction with the Susquehanna Trail, and then 0.4 mile to the parking area.

Nearby Attractions

The Doyle Hotel (717-834-6789) at 9 N. Market St. in Duncannon, Pennsylvania, an officially designated Appalachian Trail Community, is a popular layover for thru-hikers. It is a good place to stop for a meal or refreshments and to hear stories about people's experiences and encounters on the trail.

Directions

From I-81 north of Harrisburg, Pennsylvania, follow US 22/US 322 north 11.8 miles to the PA 147/Halifax exit. The parking area is on the left at the end of the exit ramp. If this area is full, overflow parking is available on the left side about 50 yards farther. The trailhead is at the obvious A.T. sign just beyond the stop sign looking north.

17 # Table Rock

LOOKING ACROSS THE CLARK CREEK VALLEY TO THIRD MOUNTAIN FROM TABLE ROCK

SCENERY: ★ ★ ★ ★
TRAIL CONDITION: ★ ★ ★ ★ ★
CHILDREN: ★ ★ ★ ★ ★
DIFFICULTY: ★
SOLITUDE: ★ ★

GPS TRAILHEAD COORDINATES: N40° 24.726' W76° 55.795'

DISTANCE & CONFIGURATION: 4.2-mile out-and-back

HIKING TIME: 2–3 hours

HIGHLIGHTS: Beautiful views from Table Rock and the power line

ELEVATION: 1,220' at trailhead, with no significant rise

ACCESS: Daily, sunrise–sunset; no fees or permits required

MAPS: Keystone Trails Association *Appalachian Trail in Pennsylvania, Sections 7 & 8: Susquehanna River to Swatara Gap;* USGS *Halifax* and USGS *Enders*

FACILITIES: None

CONTACT: Appalachian Trail Conservancy, Mid-Atlantic Regional Office, 717-258-5771, appalachiantrail.org; Susquehanna Appalachian Trail Club, satc-hike.org

COMMENTS: Exercise caution at the Table Rock overlook, especially with young children.

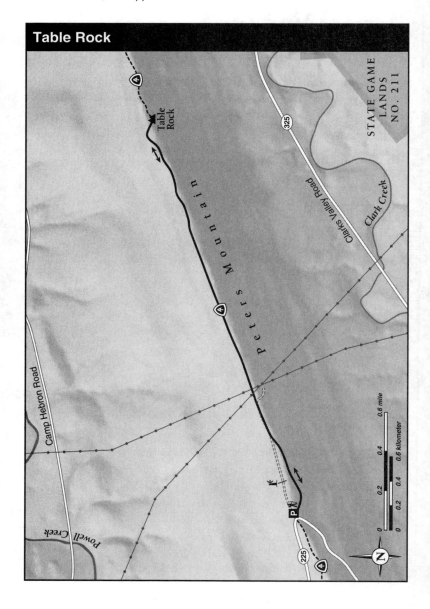

Overview

Though you will be sharing the trail with many people on the week-ends, this deservedly popular out-and-back hike along the crest of Peters Mountain provides an excellent excursion for the entire family. The overlooks at the main power line crossing and at Table Rock serve as ideal locations for a long break or a picnic.

Route Details

The hike along the Appalachian Trail (A.T.) to Table Rock is a popular short day hike in the Harrisburg area. It is an easy hike on a pleasant section of the trail with no significant elevation gain or loss. The fact that the hike begins at the A.T. parking lot on the Peters Mountain ridge is fortuitous because the elevation (predominantly consistent at 1,200 feet) provides for some wonderful views up and down the Susquehanna River Valley. This hike is good even for young kids, though parents will want to exercise great caution at Table Rock because the overlook is not fenced.

This trip is a good place to see some wildlife. It might be a bunch of turkey vultures from the overlook, a nest of squirrels or a deer, or even—as on my last trip—a whole flock of several dozen turkeys; there always seems to be something. Another nice aspect of

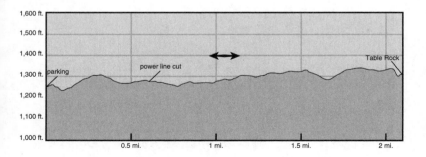

this hike is that, because it is not very long, it makes for a great late-day excursion. When the sun is low in the west, the play of light in the woods on the ridge and up the Clarks Creek valley below to the south is quite beautiful.

The hike itself couldn't be more straightforward. From the parking area, follow the A.T. northbound, heading east. At first, the trail stays to the south side of the ridge to avoid private land and some cellular towers. This initial section of trail is the most rugged, and its passage requires walking around a few rocks. At 0.4 mile, the path joins a

A SPIDER SPINS ITS WEB IN THE PERFECT PLACE TO CATCH SOME LATE-DAY SUNSHINE.

service road and follows that 0.25 mile to a power line clearing at the top of the ridge. From the trail, the view north toward Millersburg, the upper Susquehanna River Valley, and Haldeman Island (a prominent wildlife area) is excellent, even if crossed by power lines and towers. Though it requires a little scrambling, the view from the very top of the ridge to the south is equally impressive. From there, the vista takes in the Susquehanna River Valley, winding south toward Harrisburg, as well as the lay of the valley and ridge topography stretching east and west.

Here, at the power lines, I had an exciting encounter with wild turkeys. I could hear them for quite a distance before reaching the power lines, and just as I reentered the woods from the clearing, the forest exploded with all sorts of commotion. They were everywhere—up on the rocks, scrambling about the trail, and running through the woods to the ridge. A couple came right toward me and then scampered off in different directions. It was quite a treat.

From the power line, the trail remains right on top of the ridge in the woods for the next 1.5 miles to Table Rock. Table Rock is a bit of a misnomer for the geologic feature. I have always thought that Table-on-Its-Side Rock might be more accurately descriptive. The top of the outcrop consists of a few fins of quartzite that provide for rather uncertain footing. The tabletop part of the formation seems more to be the cliff face that drops precipitously for 40 or 50 feet down the hillside. Most people don't realize that the bottom of the cliff is actually a wide ledge and that a second, equally as steep and tall cliff descends from that as well. You have to peer over the edge to be able to see that, and doing so is rather vertiginous.

From the outcrop, one looks across the Clark Creek valley, a good 1,000 feet below, and across to the ridge of Stony Mountain. From the edge of the outcrop, looking west beyond a jack pine tree, the lookout tower on Stony Mountain is visible on top of the ridge. Most of that terrain across the valley is Pennsylvania State Game Lands No. 211, one of the nicest and most remote areas in all of central Pennsylvania. The A.T. enters it from Clark Creek, almost directly below the tower.

From Table Rock, follow the A.T. back to the parking area. The only potential problem area is where the A.T. leaves the service road west of the power line. It is easy to walk past the junction if you aren't paying attention.

Nearby Attractions

The Stoney Creek Inn (717-921-8056; thestoneycreekinn.com), at the intersection of Erie Street and Stony Creek Road in Dauphin borough to the south, is a nice place to grab a bite after the hike.

Directions

From I-81 north of Harrisburg, Pennsylvania, take US 22/US 322 north 6.1 miles to the PA 225/Halifax exit. Follow PA 225 north 3.8 miles to the top of Peters Mountain. The entrance to the A.T. parking area is on the right just before you pass underneath the footbridge.

AN UNOBSTRUCTED VIEW FROM PETERS MOUNTAIN TO THE SUSQUEHANNA RIVER NORTH OF HARRISBURG

SCENERY: ★ ★ ★ ★
TRAIL CONDITION: ★ ★ ★ ★
CHILDREN: ★ ★ ★
DIFFICULTY: ★ ★
SOLITUDE: ★ ★ ★ ★ ★

THE CYRUS C. STURGIS JR. MEMORIAL AT THE WEST TERMINUS OF THE HORSE-SHOE TRAIL

GPS TRAILHEAD COORDINATES:

PA 325 parking and trailhead: N40° 27.089' W76° 46.558'

PA 443 parking and trailhead: N40° 28.903' W76° 33.032'

DISTANCE & CONFIGURATION: 16.2-mile point-to-point

HIKING TIME: 8–9 hours, a nice overnight trip

HIGHLIGHTS: Historical sites including Yellow Springs townsite, the Stone Tower ruins, and the General; the beautiful Rausch Creek

ELEVATION: 577' at the Clark Creek trailhead; 492' at the PA 443 trailhead; 1,618' at 3.45 miles

ACCESS: Daily, sunrise–sunset; no fees or permits required

MAPS: Keystone Trails Association *Appalachian Trail in Pennsylvania, Sections 7 & 8: Susquehanna River to Swatara Gap;* USGS *Enders, Grantville, Indiantown Gap,* and *Tower City*

FACILITIES: Privy and water at Rausch Gap Shelter

CONTACT: Pennsylvania Game Commission, 717-787-4250, tinyurl.com/pagamelands

COMMENTS: Because this hike is entirely on Pennsylvania state game lands, regulations regarding camping apply. Camping is permitted for A.T. thru-hikers entering and exiting the game lands at different points. See page 22 in the "Introduction" for more information on Pennsylvania state game lands regulations.

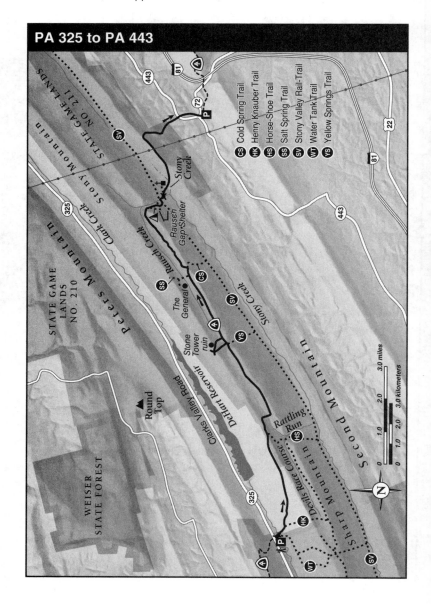

PA 325 to PA 443

GS Cold Spring Trail
HK Henry Knauber Trail
HS Horse-Shoe Trail
SS Salt Spring Trail
SV Stony Valley Rail-Trail
WT Water Tank Trail
YS Yellow Springs Trail

Overview

The section of the Appalachian Trail (A.T.) between PA 325 at Clark Creek and PA 443 near Swatara State Park to the north is the crème de la crème of the trail in Pennsylvania. This 16-mile section of trail passes through the wild country of Pennsylvania State Game Lands No. 211 and provides access to a variety of day trips and remote historical sites. An overnight trip along this stretch of trail can be completed from either direction, leaving a car at the other trailhead and camping along the way (please see the note on Pennsylvania state game lands camping regulations in the "Introduction," page 22). This profile describes a one-way overnight trip heading north-bound on the trail from PA 325. The following two hikes describe day hikes in this area.

Route Details

Leaving the parking area, the A.T. northbound crosses Clark Creek over a concrete bridge and departs from the dirt road to the south (left) just beyond the bridge. For the next 2.0 miles, it makes a steady though not excessively steep ascent to the east along the forested talus slope that forms the north side of Stony Mountain, eventually following the path of an old road dating back to the 19th

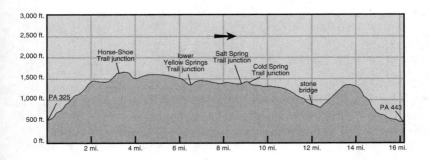

REMAINS OF THE OLD STONE TOWER ON SHARP MOUNTAIN ABOVE YELLOW SPRINGS

century. Along the way, the trail passes the trailhead for the steep and rocky Henry Knauber Trail (0.4 mile) and the remains of several old mining roads that enter and depart the trail, one of which (1.9 miles) still has part of its uphill retaining wall intact.

Just beyond a short section of downhill, the trail makes a short climb to the ridge of Stony Mountain, where it meets the western terminus of the yellow-blazed Horse-Shoe Trail. This 140-mile-long hiking and equestrian path follows foot trails, rights-of-way, and shoulders of roads east to Valley Forge National Historical Park. The beginning of the trail is marked by a yellow horseshoe that has been nailed into a tree, a trail register, and a stone emblazoned with a plaque dedicated to the memory of the late Cyrus C. Sturgis Jr., a frequent traveler from the area. Though the junction with the Horse-Shoe Trail seems a good place for a break, I recommend pushing up the next rise on the A.T. for another hundred yards or so to an even nicer place atop the hill among tall pine trees. Here you will find rocks to sit on and the ruins of some old buildings, remnants of the Rattling Run settlement that was active in this area during the coal-mining days of the 19th century.

From this point, the trail descends gently to a reliable creek, the cool and clear headwater of Rattling Run, and to what is marked on some older maps as the Rhododendron Forest. After crossing the creek, the rhododendrons become quite dense, enough so that I felt it wise to make some noise as I was traveling along so as not to surprise any wildlife that might not appreciate being surprised—namely black bears, which inhabit this area. For a long distance from the creek, the walking is mostly level and pleasant enough, with some short rocky sections. This stretch of trail, all the way east into Rausch Gap, follows the path of an old stagecoach road that connected the several mining settlements along the ridge. At times, the trail is wide and level enough to imagine a stagecoach passing over it; the abundance of rocks, however, suggests that it would have been a rough ride.

At approximately 6 miles into the hike, the A.T. begins a rocky descent into the Yellow Springs drainage, where it crosses the blue-blazed Yellow Springs Trail (6.5 miles). Downhill, this path reaches the Stony Valley Rail-Trail in about a mile (see below). Uphill and north (left) from the A.T., the Yellow Springs Trail offers a nice side trip of some historical interest. Following the bed of the old incline that extends from the top of Sharp Mountain to the old Schuylkill and Susquehanna Railroad line in the Stony Valley, the path runs straight as an arrow up to the ridge, at the top of which is a junction of several trails at a couple of cairns. The blue-blazed Yellow Springs Trail heads east (right) and after 200 yards joins a red-blazed trail that enters from the north side of Sharp Mountain. Turn right again (roughly southeast), and in a short distance the trail arrives at the Stone Tower. At 30 feet tall, this stone construction likely provided ventilation for the deep coal shafts in the immediate area. Return to the A.T. by continuing along the blue-blazed Yellow Springs Trail another 0.25 mile to the old townsite of Yellow Springs, which is identified with a sign and a white mailbox that contains the trail register.

Continuing from Yellow Springs, the walking is generally flat for several miles through open forest in a very secluded setting. At 8.8 miles, the Salt Spring Trail enters from the north (left). Another excellent side trip along this trail leads to the site of the General, an old excavator that remains from the mining days (see page 131). A quarter mile beyond the Salt Spring Trail, the Cold Spring Trail (9.1 miles) enters from the south. From this junction the A.T. northbound begins a slow, steady descent into Rausch Gap (you'll know you are getting close when you start passing piles of culm—old coal debris—on the right), where there are excellent campsites and the blue-blazed side trail (11.4 miles) for the Rausch Gap Shelter.

From Rausch Gap, the hike continues along the A.T. downhill a short distance to the Stony Valley Rail-Trail. Head east (left) and follow the rail-trail over Rausch Creek. From the bridge over the creek, a limestone diversion well is visible upstream on the east side of the creek. The first of its kind in the United States, it was constructed to divert the acidic creek water (an effect of the mining upstream) over the alkaline limestone to reduce the acidity of the water. Upstream from the well, you won't find any fish, but downstream, the water is neutralized enough to support a healthy trout population.

Once across the bridge, the A.T. leaves the rail-trail to the south (right) and follows the path into a beautiful hemlock forest and to the headwater of Stony Creek. After crossing the creek, the A.T. climbs steadily for the next 2 miles to Second Mountain and then another 2 miles down the mountain's other side to the parking area at PA 443 (see the Yellow Springs from PA 443 hike description, page 133).

Nearby Attractions

Harrisburg, Pennsylvania, about 10 miles south of the PA 325 trailhead, has an abundance of culinary and cultural establishments. Lickdale, Pennsylvania, south of the PA 443 trailhead, has gas stations and several convenience stores.

Directions

To the parking area on PA 325: From I-81 north of Harrisburg, Pennsylvania, take US 22/US 322 north 6.1 miles to the PA 225/Dauphin exit. Follow PA 225 north 1.7 miles to PA 325. Turn right and follow PA 325 east 10 miles to where the A.T. crosses the road, and park in the large parking area on the right.

To the parking area on PA 443: From Harrisburg, Pennsylvania, follow I-81 North to Exit 90 for PA 72/Lickdale. Take PA 72 North 3.5 miles to where it ends at PA 443. Turn left onto PA 443 (also called Moonshine Road). The A.T. parking and trailhead are on the left immediately after making the turn.

Cold Spring and Rausch Gap

THE GENERAL, AN OLD EXCAVATOR THAT STANDS IN THE WOODS JUST NORTH OF RAUSCH CREEK

GPS TRAILHEAD COORDINATES: N40° 28.667' W76° 37.565'

DISTANCE & CONFIGURATION: 5.9-mile loop

HIKING TIME: 3–4 hours

HIGHLIGHTS: Historical townsites of Cold Spring and Rausch Gap, beautiful creek in Rausch Gap with its many pools and pour-overs, side trip to the General

ELEVATION: 791' at trailhead; 1,392' at junction with A.T.

ACCESS: Daily, sunrise–sunset; no fees or permits required

MAPS: Keystone Trails Association *Appalachian Trail in Pennsylvania, Sections 7 & 8: Susquehanna River to Swatara Gap;* USGS *Grantville, Indiantown Gap,* and *Tower City*

FACILITIES: Privy and water at Rausch Gap Shelter

CONTACT: Pennsylvania Game Commission, 717-787-4250, tinyurl.com/pagamelands

COMMENTS: Because the road from Second Mountain to the parking area can be quite rough and is infrequently maintained, a high-clearance vehicle may be necessary to reach the trailhead. If you have doubts about whether your car can make the final mile to the trailhead, scout the road by foot first. If in doubt, park on top of Second Mountain and walk into the Stony Creek valley. Doing so will add approximately 2.4 miles to your hike, plus 500 feet of descent and ascent. This hike is entirely on Pennsylvania state game lands, so game lands regulations regarding camping and use apply (see page 22 in "Introduction").

Overview

This loop is one of my favorite excursions in central Pennsylvania. At just shy of 6 miles, it is a manageable length for the whole family. The first mile of the hike consists of a moderate ascent of 600 feet up to the Appalachian Trail (A.T.) on the ridge of Sharp Mountain, and the rest of the hike is downhill. It offers easy access to some of the notable history of the Stony Creek valley and the surrounding terrain, and the area in Rausch Gap where the creek tumbles steeply over boulders is a photographer's paradise. During the spring and fall, this hike is hard to beat.

Route Details

The hike begins at the parking area next to the old townsite of Cold Spring. Originally a popular summer resort during the 19th century, the ruins of the spring and the foundations of the old hotel and the caretaker's house still remain. From the parking area, walk north past the gate across the service road and follow the road around to the west (left). At the intersection with another service road heading north (and which you will follow to the rail-trail) stand the ruins of the caretaker's house and, across the road, the hotel, with the large spruce trees across what must have been its facade. If you have interest in visiting the spring, continue along the road in front of the hotel and follow it downhill to where the spring and pools are located.

Return to the hotel and the caretaker's house and follow the service road north and out to the Stony Valley Rail-Trail, about 0.25 mile. Head east on the rail-trail and walk along it 0.25 mile to where the Cold Spring Trail crosses it. A sign on the left indicates that the A.T. is 1.0 mile uphill from this spot. Follow the blue-blazed trail uphill (north) through the woods. The track is a little rocky but not especially steep. Near the top of the ridge, the path joins an old road and traverses a steep hillside just before gaining the ridge. Once you're on the ridge, the A.T. is 75 feet dead ahead.

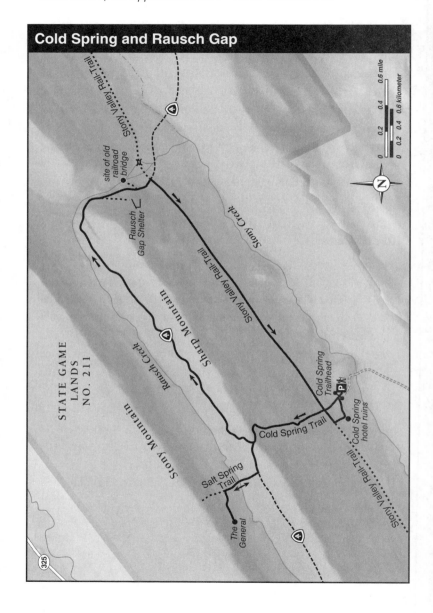

Cold Spring and Rausch Gap

Stony Valley Rail-Trail

site of old railroad bridge

Rausch Gap Shelter

Stony Creek

Stony Valley Rail-Trail

Sharp Mountain

Rausch Creek

STATE GAME LANDS NO. 211

Stony Mountain

Cold Spring Trailhead

Cold Spring Trail

Cold Spring hotel ruins

Stony Valley Rail-Trail

Salt Spring Trail

The General

325

0.2   0.4   0.6 mile
0.2   0.4   0.6 kilometer

N

Before following the A.T. down into Rausch Gap, you can make an interesting side trip to visit the General, the remains of an old excavator from the mining days in the region that was probably used for excavating gravel from a nearby pit. Its presence in the middle of the woods is striking and a testament to the extent of the mining activity that took place in this area. To visit the General, head southbound (left) on the A.T. and follow it west 0.25 mile to the junction with the Salt Spring Trail, entering from the north. Follow the Salt Spring Trail north through dense rhododendrons to Rausch Creek. Crossing Rausch Creek should not be a big deal unless there have been recent heavy rains, as was the case the last time I was there. In this case, head upstream 50 or 100 feet and see if you can find a place to balance your way across from rock top to rock top. If not, the only other choices are to get your feet wet or come back another time.

Once across the stream, continue along the Salt Spring Trail, keeping a lookout for a trail departing to the west (left). At one time, a sign existed marking the beginning of the side trail. I was unable to locate the sign the last time I was there, but a piece of old machinery is nailed to a tree at the junction. The trail is 0.3 mile from the A.T. (N40° 29.342' W76° 38.332'). If the Salt Spring Trail starts climbing steeply, you have gone too far. Follow the trail and some occasional old red blazes west into the woods for another 0.3 mile. The General stands rusting away among the trees (N40° 29.294' W76° 38.555').

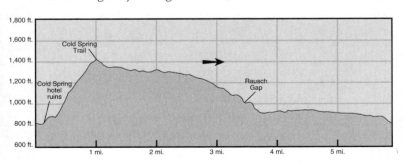

After visiting the General, return to the A.T. and hike east. The trail offers easy walking and descends gently in the direction of Rausch Gap. About 2 miles along the A.T., piles of culm, old coal debris, on the right side of the trail indicate that Rausch Gap is not far, and the trail bends toward the south. Soon, the A.T. enters Rausch Gap proper, where there are plenty of places to hang around and enjoy the scenery along the banks of Rausch Creek. From Rausch Gap, follow the A.T. downhill another 0.5 mile to the rail-trail. Head west (right) on the rail-trail and follow it 2.0 miles back to the Cold Spring Trail. Turn left (south) onto it and return to the parking area. If you should miss the Cold Spring Trail, simply turn left on the road marked COLD SPRING (about 0.25 mile beyond the trail), which will take you back to the hotel area.

Nearby Attractions

If you have an inclination, you might drive over to Hershey, Pennsylvania, after your hike and visit Chocolate World to see how Hershey makes its candy bars. Follow I-81 east toward Harrisburg to the second exit for Hershey, Exit 77, PA 39. Follow PA 39 south 6 miles, past the Giant Center arena. Chocolate World will be on your left.

Directions

From I-81 north of Harrisburg, Pennsylvania, take Exit 85B for PA 934/Fort Indiantown Gap. Drive north on PA 934 0.5 mile and turn left onto Asher Miner Road, which joins PA 443 in 1.1 miles. Follow PA 443 an additional 1.1 miles into the prominent water gap (Indiantown Gap), and turn left onto McLean Road/Ammo Road, following signs for the Second Mountain Hawk Watch. In 0.4 mile turn right onto Cold Spring Road, and follow this 0.5 mile through the military reservation, over the top of Second Mountain, and down to the Cold Spring parking area in a large field in the Stony Creek valley. A high-clearance vehicle is recommended for the descent from Second Mountain to the parking area.

Yellow Springs from PA 443

> **SCENERY:** ★ ★ ★ ★
> **TRAIL CONDITION:** ★ ★
> **CHILDREN:** ★
> **DIFFICULTY:** ★ ★ ★ ★ ★
> **SOLITUDE:** ★ ★ ★ ★ ★

THE APPALACHIAN TRAIL SHARES THE PATH WITH THE STONY VALLEY RAIL-TRAIL FOR A SHORT DISTANCE NEAR RAUSCH GAP.

GPS TRAILHEAD COORDINATES: N40° 28.903' W76° 33.032'

DISTANCE & CONFIGURATION: 19.2-mile balloon

HIKING TIME: 10–12 hours

HIGHLIGHTS: Historical townsites of Rausch Creek, Yellow Springs, and Cold Spring; the beautiful creek in Rausch Gap with its many pools and pour-overs; several optional side trips to sites with interest regarding the 19th-century coal mining operations in the area

ELEVATION: 492' at the trailhead on PA 443; 1,325' atop Second Mountain; 1,450' at Yellow Springs

ACCESS: Daily, sunrise–sunset; no fees or permits required

MAPS: Keystone Trails Association *Appalachian Trail in Pennsylvania, Sections 7 & 8: Susquehanna River to Swatara Gap;* USGS *Grantville, Indiantown Gap,* and *Tower City*

FACILITIES: Privy and water at Rausch Gap Shelter

CONTACT: Pennsylvania Game Commission, 717-787-4250, tinyurl.com/pagamelands

COMMENTS: Because this hike is entirely on Pennsylvania state game lands, regulations regarding camping apply. This hike must be completed in a single day. See page 22 in the "Introduction" for more information on Pennsylvania state game lands regulations.

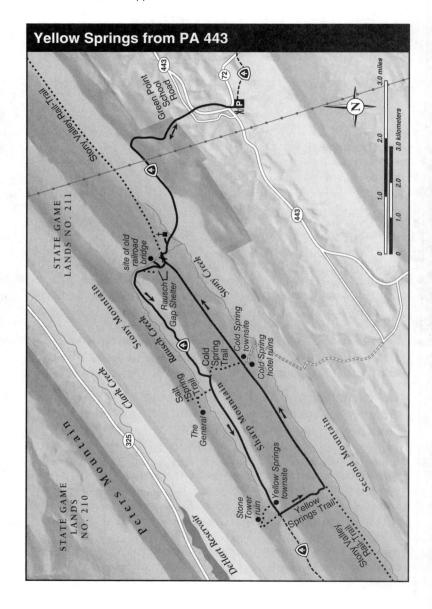

Yellow Springs from PA 443

Overview

This would be a perfectly reasonable day trip if it weren't for the presence of Second Mountain, which adds 4 miles and a significant ascent and descent to both the beginning and end of your day. At 19.2 miles, with 2,500 feet of elevation gain and loss, this is a mighty hike that will challenge even the hardiest of hikers. Add in all of the various side trips that one can visit along the way, and the trip can go as long as 22 miles or more. The hike is best done during the summer, when the days are long. Because of Pennsylvania state game lands regulations, which state that you can only camp along the Appalachian Trail (A.T.) if you enter and exit from different trailheads, the hike needs to be completed in a single day.

Route Details

I had wanted to make this trek for years and had hiked all sections of it except the initial 4 miles over Second Mountain. After working on this book for a couple of months, I thought that I was in good enough shape to take it on. So on Halloween, I left the trailhead at PA 443 at 7 a.m. before the sun had come up over Blue Mountain and melted the frost that covered all of the low bushes alongside the trail. As you follow the A.T. southbound, it initially crosses PA 443

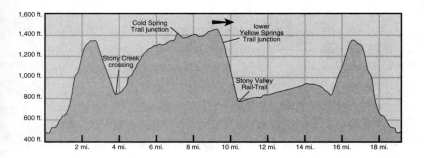

from the parking lot, passes through a small meadow, and follows a creek, Trout Run, underneath PA 443 east of the trailhead. Beyond the overpass, the trail veers to the left, crosses the creek on a log, follows some planks through a marshy area, and then traverses a south-facing hillside, climbing easily until it comes out to PA 443 once again at 0.7 mile. Here the trail crosses the road and then immediately crosses Green Point School Road, after which it enters the woods for a short distance and then passes through a very beautiful meadow. The day I did this hike also turned out to be the first day of gobbler season, and I was very glad to be wearing blaze orange when I saw four hunters stalking game in the fields (see page 22 for regulations regarding the use of blaze orange on Pennsylvania state game lands).

After passing through the field and entering the forest again in the area of some large oak trees at 0.6 mile, the trail begins to ascend Second Mountain. Though only moderately steep, the climb is continuous for 1.5 miles to the ridge of Second Mountain (2.1 miles).

A FEW OLD GRAVESTONES DATING TO THE 19TH CENTURY STILL STAND AT THE RAUSCH GAP CEMETERY.

For about the next mile and a half, the trail stays to the ridgetop. At 3.0 miles, a power line cut offers a view toward Sharp Mountain across the valley to the north, and shortly thereafter the trail reaches a saddle where several old roads cross. The A.T. follows the old forest road to the west and descends the north slope of Second Mountain until it curves around to the north, entering a lovely hemlock forest in the bottom of the valley at a stream crossing, the headwaters of Stony Creek. Cross the creek and follow the level path 0.4 mile out to the Stony Valley Rail-Trail.

Before reaching the rail-trail, after 0.2 mile, a side trail marked by a sign that says CEMETERY departs to the right. The cemetery is the old burial ground for the village of Rausch Gap, which existed in this area 1828–1910, the heyday of coal and iron ore mining in the area. Presently, a half dozen headstones remain, dating back to the 1850s.

After visiting the cemetery, walk out to the rail-trail, and follow the A.T. west over Rausch Creek for 100 yards and then to the north up toward Rausch Gap, leaving the rail-trail behind. Though the A.T. climbs onto Sharp Mountain from the rail-trail, the ascent is quite gradual and the hiking is very pleasant. At 4.9 miles, about 0.5 mile from the rail-trail, the Rausch Gap Shelter trail heads off to the left. Here the A.T. passes through the heart of Rausch Gap. Both sides of the gap are steep and rocky, and the creek tumbles over large boulders among the steep-sided ravine.

Continuing southbound, the A.T. emerges from the gap and for a long distance climbs very gently to the west just north of the Sharp Mountain ridge. It follows the path of an old stagecoach road through beautiful forest with an understory of rhododendrons. This area is referred to on some maps as St. Anthony's Wilderness, and very few areas that are this secluded exist in central Pennsylvania. At 7.1 miles, the Cold Spring Trail enters from the south. The Cold Spring Trail descends 1.0 mile to the rail-trail. If you question your ability to complete the entire hike, or if you have an emergency, this trail offers an escape route or a shortcut. Following it to the rail-trail, and following that east back to the A.T., will knock about 4.5 miles off the hike. A game lands parking area (the trailhead for hike 19, Cold Spring and Rausch Gap) is located at the end of the trail, just beyond the rail-trail (see page 128), and you might be able to get a ride out from there if you have problems.

Continuing west (southbound) along the A.T., the Salt Spring Trail enters from the north after 0.25 mile. The Salt Spring Trail offers a side trip of about 1.5 miles round-trip to the General, an old steam-powered excavator that remains from the mining era (see page 131 for the route description to the General). From the Salt Spring Trail, the A.T. continues west along the old stagecoach road to the townsite of Yellow Springs. As I was closing in on Yellow Springs, I was arrested in my tracks by the sight of the blackest tree stump I had ever seen just off the trail about 75 yards ahead. When it stood up on its hind legs and began sniffing around, I realized that it was no stump. I stood still on the trail for several minutes while the bear looked around, got on all fours, and ambled off in the woods toward the ridge.

The Yellow Springs townsite is identified by a sign, a trail register housed in a white mailbox, and a couple of campsites. Like Rausch Gap, Yellow Springs was a community in this area during the 1800s, and judging by the abundance of old foundations in the woods and the fact that a stagecoach ran by, it must have been a thriving community. Another interesting side trip can be had from Yellow Springs by following the blue-blazed trail that begins at the townsite, up the ridge to the north to the Stone Tower ruin (see page 121).

The hike continues along the A.T. west for another 0.25 mile, lined with old paving stones and steps as it descends into the Yellow Springs creek bed. Some water typically flows in the creek, and immediately after crossing it and climbing a small embankment, the A.T. meets the blue-blazed Yellow Springs Trail, which this hike follows downhill and south for a mile back to the rail-trail. This next mile is definitely the most difficult section of the hike. The trail originally followed the grade of the old incline that ran from the top of the mountain down to the Stony Valley. Uphill from the A.T., the incline runs straight up the hillside. Downhill, it is difficult to discern, and the trail more or less threads its way through trees and boulders along the west side of the creek. The rugged nature of the trail exists, I am told, as a result of Hurricane Ivan, which in 2004 dumped up to 8 inches of rain in central Pennsylvania and washed out much of the lower incline.

So this is all to say, don't count on sprinting down it to the rail-trail; this is a good place to bust an ankle! At times the footing is difficult and the trail not at all clear. Blue blazes mark a path all the way to the rail-trail, but the path can be a little difficult to follow, especially near the bottom where it leaves the creek. Once on the rail-trail, head east (left), and begin the flat walk back to the A.T. at Rausch Gap, 4.2 miles distant. Of interest along the way is the townsite of Cold Spring, which is located 0.25 mile south of the rail-trail along a service road marked with a trail sign that says COLD SPRING (2.0 miles from the Yellow Springs Trail; see page 133). Upon rejoining the A.T. at the bridge over Rausch Creek, you have completed the loop section of the hike. It's only 4.4 miles (over Second Mountain) back to the car. It should come as some consolation that the ascent of Second Mountain from this side is less steep and involves less of an elevation gain than from the trailhead.

Nearby Attractions

Swatara State Park, which is only partially developed, has picnic grounds and an excellent rail-trail open to hikers and bicyclists. Access to the park is gained from PA 443 north of the parking lot on signed roads departing to the right, as well as south on PA 72 about 0.25 mile from the parking lot.

Directions

From Harrisburg, Pennsylvania, follow I-81 North to Exit 90 for PA 72/Lickdale. Take PA 72 North 3.5 miles to where it ends at PA 443. Turn left onto PA 443 (also called Moonshine Road). The A.T. parking and trailhead are on the left immediately after making the turn.

Round Head and Shikellamy Overlook

A COUPLE ENJOYS A LATE-DAY BREAK AT THE SHIKELLAMY OVERLOOK.

SCENERY: ★ ★ ★ ★
TRAIL CONDITION: ★ ★ ★
CHILDREN: ★ ★ – ★ ★ ★
(depending on distance)
DIFFICULTY: ★ ★ ★
SOLITUDE: ★ ★ ★

GPS TRAILHEAD COORDINATES: N40° 30.756' W76° 20.664'

DISTANCE & CONFIGURATION: 10.8-mile out-and-back

HIKING TIME: 5–6 hours

HIGHLIGHTS: Nice views from Round Head and the Shikellamy Overlook, the Showers Steps

ELEVATION: 1,461' at trailhead; 1,620' at the top of Round Head

ACCESS: Daily, sunrise–sunset; no fees or permits required

MAPS: Keystone Trails Association *Appalachian Trail in Pennsylvania, Sections 1–6: Delaware Water Gap to Swatara Gap;* USGS *Swatara Hill*

FACILITIES: None

CONTACT: Pennsylvania Game Commission, 717-787-4250, tinyurl.com/pagamelands

Overview

In addition to a nice walk in the woods, this day trip offers outstanding views of the valley to the south at the two overlooks. From the overlook on the south side of Round Head, a blue-blazed trail follows the remains of the Showers Steps (a series of several stone steps built into the hillside by Lloyd Showers) downhill until it ends at private property. The Shikellamy Overlook provides an excellent lunch spot and destination.

Route Details

This hike begins at the large parking area located where the Appalachian Trail (A.T.) crosses PA 501 at the top of the ridge. This ridge extends west to east for 75 miles from Swatara Gap to the Delaware Water Gap, broken only by the Schuylkill and Lehigh River Gaps, and is referred to as Blue Mountain all the way to Wind Gap, Pennsylvania, an officially designated Appalachian Trail Community 16 miles short of the New Jersey state line. The A.T. generally follows the crest for its entire length.

The A.T. crosses the road immediately south of the parking area. Follow it northbound, heading east from the road. The hike starts out with some tramping over stone treads, which, in wetter years, help hikers navigate a bit of soggy ground. For a distance beyond the treads, the hiking is awkward, verging on unpleasant because the trail is extremely rocky, and many of the rocks are like little pyramids and blocks. A sturdy pair of boots is an asset for this section of trail. But at 0.35 mile, the trail crosses a significant old road cut (the second of several), and afterward the quality of the trail surface improves dramatically. Shortly beyond that road cut, a blue-blazed trail departs to the left to a campsite. A sign indicating a spring points right. The trail continues through the forest to the east, crossing a few more old paths, for another mile, at which point (1.3 miles) the trail curves southeast and out to the edge of the ridge.

Round Head and Shikellamy Overlook

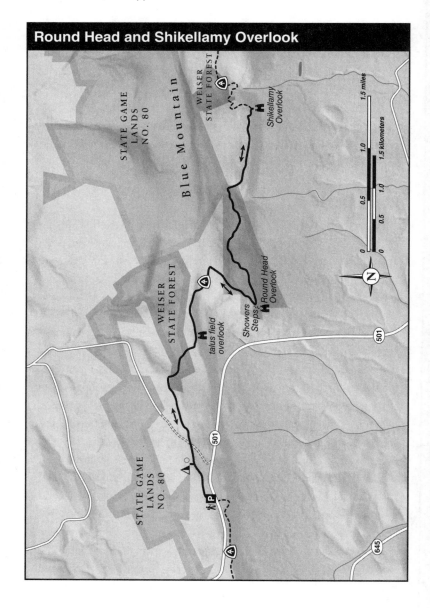

STATE GAME
LANDS
NO. 80

WEISER
STATE FOREST

Blue Mountain

Shikellamy
Overlook

WEISER
STATE FOREST

Round Head Overlook

Showers Steps

talus field
overlook

STATE GAME
LANDS
NO. 80

501

501

645

1.5 miles

1.0

0.5

0

1.5 kilometers

1.0

0.5

0

N

At 2.0 miles, the A.T. reaches a small overlook that offers a view south toward Round Head. A short distance beyond is a second larger overlook at a small talus field that offers a broader view and plenty of big flat rocks on which to sit (2.2 miles). From there, the A.T. continues to the east, climbing gently until 2.6 miles, where it makes a sharp turn to the southwest. If you look around at this point, you'll notice an old, disused trail that heads off to the north and is blocked from use by a pile of logs and debris. According to one of the aged maps I have, that is the old path of the A.T., which has now been rerouted to the south. I hiked that old trail from the east some years ago. It was tough going then, and it doesn't appear to have gotten better with time.

From this point, a pleasant walk along the main trail through rhododendrons and some mixed pine and oak forest leads to the overlook at Round Head and a pleasant vista of the Berks County countryside. This overlook is a popular destination for area hikers, so much so that I've never had it to myself. From the overlook, a blue-blazed trail descends steeply to the south, following the talus field directly below the overlook. This trail follows the path of the old Showers Steps. Originally conceived and largely constructed by Lloyd Showers, an area resident, 500 very steep rock steps guided hikers from PA 501 up to the overlook, probably because the original route of the A.T. bypassed the overlook. I thought I would take a walk at least partway down to check out their condition, and they appear

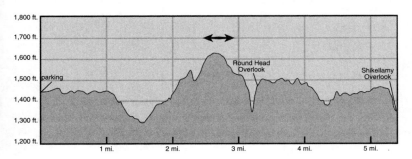

to have not been maintained for many years. If any reader should decide to follow them downhill, I recommend exercising extreme caution. Especially near the top, the trail is quite steep and slippery and abounds with loose rock. The trail ends at private property, and it is no longer possible to reach the highway via the path.

Continuing northbound on the A.T., the trail remains fairly level for the next couple of miles out to the Shikellamy Overlook (5.4 miles). Though there is no single feature along this section of trail that stands out as especially remarkable, the walk through the woods is extremely pleasant and well worth doing. Along the way, I ran into a young boy, Cade, and his father, who told me about seeing a deer and an eagle along the trail. Arriving at the overlook, a pretty outcrop surrounded by trees, I met a couple who were taking in the view of Berks County. They were out hiking for a week and recommended some places to visit along the trail farther north.

On my return to the parking area, the sun dropped low on the horizon, and at times, I could look at the great golden disk behind a silhouette of tree trunks—a wonderful way to end the day.

Nearby Attractions

South of I-78 at Exit 23, east toward Allentown from the exit for the hike, is Roadside America (610-488-6241; roadsideamericainc.com). A classic piece of Americana, it boasts "the world's greatest indoor miniature village." Essentially a huge electric train display, it's worth seeing at least once in your lifetime.

Directions

From I-78 west of Allentown, Pennsylvania, take Exit 13 for PA 501/ Bethel. Follow PA 501 North 4.3 miles to the top of the main ridge. A large parking area occupies the top of the ridge, and the A.T. crosses the road at its south edge.

Pulpit Rock
and the Pinnacle

SCENERY: ★ ★ ★ ★ ★
TRAIL CONDITION: ★ ★ ★ ★ ★
CHILDREN: ★ ★ ★
DIFFICULTY: ★ ★ ★
SOLITUDE: ★ ★

**HIKERS ADMIRE A VIEW OF THE GREAT VALLEY IN BERKS COUNTY
FROM THE PINNACLE.**

GPS TRAILHEAD COORDINATES: N40° 34.975' W75° 56.525'

DISTANCE & CONFIGURATION: 8.7-mile balloon

HIKING TIME: 5–6 hours

HIGHLIGHTS: Pulpit Rock, the Pinnacle

ELEVATION: 775' at the trailhead; 1,523' at Pulpit Rock; 1,581' at the Pinnacle

ACCESS: Daily, sunrise–sunset; no fees or permits required

MAPS: Keystone Trails Association *Appalachian Trail in Pennsylvania, Sections 1–6: Delaware Water Gap to Swatara Gap;* USGS *Hamburg*

FACILITIES: Privy at the Windsor Furnace Shelter

CONTACT: Borough of Hamburg, 610-562-7821, hamburgboro.com

COMMENTS: The hike is through the Hamburg Municipal Watershed, so hikers should be sure to follow posted regulations regarding pets, fires, and access to water.

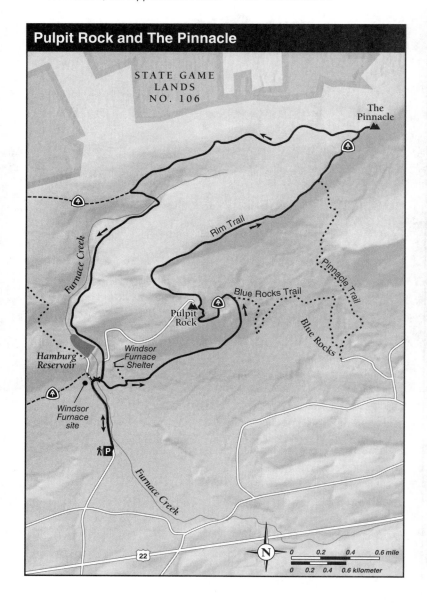

Overview

One of the most popular Appalachian Trail (A.T.) hikes in Pennsylvania, the overlooks at Pulpit Rock and the Pinnacle provide excellent photo ops. The descent along Furnace Creek passes through a remarkable forest of hemlocks and rhododendrons.

Route Details

Great hike? Definitely. Solitude? Not so much. The Pulpit Rock and Pinnacle hike is very popular, and it can be very busy on weekends any time of the year. Even during the week, you probably won't be alone. At almost 9 miles in length, the loop described here offers a variation to the standard out-and-back trip and covers enough terrain to provide some solitude.

From the parking lot, pass the main gate and follow the wide access road for the Hamburg Reservoir to the north. Because much of the hike lies on land administered by the Hamburg Water Authority, you must stay on the trails and respect regulations regarding water usage. The Hamburg borough has posted many signs with regulations and has provided signs with a map that has all of the trails in the watershed indicated. Though you may encounter several yellow gates across access roads to the reservoir adorned with NO TRESPASSING signs, hiking is permitted on the trails that pass by these gates.

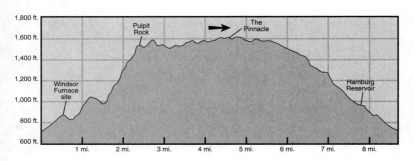

Follow the wide access road toward the reservoir 0.5 mile to where it joins the A.T. at a large clearing below the dam. This area was the site of the Windsor Furnace, one of the many Pennsylvania iron furnaces that were constructed during the 18th and 19th centuries in response to demand for iron products (especially during the Revolutionary War). With vast deposits of iron ore, forests that supplied wood (and consequently charcoal) to fuel the furnaces, and streams for power, a couple hundred furnaces were in operation throughout the

IT'S TOUGH TO MISS THE JUNCTION WITH THE PINNACLE TRAIL; JUST LOOK FOR THE WORLD'S BIGGEST CAIRN!

state by the mid-1800s. Remains of some of the old stonework from the Windsor Furnace can be seen just north of the trail.

From the furnace site, follow the A.T. northbound (turn right), across the bridge over the creek, and to the east (right) along an old forest road for 0.25 mile. At the junction with the blue-blazed side trail for the Windsor Furnace Shelter on the left (0.8 mile), the A.T. leaves the road to the east and becomes a footpath. Walking along the trail is quite pleasant as it climbs gently along the southern flank of the Pulpit Rock ridge and at 1.8 miles meets the side trail to the Blue Rocks Family Campground on the right. An alternate start to the hike, Blue Rocks is a commercial campground accessed from Mountain Road near PA 143. Beyond the junction with that side trail, the A.T. gets moderately steep for a short distance as it swings around to the west and then levels off beneath a large talus field. Pulpit Rock is located atop the talus field.

Follow the A.T. past the talus field and around the ridge to a point where it makes a sharp turn east (right) and climbs over rocks through the woods. At 2.4 miles from the parking lot, the trail reaches the ridge near a private observatory, the Pulpit Rock Astronomical Park, which is run by the Lehigh Valley Amateur Astronomical Society. Pulpit Rock is 50 yards farther along the trail, and it offers an excellent view of Berks County and the Lehigh Valley to the south and east.

The Pinnacle, which offers a view that exceeds in quality even that of Pulpit Rock, is located at the end of the ridge extending east for an additional 2 miles. Also referred to as the Rim Trail between Pulpit Rock and the Pinnacle, the A.T. generally hugs the southern edge of the ridge the whole way across. Within a hundred feet or so of Pulpit Rock, the character of the trail for the next mile heading to the Pinnacle becomes obvious. *Rocky* seems almost an understatement because the crest of the ridge is often little more than a talus field wending through the woods. The rocks, however, are all quite large and stable, so it is easy to balance from one to the next. After about a mile of this, the trail becomes more trail-like and pleasant to walk.

At 4.5 miles, the blue-blazed side trail to the Pinnacle departs to the east, and the A.T. makes a sharp bend to the west. Missing this side trail is darn near impossible, for not only is it blazed, but the junction is also identified by what might be the world's largest cairn. I estimate it to be approximately 10 feet tall with a circumference at the base of 30–40 feet. The Pinnacle is 80 yards off the A.T. to the east. Formed by an expansive outcrop of flat slabs of sandstone, the Pinnacle is a broad cliff band defining a sharp east–west bend in the ridge of Blue Mountain. It offers one of the best views I have seen in Pennsylvania. The Lehigh Valley, which it overlooks, is dappled with fields and furrowed with rolling hills reaching out to the horizon. Pulpit Rock is visible to the west, and between it and the Pinnacle, a ridge descends southward to a small conical hill covered with trees.

BENEATH THIS TREE IS PROBABLY NOT THE BEST PLACE TO SET UP CAMP.

From the Pinnacle, the trip back to the parking area is quite easy. Hike back to the A.T. and turn right, continuing along the trail northbound. After 0.4 mile, the trail joins an old service road, and the hiking couldn't be more pleasant. Though the white blazes aren't abundant, the A.T. follows this road to, and beyond, a large clearing, which is used for landing helicopters. At the helipad, a water authority map like the one near the trailhead, complete with the words YOU ARE HERE marked on it, stands at the head of a blue-blazed service road that descends to the south, leaving the A.T. behind.

Follow this road 1.5 miles through an extraordinarily beautiful valley to the reservoir. The road generally stays above Furnace Creek, which tumbles over rocks below. At first, the valley is filled with hemlocks and the creek lined with rhododendrons. The hemlocks eventually give way to hickories, and the rhododendrons become remarkably thick all along the creek in the bottom of the valley. At the reservoir, the trail follows the east shore to and past a yellow gate and down a service road back to the A.T. where it crosses the creek at the Windsor Furnace site.

Nearby Attractions

Cabela's in nearby Hamburg has many of the supplies one might need for camping and hiking, as well as a large display of trophy mammals and a freshwater aquarium. It is located just north of I-78 at Exit 29 for Hamburg.

Directions

Take I-78 West from Allentown, Pennsylvania, or I-78 East from Harrisburg, Pennsylvania, to Exit 35 for PA 143/Lenhartsville. Follow PA 143 North 0.7 mile. Turn left (west) onto Mountain Road and follow it 2.9 miles, and turn right onto Reservoir Road. Be aware that at the junction with Monument Road, Mountain Road continues straight (it appears to be a right turn). If you go underneath I-78, you have just passed it. Follow Reservoir Road 0.4 mile to the parking area near the gate.

23 **PA 309 to Bear Rocks**

THE SNOW BEGINS TO FALL ON BEAR ROCKS.

SCENERY: ★ ★ ★ ★ ★
TRAIL CONDITION: ★ ★ ★ ★
CHILDREN: ★ ★
DIFFICULTY: ★ ★
SOLITUDE: ★ ★ ★ ★

GPS TRAILHEAD COORDINATES: N40° 42.468' W75° 48.465'

DISTANCE & CONFIGURATION: 7.0-mile out-and-back

HIKING TIME: 4 hours

HIGHLIGHTS: Knife Edge, Bear Rocks

ELEVATION: 1,385' at trailhead; 1,568' at Bear Rocks

ACCESS: Daily, sunrise–sunset; no fees or permits required

MAPS: Keystone Trails Association *Appalachian Trail in Pennsylvania, Sections 1–6: Delaware Water Gap to Swatara Gap;* USGS *New Tripoli*

FACILITIES: None

CONTACT: Pennsylvania Game Commission, 717-787-4250, tinyurl.com/pagamelands

COMMENTS: Because this hike passes through state game lands, you must wear at least 250 cubic inches of blaze orange November 15–December 15.

Overview

Both the exposed Knife Edge section of the trail and the stunning Bear Rocks outcrop make this an exciting and rewarding hike. The hiking is interesting and the views are wonderful.

Route Details

Bear Rocks is a towering formation of quartzite surrounded by forest along the ridge of Blue Mountain. It is an excellent hiking destination because of its view as well as the geologic interest of the rocks. The spelling and origin of the name of the outcrop is, if not disputed, at least quite inconsistent. The official Appalachian Trail (A.T.) map published by the Keystone Trails Association, as well as the sign at the blue-blazed access trail to the formation, refers to the outcrop as Bear Rocks. Other maps, including the U.S. Geological Survey map, refer to the outcrop as Bears Rocks, with an s. Both of these spellings suggest that it was named for a common inhabitant of Penn's woods. I have also seen it referred to as Baers Rocks and have read that it was named for a past landowner. Wherever the name comes from, I've used Bear Rocks to be consistent with usage on A.T. maps.

The hike begins from the Pennsylvania State Game Lands No. 106 parking area located on the left off a power company access road just east of PA 309 at the crest of Blue Mountain. From the parking area, follow the blue-blazed access trail south about 75 feet to the A.T., onto which you will turn left and follow it northbound (generally northeast) along the crest of Blue Mountain. Initially, the A.T. follows a forest road with no appreciable elevation gain or loss for 1.25 miles. When the road forks, continue along the right fork (white blazed). In a short distance, the road approaches the south edge of the Blue Mountain crest, affording an excellent view of the patchwork of fields and meadows across the Great Valley.

At 1.8 miles, the road ends at a power line clearing. A nice campsite is located to the left of the trail just before the power lines, and the clear-cut area around the towers offers a very pretty

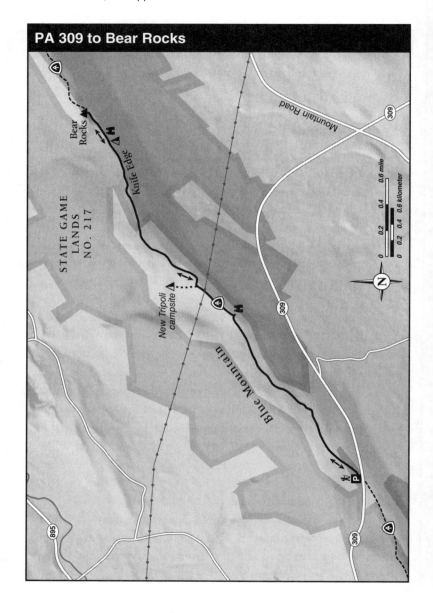

PA 309 to Bear Rocks

Bear Rocks

Knife Edge

STATE GAME
LANDS
NO. 217

New Tripoli campsite

Blue Mountain

Mountain Road

309

309

309

895

0   0.2   0.4   0.6 mile
0   0.2   0.4   0.6 kilometer

N

view along a drainage to the north. Continuing northbound from the clearing, the A.T. enters the woods as a footpath. A blue-blazed side trail to the New Tripoli campsite immediately departs the main trail to the left. From here, the walking becomes a little rough going, at times crossing over talus fields, at times just plain old rocky and awkward to pass. Around 2.75 miles, a long and tall outcrop of rock rises to the south of the trail. This is a very interesting geological feature because you can see the layering of sedimentary plates at various places along it. Just beyond this begins the section of the hike referred to as the Knife Edge.

While the name is something of an overstatement about the nature of the passage, the Knife Edge is a 150-yard-long outcrop of folded sandstone that forms the ridgecrest above the tops of the surrounding trees. Here the A.T. leaves the shelter of the trees and passes right along the top of the outcrop. The rocks drop off steeply to the north and south to the forest floor about 75 feet below. The trail weaves its way across the top of the rocks through cracks and crevices and past a couple of pines. Though the hiking is never diffi-cult, the setting is spectacular, with great views over the surrounding treetops to the south and north. In fact, about 100 feet along the ridge, you'll pass a nice, flat boulder in the shade of a pine that pro-vides a great vantage point and place to sit. Making your way across the Knife Edge, you will need to use your hands to get up and over

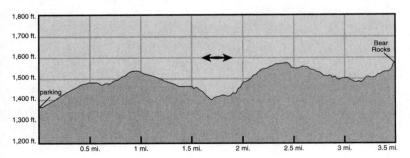

some steps at times. The descent from the outcrop (in both directions) deserves some care, especially when wet, because you are walking right along the sloped edge of the geologic plates.

Once beyond the Knife Edge, the A.T. drops back into the woods, passes a small campsite located to the right of the trail, and soon afterward a small overlook at an outcrop of rocks surrounded by some hemlocks (3.25 miles). To be sure, this is not your destination.

TRAVERSING THE KNIFE EDGE OFFERS A FUN BIT OF HIKING ALONG THE TOP OF BLUE MOUNTAIN.

It is about 0.25 mile beyond the overlook, and it consists of a significant outcrop of rocks 75 feet tall or so to the north of the trail. The A.T. passes beneath the better part of the outcrops before a blue-blazed side trail leading to the top of the rocks departs at a sign that reads BEAR ROCKS.

From the A.T., the blue-blazed trail climbs up, over, and around boulders on its way to the crest of the ridge. While the highest point of the rocks is 75 yards or so to the west of the end of the access trail, the view from that point is somewhat obstructed by trees. When I was last there on a weekend in early April, it made no difference; by the time I reached the rocks, the snow had begun to fall, and I was unable to see more than a couple of hundred feet in any direction. View or not, Bear Rocks is a nice place and a worthy destination for a day trip.

Nearby Attractions

If you are hungry, drive 3 miles north on PA 309 and turn right onto PA 895 (Lizard Creek Road). Happy's Diner (570-386-4333) is on the left.

Cabela's is located just off I-78 in Hamburg. Not only will you find just about all of the supplies you might need for hiking there, the store has an extensive array of trophy wildlife and a tank with sport fish. The address is 100 Cabela Drive, Hamburg, PA 19526 (610-929-7000; cabelas.com).

Directions

From Hamburg, Pennsylvania, follow I-78 East to Exit 35 for PA 143 and Lenhartsville. Follow PA 143 North 13.4 miles to PA 309. Turn left onto PA 309 and follow it to the crest of Blue Mountain, 4.9 miles. Turn right onto the power company access road at the top of Blue Mountain. The Pennsylvania state game lands parking area is on the left.

THE VIEW INTO THE DELAWARE WATER GAP AND ACROSS TO MOUNT TAMMANY
FROM LOOKOUT ROCK

GPS TRAILHEAD COORDINATES: N40° 58.796' W75° 8.517'

DISTANCE & CONFIGURATION: 5.0-mile balloon

HIKING TIME: 3 hours

HIGHLIGHTS: Mount Minsi, Delaware Water Gap

ELEVATION: 571' at trailhead; 1,445' at Mount Minsi

ACCESS: Open 24/7; no fees or permits required

MAPS: Keystone Trails Association *Appalachian Trail in Pennsylvania, Sections 1–6: Delaware Water Gap to Swatara Gap*; USGS *Stroudsburg*

FACILITIES: None

CONTACT: Delaware Water Gap National Recreation Area, 570-426-2452, nps.gov/dewa

COMMENTS: Break-ins have become increasingly common in the parking area, so be sure not to leave valuables in your car.

Overview

This hike makes use of the Appalachian Trail (A.T.) and side trails to make a loop over Mount Minsi. The hike offers beautiful views of the Delaware Water Gap on the way up and passes through a forest of hemlocks and thick rhododendrons on the descent. Table Rock, near Lenape Lake, is an impressive feature of the local geology.

Route Details

In addition to experiencing a beautiful rhododendron and hardwood forest, this delightful easternmost A.T. hike in Pennsylvania rewards hikers with excellent views of the Delaware Water Gap. The A.T. for this hike follows trails and roads that were constructed in the late 1800s when the area was a resort destination for visitors from New York. The trailhead for the hike is located at the Lenape Lake parking area just outside of downtown Delaware Water Gap, Pennsylvania, an officially designated Appalachian Trail Community. From the parking lot, walk east, passing a gate and an A.T. sign, and follow the trail along an old paved roadbed past the east edge of Lenape Lake. The lake is quite pretty, surrounded by cliffs, rhododendrons, and hemlocks.

After climbing along the roadbed for about 0.4 mile, the A.T. leaves the road behind and enters the woods on the left, becoming a footpath. The trail traverses the hillside above the Delaware Water Gap, through some thick rhododendrons at times, climbing all the way. Occasionally, an opening in the foliage offers a good view of the water gap and Mount Tammany across the river, the first of which is at Council Rock, identified by a sign. At a little beyond a mile, the trail crosses Eureka Creek, a small, pretty tributary of the Delaware River that flows past the trail over red sandstone slabs and through thick rhododendrons. A few minutes beyond the creek, the A.T. makes a sharp turn to the right, up steps and switchbacks to Lookout Rock, which offers yet another impressive view.

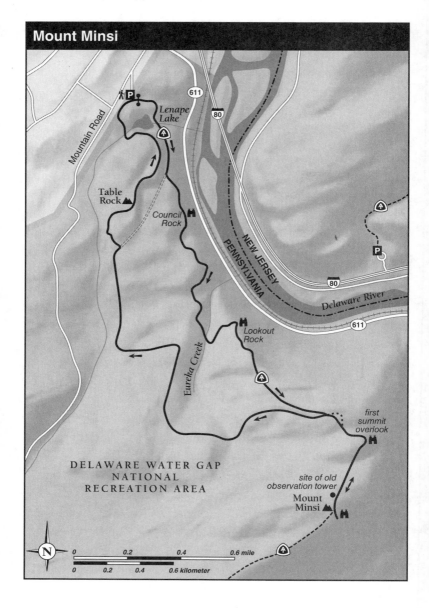

Mount Minsi

Lenape Lake

Mountain Road

Table Rock

Council Rock

Eureka Creek

Lookout Rock

NEW JERSEY

PENNSYLVANIA

Delaware River

first summit overlook

site of old observation tower

Mount Minsi

DELAWARE WATER GAP
NATIONAL
RECREATION AREA

N

| 0 | 0.2 | 0.4 | 0.6 mile |

| 0 | 0.2 | 0.4 | 0.6 kilometer |

The trail climbs from the overlook for 0.7 mile before leveling out quite suddenly at an old forest road. Cross the forest road, and follow the A.T. past a flat area and up a small hill to the first of two lookouts on the Mount Minsi ridge. This looks east over the water gap toward Mount Tammany and Kittatinny Mountain, reaching across northern New Jersey. About 0.2 mile beyond that is the top of Mount Minsi proper and the site of the old observation tower that used to grace its summit. Now all that is left of the tower is a few of the old stone entry steps. Continue along the A.T. 50 yards, and walk out to the second overlook on the south edge of the ridge (2.3 miles). This spot features a great view and nice comfortable rocks on which to sit and soak up the sun.

Rather than retracing the A.T. from Mount Minsi back to the parking area, I recommend taking an alternate route down the mountain. From the top of Mount Minsi, follow the A.T. back past the first summit overlook and down to the forest road you crossed at the top of the steep climb. Turn left onto the forest road, and follow it westward along the north side of Mount Minsi. It can be a little rocky in places, and it descends at a considerably easier rate than does the Appalachian Trail. For the next 1.5 miles, the road curves through a pretty rhododendron forest until it comes to a significant road that departs to the left—the first road of any consequence that departs

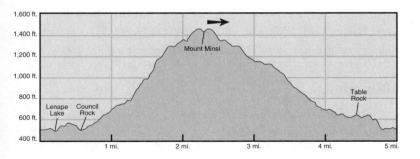

to the left. At the time of this writing, a piece of old culvert pipe was lying on the ground on the right at the junction.

Turn left and follow this road downhill past a small creek out to Table Rock (4.5 miles), a large, flat, red sandstone outcrop that ends abruptly at a cliff on its eastern edge. An old fence runs along the edge of the cliff. Though Table Rock offers a great view to the east, I found the presence of the rock itself as a geological feature, as well as the hiking that follows, to be most interesting. The road ends at Table Rock, so to return to Lenape Lake, walk out to the edge of the cliff and follow the edge north. As the rock gives way to woods and grass, a good foot trail appears. Follow it back to Lenape Lake. Above the lake, the trail veers to the west, descending toward the inflow of the lake, and makes a short, steep descent through the rhododendrons to the level of the lake. Continue along the path to the west, over what appears to be an old dam along the edge of the lake. After the dam, the trail becomes more of an old roadbed that ends at the upper section of the Lenape Lake parking lot. Turn right and follow the gravel road back to the main parking area.

Nearby Attractions

Delaware Water Gap, Pennsylvania, an officially designated Appalachian Trail Community, has bike rentals and the small Antoine Dutot Museum (570-476-4240; dutotmuseum.com), which has information on the history of the town. Along PA 611, the Village Farmer and Bakery (570-476-9440; villagefarmerbakery.com) has pies and all sorts of goodies, as well as a café that serves an excellent breakfast.

Directions

From I-80, take Exit 307 in Stroudsburg, Pennsylvania, and head south on PA 611 into Delaware Water Gap, Pennsylvania. In 2.5 miles, make a slight right to remain on PA 611. In another 0.7 mile, at the edge of town, turn right onto Mountain Road. The access road to the parking area is in 0.1 mile, the first left off Mountain Road.

A SMALL WATERFALL AND RHODODENDRONS ALONG THE HIKE TO MOUNT MINSI

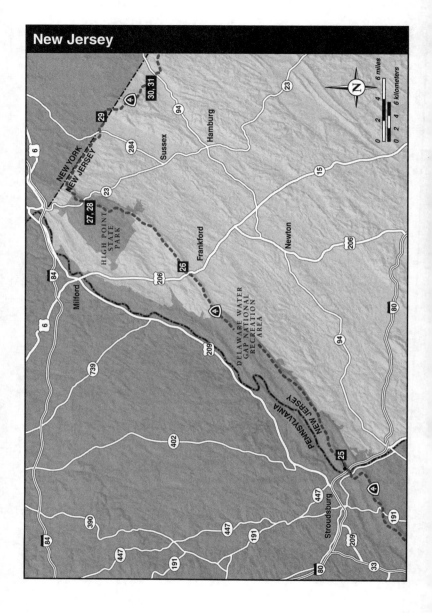

New Jersey

THE POCHUCK BOARDWALK IN NORTHERN NEW JERSEY OFFERS A PLEASANT
MILE OF BEAUTIFUL HIKING ALONG THE APPALACHIAN TRAIL.
(See Hike 30, page 191.)

25 SUNFISH POND p. 166

26 CULVERS FIRE TOWER OVERLOOK p. 171

27 LAKE RUTHERFORD p. 176

28 NEW JERSEY HIGH POINT p. 181

29 WALLKILL RIVER NATIONAL WILDLIFE REFUGE:
    LIBERTY LOOP TRAIL p. 186

30 POCHUCK BOARDWALK p. 191

31 WAWAYANDA MOUNTAIN p. 196

25 # Sunfish Pond

SCENERY: ★ ★ ★ ★ ★
TRAIL CONDITION: ★ ★ ★
CHILDREN: ★
DIFFICULTY: ★ ★ ★ ★ ★
SOLITUDE: ★ ★

PROBABLY THE BEST VIEW OF SUNFISH POND IS HAD FROM THE TURQUOISE TRAIL ALONG THE POND'S EASTERN EDGE.

GPS TRAILHEAD COORDINATES: N40° 58.312' W75° 7.528'

DISTANCE & CONFIGURATION: 9.6-mile figure eight with short out-and-back

HIKING TIME: 5–6 hours

HIGHLIGHTS: Sunfish Pond, the southernmost glacial pond on the A.T.; Dunnfield Creek Natural Area

ELEVATION: 348' at trailhead; 1,434' at east edge of Sunfish Pond

ACCESS: Open 24/7; no fees or permits required

MAPS: Appalachian Trail Conservancy *New York–New Jersey, Maps 3 & 4: New York 17A to Delaware Water Gap, Pennsylvania;* USGS *Bushkill, Portland,* and *Stroudsburg*

FACILITIES: None

CONTACT: Delaware Water Gap National Recreation Area, 570-426-2452, nps.gov/dewa; Worthington State Forest, 908-841-9575, www.state.nj.us/dep/parksandforests/parks /worthington.html

COMMENTS: Break-ins have occurred in the parking lot, so be sure to take any valuables with you. The stream crossings on the Dunnfield Creek Trail may not be passable after heavy rain.

Overview

This New Jersey hike provides hikers with the opportunity to visit the southernmost glacial pond along the Appalachian Trail (A.T.). Sunfish Pond, the destination, is in effect a 44-acre glacial tarn carved out of the surrounding bedrock during the last glacial period of the ice age around 10,000 years ago. A loop around the lake provides access to several excellent places to have a picnic or a long break. The descent for this hike along the Dunnfield Creek Trail passes through a remarkable hemlock- and rhododendron-filled gorge carved through the uplifted layers of sandstone and quartzite that form Kittatinny Mountain. Due to its 9.6-mile length, plan on a full day out and a lot of varied scenery.

Route Details

Follow the trail out of the back of the parking lot, passing the sign for the A.T. and the Dunnfield Creek Natural Area. Cross the creek over a footbridge, and begin climbing along the north side of the creek. At 0.4 mile, the blue-blazed Dunnfield Creek Trail diverges to the right, descending to the level of the creek. Continue northbound along the A.T., which climbs a little more steeply from this point.

At 1.5 miles, the A.T. passes the Holly Springs Trail (red blazed), which branches off to the right, and the yellow-blazed Beulahland Trail, which departs to the north. The latter descends 1.3 miles to the Fairview parking area on Old Mine Road along the Delaware River. Up to this point and for the next 0.75 mile, the A.T. is pretty rocky and at times seems more like a dry creek bed than an actual footpath. I would recommend a sturdy pair of hiking shoes for this hike.

As the trail continues to climb, it works over to the north side of the main ridge. A little past 3 miles, it crosses a seasonal creek, and about 100 yards beyond that, you'll see the large sign indicating access to the backpackers' sites, located in the woods to the north of the trail. Camping is permitted here only for thru-hikers. The ridge is quite sparsely forested with an understory of scrubby oak and rhododendron. Beyond the backpackers' sites, in fact, many standing

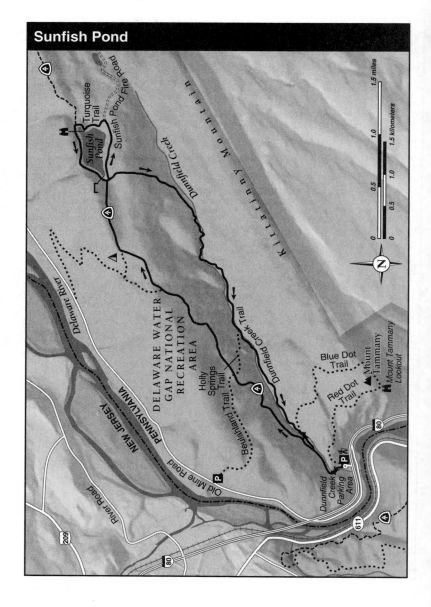

dead trees along the north side of the trail lend a kind of surreal ambience to the terrain. The trail levels out somewhat, taking on more of the character of an old forest road, and at 3.8 miles it reaches the west edge of Sunfish Pond. A bench sits at the water's edge, and a sign and monument provide some area history. If you are up for the effort, make the 1.5-mile-long, mostly easy and level loop around the pond by following the Sunfish Pond Fire Road (it heads directly east) south of the pond 0.6 mile to the Turquoise Trail, marked with blazes the color of its name. A cairn on the left identifies the trail-head. Follow that trail downhill to the northeast corner of the pond, where you'll find a nice pondside overlook at an open rock shelf. The A.T. is another hundred yards or so along the Turquoise Trail beyond the overlook. Turn left on the A.T. and follow it over uneven and rocky terrain along the edge of the pond.

Upon returning to the west edge of the pond, turn toward the Sunfish Pond Fire Road and follow the rocky footpath to the right of the road uphill and directly south through rhododendrons. After a short climb and a level stretch, the trail descends, quite steeply at first, into the Dunnfield Creek drainage. The upper part of the drainage consists of a broad, open valley with few trees and a fair amount of understory. The trail is marked with green blazes and is not at all difficult to follow, though the ground can be rather damp in sections.

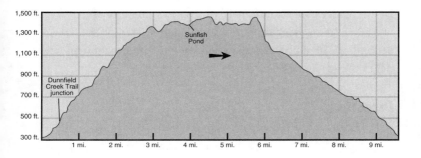

When you are 1.2 miles from Sunfish Pond, you'll make the first of many creek crossings, and the valley narrows into a steep-sided gorge. Each crossing is quite obviously marked, and several signs advise hikers to stay on the trail. It is advice worth heeding, as trying to skip a crossing by traversing will in every case result in getting stopped by a cliff. For the most part, the trail proceeds very close to the creek. Rugged cliffs bursting with rhododendrons hem the creek on one side or the other; tall hemlocks line the valley floor.

A half mile after the first crossing, the trail crosses back to the north side of the creek and then almost immediately afterward to the south side. A half mile or so farther, the trail crosses back to the north, passes the southern terminus of the red-blazed Holly Springs Trail, and shortly afterward crosses back to the south side of the creek, where it stays for 0.75 mile. Just beyond a steep descent, the Blue Dot Trail departs to the left and leads to the Mount Tammany Mountain, about 1 mile and 1,000 feet of elevation to the south. Just beyond the junction, you'll cross the creek one more time on a significant footbridge. Walk up to the A.T. and follow that to the parking area in about 0.4 mile.

Nearby Attractions

The Delaware Water Gap National Recreation Area offers opportunities for more hiking, camping, biking, nature study, and float trips on the Delaware River. The Kittatinny Point Visitor Center is on the west side of I-80 within walking distance of the Dunnfield Creek Natural Area parking lot. The staff there can provide you with information on activities in the gap in both New Jersey and Pennsylvania.

Directions

From Stroudsburg, Pennsylvania, follow I-80 east over the Delaware River. Take the first exit east of the river, and follow signs for the Kittatinny Visitor Center. Pass the visitor center, and in 0.4 mile turn left underneath 1-80. Turn left again and the parking area is on the right.

Culvers Fire Tower Overlook

SCENERY: ★ ★ ★ ★ ★
TRAIL CONDITION: ★ ★ ★ ★ ★
CHILDREN: ★ ★ ★ ★
DIFFICULTY: ★ ★
SOLITUDE: ★ ★

AT THE SHOULDER OF THE RIDGE APPROACHING THE CULVERS FIRE TOWER

GPS TRAILHEAD COORDINATES: N41° 10.812' W74° 47.268'

DISTANCE & CONFIGURATION: 3.4-mile out-and-back

HIKING TIME: 2 hours

HIGHLIGHTS: Excellent view toward the Acropolis from the ridge and of the Pocono Mountains from the overlook area

ELEVATION: 947' at trailhead; 1,467' at overlook

ACCESS: Open 24/7; no fees or permits required

MAPS: Appalachian Trail Conservancy *New York–New Jersey, Maps 3 & 4: New York 17A to Delaware Water Gap, Pennsylvania*; USGS *Culvers Gap*

FACILITIES: Picnic table at the fire tower

CONTACT: Stokes State Forest, 973-948-3820, tinyurl.com/stokessf

COMMENTS: Culvers Fire Tower is closed to the public.

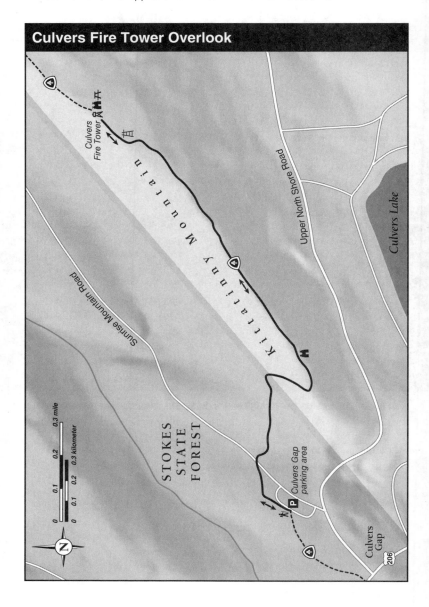

Culvers Fire Tower Overlook

Culvers Fire Tower

Kittatinny Mountain

Upper North Shore Road

Culvers Lake

Sunrise Mountain Road

STOKES STATE FOREST

Culvers Gap parking area

Culvers Gap

206

0.3 mile

0.2

0.1

0.3 kilometer

0.2

0.1

0

0

N

Overview

This short hike makes for an excellent late-day and early-evening trip. As the sun begins to drop in the west, the light casts long shadows on the ridge and across the rolling forest to the north. A picnic table at the overlook near the fire tower makes a nice place for a picnic even nicer.

Route Details

From the Culvers Gap parking area, gain the Appalachian Trail (A.T.) by walking out of the northeast corner of the lot, where you should see a sign for the trail. It doesn't actually meet the parking lot but passes about 50 feet or so north of the lot in the woods. If you are at all disoriented, follow Sunrise Mountain Road to the northeast from the lot, and the A.T. will cross it in about 0.25 mile. You'll need to be looking for that crossing because no sign marks it, only the white blazes. Once you pick up the A.T., follow it northbound from Sunrise Mountain Road and uphill for 0.4 mile to the crest of Kittatinny Mountain. The ascent gets steeper as you go along but never unpleasantly so. About two-thirds of the way up, it makes a switchback to the south.

When you attain the ridge, you'll come to a clearing that greets you with an excellent view to the north and west over Culvers Gap.

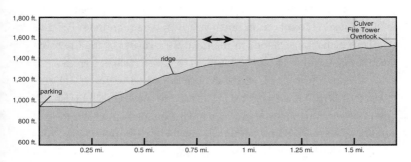

According to V. Collins Chew in his book *Underfoot: A Geologic Guide to the Appalachian Trail,* the gap was formed by the action of an old river that once crossed the ridge. As surrounding creeks eroded the nearby terrain, they drained the river of its flow, leaving only the notch in the ridge. This type of depression in the ridge is classified as a wind gap, as opposed to a water gap like those found in Pennsylvania that have rivers and creeks flowing through them. The only thing that blows through Culvers Gap is the wind and the din of automobiles along US 206.

At the clearing on the shoulder of the ridge, some slabs and a few blocks of polished quartzite provide nice places to rest and have a drink after the ascent, as well as an excellent place to watch the sunset. From the clearing, follow the A.T. as it works its way northeast along the ridge. The forest consists of oak and pine trees and is fairly open for most of the mile-long walk out to the fire tower, occasionally providing some partially obstructed views to the south. The path is mostly level, and the walking is quite pleasant.

You'll know you are close to your destination when the trail passes a tall cellular tower to the south side of it and the landscape becomes more densely forested, especially with shrubs and bushes. Five minutes beyond that tower, you'll see the fire tower standing about 70 feet tall and above the trees. Emerging from the trees, the trail enters a clearing that is open to the north. It is pretty obvious why the fire tower was built in this location: it commands a sweeping view of the Pocono Mountains in northwest New Jersey and into Pennsylvania. A picnic table stands in the northwest corner of the fire tower clearing, and you can't beat it as a place to have a meal or a snack.

Though not gated, the fire tower is posted with a NO TRESPASSING sign. I have been told that the fire tower is still in use and that, when someone is there, you might be allowed to climb it. It serves as part of a system of 21 fire towers distributed among three divisions throughout the state. According to the New Jersey Forest Fire Service (NJFFS) website, at least one tower in each division is staffed during periods of low rain and high risk of fires. All 21 towers are staffed during the months of March, April, May, October, and November. The use of fire towers has historically proven to be quite an effective method for monitoring the forest. About half of all forest fires are spotted and located from the towers. The NJFFS website also has very interesting information on how the tower staff are able to determine the location of fires, as well as lots of information about wildfire prevention and education. You can visit the website at tinyurl.com/nj-firetowers.

After you have had your fill of the scenery, follow the A.T. back to the parking lot.

Nearby Attractions

Visit the Space Farms Zoo & Museum in nearby Sussex, New Jersey (973-875-5800; spacefarms.com). It has a zoo with more than 100 species of animals and an eclectic museum of Americana. It's a great place to go with the kids.

Directions

From Sussex, New Jersey, follow Loomis Avenue and then County Road 565 south 8.5 miles to US 206. Turn right onto US 206 and follow it 6.2 miles to Culvers Gap at the top of Kittatinny Mountain. Turn right onto CR 636, and in 0.2 mile, turn left onto Sunrise Mountain Road. The parking lot is on the left. If you begin to go downhill on CR 636, you have gone too far.

THOUGH CLIMBING THE CULVERS FIRE TOWER IS FORBIDDEN, THE VIEW FROM THE CLEARING BENEATH IT IS MARVELOUS.

Lake Rutherford

SCENERY: ★ ★ ★ ★
TRAIL CONDITION: ★ ★ ★ ★
CHILDREN: ★ ★
DIFFICULTY: ★ ★ ★
SOLITUDE: ★ ★ ★

SOME OF THE TALL CLIFFS NEAR THE BEGINNING OF THE LAKE RUTHERFORD HIKE

GPS TRAILHEAD COORDINATES: N41° 18.152' W74° 40.048'

DISTANCE & CONFIGURATION: 6.5-mile loop

HIKING TIME: 4–5 hours

HIGHLIGHTS: Excellent views from the ridge above Lake Rutherford, Lake Rutherford environs

ACCESS: Open 24/7; no fees or permits required

MAPS: Appalachian Trail Conservancy *New York–New Jersey, Maps 3 & 4: New York 17A to Delaware Water Gap, Pennsylvania;* USGS *Port Jervis South;* New York–New Jersey Trail Conference *High Point State Park*

FACILITIES: Restrooms and water at the park office

CONTACT: High Point State Park, 973-875-4800, tinyurl.com/njhighpointsp; Stokes State Forest, 973-948-3820, tinyurl.com/stokessf

COMMENTS: Though the A.T. passes right by the park office at High Point State Park, please be sure to begin this hike from the designated A.T. parking area. The lot is located about 0.25 mile south of the park office on the west side of NJ 23, and the A.T. is gained via a short blue-blazed connector trail heading south from the parking area.

Overview

This hike makes use of several of the secondary trails in High Point State Park along with the Appalachian Trail (A.T.) to create a nice loop along the ridge of Kittatinny Mountain and along the banks of Lake Rutherford.

Route Details

From the A.T. parking lot, follow the blue-blazed connector trail to the south and uphill as it bends around to the east. In about 0.25 mile, it joins with the red-blazed Iris Trail. This junction marks the end of the loop this hike makes. Turn right onto the Iris Trail and follow that north another 0.25 mile to the A.T., onto which you will turn left and head southbound. Be careful here that you get on to the Appalachian Trail. The yellow-blazed Mashipacong Trail also departs from this junction to the north.

From the Iris Trail, the A.T. climbs a short distance and joins an old roadbed beneath quite a significant cliff face. Soon afterward, the trail attains the crest of the ridge in a forest of Gambel oak and comes to a junction with the Blue Dot Trail departing to the northwest. That trail descends to Sawmill Pond, which you'll be able to see below you. Just beyond that junction, the A.T. makes a sharp left bend and heads southeast through the head of a high hollow. After passing the hollow, the path climbs onto another ridge and makes a sharp bend to the right (southwest) at a couple of nice vantage points overlooking Lake Rutherford. From here, you will get a good sense of the terrain that you'll cover as you make your way to the south end of the lake and back along its west shore.

Continue following the trail along the ridge with frequent views to the east for a good mile or so, passing at times over and along large slabs of glacial-polished quartzite. The most prominent of these you'll encounter just before the trail leaves the ridge heading south. This is called Dutch Shoe Rock, and it is marked as a viewpoint on the High Point State Park map available at the visitor center.

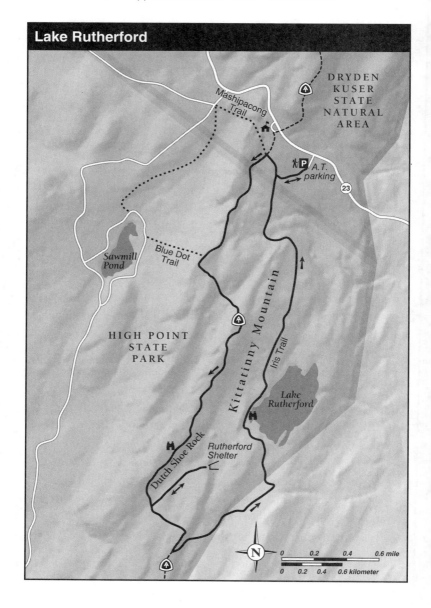

Lake Rutherford

DRYDEN
KUSER
STATE
NATURAL
AREA

Mashipacong
Trail

A.T.
parking

23

Sawmill
Pond

Blue Dot
Trail

HIGH POINT
STATE
PARK

Kittatinny Mountain

Iris Trail

Lake
Rutherford

Dutch Shoe Rock

Rutherford
Shelter

N

| 0 | 0.2 | 0.4 | 0.6 mile |

| 0 | 0.2 | 0.4 | 0.6 kilometer |

After descending from the main ridge, the blue-blazed side trail to the Rutherford Shelter departs to the left in the bottom of a hollow. The hike out to the shelter is longer than you might expect, about 0.4 mile. The shelter is situated at the back of a clearing near the edge of a large pond (not visible from the shelter) and swampy area. It certainly has a kind of rustic quality to it. For me, it offered a nice place to take a break, but there are other even nicer places farther along the hike.

From the shelter trail, continue southbound along the A.T., and in 0.25 mile it will join an old road that bends to the right. Just beyond that, a trail blazed with red dots joins the A.T. from the left. That is the Iris Trail, and *you want to be sure to turn left* and follow it northward. (I passed it and walked 0.25 mile before I got the sense that something wasn't quite right.) Initially, the Iris Trail passes through a lovely hollow along an old road grade bordered by swampland. Then it reaches private property and turns left, heading west on another old road grade. The road forks, and you'll stay right, and in a few minutes, you'll reach a bridge over the inflow to Lake Rutherford. Continue past the bridge up a short hill, and you'll find a nice place to sit down on a rock outcrop to the right side of the trail. Here you can take in a view of the lake and the lowlands beyond to the southeast. Those lowlands are part of the Great Valley that runs along the east

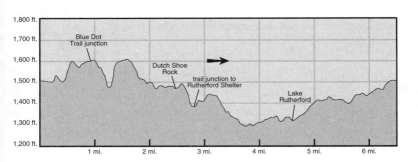

side of the Ridge and Valley Physiographic Province north and south along the entire Appalachian Mountain chain. Far off to the east you can see ski trails along the hills that rise on the other side of it.

From the lake, the hike is just a nice walk in the woods back to the car. The Iris Trail stays on the old road grade for most of the way back to the blue-blazed connector trail that accesses the parking area. If the weather has been wet, the trail may get rather mucky in places, especially reaching the end of the hike. Be sure to keep your eyes open for the blue blazes, as they are probably also easy to walk past.

Nearby Attractions

If you don't feel like walking anymore after completing the hike, drive over to the New Jersey High Point Monument across NJ 23. The views are outstanding. High Point State Park is more than just a monument. The park has an interpretive center, picnic areas, a campground, a swimming area on Lake Marcia, and playgrounds. Boating and fishing are permitted on its Sawmill and Steeny Kill Lakes.

Directions

From Sussex, New Jersey, follow NJ 23 north 7.6 miles to the park. The A.T. parking lot is on the left. From Port Jervis, New York, follow NJ 23 south 5.0 miles. The park office and the main entrance to the park are located on NJ 23. The A.T. parking lot is located about 0.25 mile south of the park office on the west side of NJ 23.

New Jersey High Point

SCENERY: ★ ★ ★ ★ ★
TRAIL CONDITION: ★ ★ ★ ★
CHILDREN: ★ ★ ★
DIFFICULTY: ★ ★
SOLITUDE: ★ ★

A VIEWING PLATFORM ON THE APPALACHIAN TRAIL EN ROUTE TO THE NEW JERSEY HIGH POINT MONUMENT

GPS TRAILHEAD COORDINATES: N41° 18.152' W74° 40.048'

DISTANCE & CONFIGURATION: 4.0-mile out-and-back

HIKING TIME: 2 hours

HIGHLIGHTS: New Jersey High Point Monument, excellent panoramic views from monument and viewing platform en route

ELEVATION: 1,374' at trailhead; 1,785' at New Jersey High Point Monument

ACCESS: Daily, 8 a.m.–8 p.m.; no fees or permits required

MAPS: Appalachian Trail Conservancy *New York–New Jersey, Maps 3 & 4: New York 17A to Delaware Water Gap, Pennsylvania;* USGS *Port Jervis South;* New York–New Jersey Trail Conference *High Point State Park*

FACILITIES: Restrooms and water at the park office

CONTACT: High Point State Park, 973-875-4800, tinyurl.com/njhighpointsp; Stokes State Forest, 973-948-3820, tinyurl.com/stokessf

COMMENTS: Though the A.T. passes right by the park office at High Point State Park, please be sure to begin this hike from the designated A.T. parking area. It is located about 0.25 mile south of the park office on the west side of NJ 23, and the A.T. is gained via a short blue-blazed connector trail heading south from the parking area.

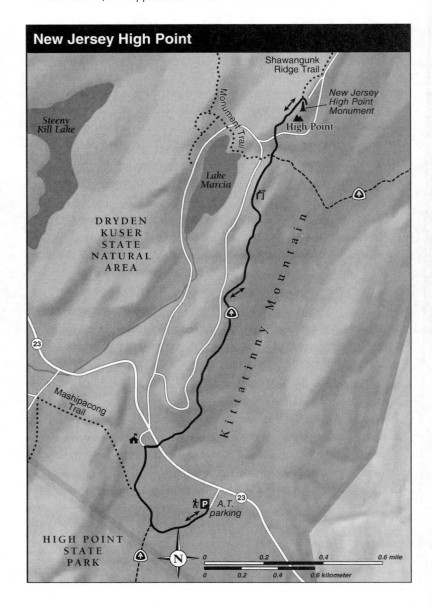

New Jersey High Point

Shawangunk
Ridge Trail

New Jersey
High Point
Monument

High Point

Steeny
Kill Lake

Monument Trail

Lake
Marcia

DRYDEN
KUSER
STATE
NATURAL
AREA

Kittatinny Mountain

23

Mashipacong
Trail

A.T.
parking

23

HIGH POINT
STATE
PARK

N

0   0.2   0.4   0.6 mile
0   0.2   0.4   0.6 kilometer

Overview

This short hike follows the Appalachian Trail (A.T.) 2 miles out to the New Jersey High Point Monument, passing a viewing platform along the way. The views in all directions are outstanding.

Route Details

At about 4 easy miles round-trip from the car, this hike's distinguishing feature is that it takes you to the highest point in New Jersey, which is capped by a significant monument that can be seen from many miles away. Though it's not Denali or Mount Washington or one of the big peaks that top any number of states in the West or along the Appalachian Trail, I was surprised at how hard the wind can blow up there. When I did the hike in February, I could barely stand up against the wind and spent most of the time on top hiding on the lee side of the monument.

From the A.T. parking lot, follow the blue-blazed connector trail to the south and uphill as it bends around to the east. In about 0.25 mile, it joins with the red-blazed Iris Trail. Turn right onto the Iris Trail and follow that north another 0.25 mile to the A.T., onto which you will turn right and head northbound. Follow the A.T. out past the High Point State Park office parking lot and across NJ 23.

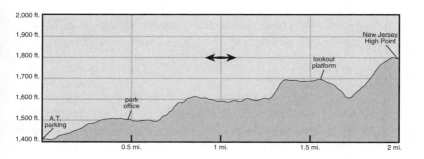

Once across the road, the A.T. passes through a grassy field and enters the woods. The trail stays to the east side of the crest of the Kittatinny Mountain ridge and weaves its way through rocks and trees for about a mile from the park office. The rocks along this stretch of trail are interesting. Not only will you find the hard, gray quartzite that stretches all the way across Kittatinny Mountain, but outcrops of conglomerate are also present in places along the path.

After the trail makes a bend to the west, it reaches an observation platform that stands about 25 feet high in the area of some lovely pine trees. Take the stairs up to the platform and check out the view. To the south and east, you are looking over the Great Valley through which the Wallkill River runs (see page 186) and toward the Hudson Highlands. On the far side of the valley stands Wawayanda Mountain (see page 196), and to the south of it, the ridge is etched by the runs of the Mountain Creek ski resort. To the northwest, you are looking out over the northern Pocono Mountains east of Scranton, Pennsylvania, and you should be able to make out the slopes of Ski Big Bear directly north.

A quarter of a mile beyond the observation platform, the A.T. meets the blue-blazed Shawangunk Ridge Trail and the Monument Trail (green and red blazes) that together lead to the monument. The A.T. takes a sharp bend toward the south here and leaves the crest of Kittatinny Mountain, which it picked up many miles back in Pennsylvania. From the junction of the trails, leave the path of the A.T. and follow the Monument and Shawangunk Ridge Trails. They climb a little bit, then cross the park road. From the road crossing, another 5 minutes of walking uphill along the trail takes you to the base of the monument.

Constructed as a memorial to veterans of all wars, the 220-foot-tall monument offers a commanding view in all directions. In addition to the vistas you get from the observation platform along the trail, from the monument you can also see north to New York's Catskill Mountains. If you are interested in going up the monument, it is open Memorial Day–late June, Saturday–Sunday and holidays, and then daily until Labor Day. From Labor Day to Columbus Day, it is open Saturday–Sunday and holidays.

Nearby Attractions

High Point State Park is more than just a monument. The park has an interpretive center, picnic areas, a campground, a swimming area on Lake Marcia, and playgrounds. Boating and fishing are permitted on its Sawmill and Steeny Kill Lakes.

Directions

From Sussex, New Jersey, follow NJ 23 north 7.6 miles to the park. The A.T. parking lot is on the left. From Port Jervis, New York, follow NJ 23 south 5.0 miles. The park office and the main entrance to the park are located on NJ 23. The A.T. parking lot is located about 0.25 mile south of the park office on the west side of NJ 23.

PORT JERVIS AND THE DELAWARE RIVER FROM THE NEW JERSEY HIGH POINT

Wallkill River National Wildlife Refuge:
Liberty Loop Trail

SCENERY: ★ ★ ★ ★
TRAIL CONDITION: ★ ★ ★ ★ ★
CHILDREN: ★ ★ ★ ★ ★
DIFFICULTY: ★
SOLITUDE: ★ ★ ★

A HIKER WALKS ALONG THE APPALACHIAN TRAIL IN SEARCH OF A GOOD VANTAGE POINT FOR PHOTOGRAPHING BIRDS.

GPS TRAILHEAD COORDINATES: N41° 17.002' W74° 31.567'

DISTANCE & CONFIGURATION: 2.7-mile loop

HIKING TIME: 1.5 hours

HIGHLIGHTS: Wildlife refuge environs, excellent birding

ELEVATION: 329' at trailhead; no appreciable elevation gain or loss

ACCESS: Daily, sunrise–sunset, no fees or permits required

MAPS: Appalachian Trail Conservancy *New York–New Jersey, Maps 3 & 4: New York 17A to Delaware Water Gap, Pennsylvania;* USGS *Unionville*

FACILITIES: None

CONTACT: Wallkill River National Wildlife Refuge, 973-702-7266, fws.gov/refuge/wallkill_river

COMMENTS: Dogs are permitted, but they must remain on a leash. Bring insect repellent; the mosquitoes can be a nuisance.

Overview

This pleasant hike makes a loop around a wetlands area in the Wallkill River National Wildlife Refuge. Though short, it packs in a lot of opportunity for bird-watching and photography. Bring binoculars and long lenses.

Route Details

At 2.7 miles, this loop hike is both short and easy. You could, however, conceivably spend hours walking it. The loop straddles the New York and New Jersey state line as it circumnavigates a broad wetlands section of the Wallkill River National Wildlife Refuge. The complete refuge encompasses a 9-mile stretch of the Wallkill River, and it provides habitat for an enormous variety of birdlife that includes geese, herons, hawks, and owls, as well as martins, buntings, finches, and a host of other songbirds. You would be wise to bring binoculars and a field guide with you.

Though the Appalachian Trail (A.T.) has now left the Kittatinny Mountain ridge to the south, it is interesting to note that the Wallkill Valley is still part of the Ridge and Valley Physiographic Province that the A.T. has followed through Maryland, Pennsylvania, and New Jersey. As the U.S. Fish and Wildlife Service (the administrating agency) brochure on the refuge explains, the Wallkill Valley is a section of the Great Valley (referred to as the Cumberland Valley in Pennsylvania) that extends from the southeastern United States all the way into Canada. The wetlands habitat here was formed by the retreat of the glaciers during the most recent glacial period of the ice age.

The hike begins at the Liberty Loop Trail parking area on Oil City Road just west of County Road 667. The hike has no elevation gain to speak of, and you should let your own preference determine whether you will walk the loop clockwise or counterclockwise. I walked it counterclockwise because the day was getting on, and I thought the evening light on the hills to the east would make for some nice photographs. I describe the hike going in that direction.

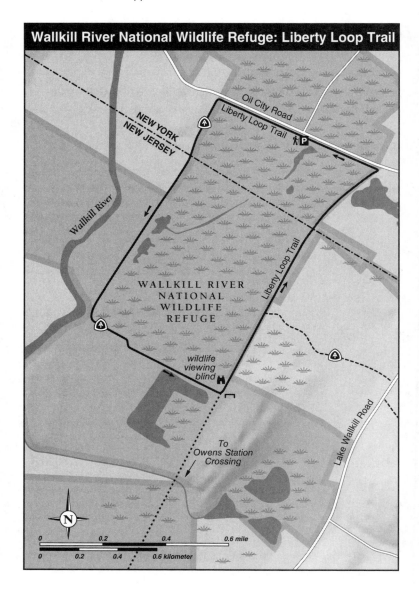

Wallkill River National Wildlife Refuge: Liberty Loop Trail

From the parking area, follow the Liberty Loop Trail west along the north edge of the wetlands. At 0.3 mile, the Liberty Loop Trail joins the A.T. at the edge of the first pond and makes a perpendicular turn to the south. The path along the west edge of the wetlands is wide and soft. All along the west side of the wetlands, you'll have great views of the rising hills to the east, the beginning of the Hudson Highlands. After 0.75 mile, the trail makes another 90-degree turn to the left and passes between two sections of the wetlands along the top of a swale bank.

At 1.5 miles into the loop, the trail comes to a T intersection. Turning to the south (right), the trail heads out to the Owens Station Crossing at CR 642 and continues beyond as the Timberdoodle Trail. The A.T. and the Liberty Loop Trail head to the north along the east side of the wetlands. A small wildlife viewing blind sits at the southeast corner of the loop, and there you will also find a bench. Continue north along the A.T. and Liberty Loop for 0.25 mile farther, and the A.T. leaves the wide path to the east into the woods at a sign for the Pochuck Shelter. Continue north along the loop trail back to Oil City Road (about 2.3 miles total). Turn left and follow the path another 0.25 mile farther back to the parking lot.

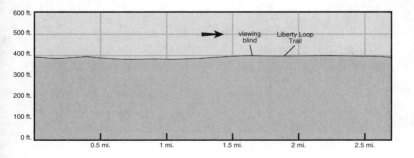

Nearby Attractions

For a rather different experience of wildlife, visit the Space Farms Zoo & Museum in nearby Sussex, New Jersey (973-875-5800; space farms.com). It has a zoo with more than 100 species of animals and an eclectic museum of Americana. It's a great place to go with the kids.

Directions

From Sussex, New Jersey, follow NJ 284 (Unionville Avenue) north 5.8 miles. Turn right onto Oil City Road and follow that 0.7 mile to State Line Road. Turn right again. State Line Road is also Oil City Road after the turn. The parking area for the Liberty Loop Trailhead will be on the right in 1.1 miles.

CANADA GEESE ARE COMMON VISITORS TO THE WALLKILL RIVER NATIONAL WILDLIFE REFUGE.

Pochuck Boardwalk

A COUPLE OF HIKERS ENJOYING A MORNING STROLL ALONG THE POCHUCK BOARDWALK

> **SCENERY:** ★ ★ ★ ★
> **TRAIL CONDITION:** ★ ★ ★ ★ ★
> **CHILDREN:** ★ ★ ★ ★
> (★ ★ ★ ★ ★ if beginning at
> CR 517 and only walking boardwalk)
> **DIFFICULTY:** ★
> **SOLITUDE:** ★ ★

GPS TRAILHEAD COORDINATES: *NJ 94 trailhead:* N41° 13.161' W74° 27.303'

CR 517 trailhead: N41° 14.147' W74° 28.827'

DISTANCE & CONFIGURATION: 5.0-mile out-and-back

HIKING TIME: 2.5 hours

HIGHLIGHTS: Pochuck Boardwalk, swamplands along Wawayanda Creek

ELEVATION: 434' at trailhead on NJ 94; no appreciable elevation gain or loss

ACCESS: Open 24/7; no fees or permits required

MAPS: Appalachian Trail Conservancy *New York–New Jersey, Maps 3 & 4: New York 17A to Delaware Water Gap, Pennsylvania;* USGS *Hamburg* and *Wawayanda*

FACILITIES: None

CONTACT: Wawayanda State Park, 973-853-4462, tinyurl.com/wawayandasp

COMMENTS: Bring binoculars and a field guide to birds with you on this hike. Also bring insect repellent; the mosquitoes can be a nuisance.

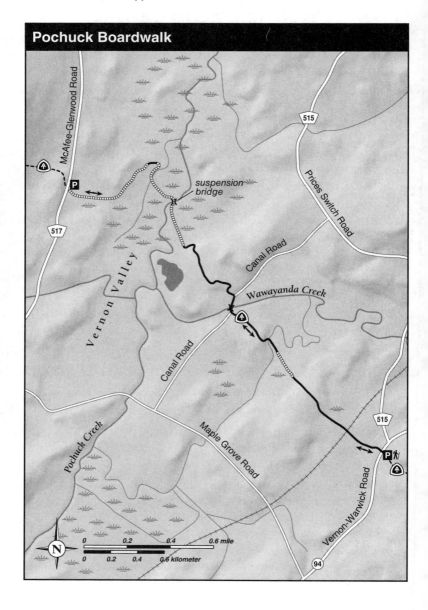

Pochuck Boardwalk

suspension
bridge

McAfee-Glenwood Road

515

Prices Switch Road

Canal Road

Wawayanda Creek

Canal Road

Vernon Valley

517

Pochuck Creek

Maple Grove Road

515

Vernon-Warwick Road

94

N

| 0 | 0.2 | 0.4 | 0.6 mile |

| 0 | 0.2 | 0.4 | 0.6 kilometer |

Overview

From the Appalachian Trail (A.T.) parking lot on NJ 94, you'll follow the trail through a pasture and over some old moraines out to the wetlands surrounding Wawayanda Creek. The Pochuck Boardwalk winds its way through the wetlands for a mile to NJ 517.

Route Details

This hike is one of those places I just can't wait to get back to.'This out-and-back hike is 2.5 miles each direction, a full mile of which is along a beautifully constructed wooden boardwalk that passes through the wetlands surrounding Wawayanda Creek. One of the more prominent man-made features of the A.T. designed for hiking, the boardwalk and the suspension bridge over the creek near the middle of the boardwalk took seven years to build. The name Pochuck means "out of the way place" in the language of the Lenni-Lenape tribe. The name is a bit inconsistent with the character of the hike because this is a very popular section of trail. If you would like some solitude, your best bet would be to do this hike early on a weekday.

You can begin this hike from either County Road 517 (McAfee-Glenwood Road) to the west or from NJ 94 (Vernon-Warwick Road) to the east. Beginning from the west, you'll need to park on the wide

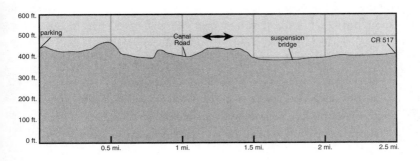

shoulder alongside the road. The benefit of beginning here is that you can just walk the boardwalk, if you so choose, because it begins just below the level of the road. From here, you can link this and the next hike up Wawayanda Mountain for an out-and-back trek of about 7.5 miles. The better parking, however, is at the A.T. crossing on NJ 94. There you will find a small A.T. parking lot with room for about 10 cars or so and additional parking in a lot just to the north. Use extra caution when using the A.T. lot on NJ 94, as it is on a blind curve, and the road is rather busy. From this lot, you can still do both the boardwalk and Wawayanda Mountain, though as two out-and-back hikes.

From the parking area on NJ 94, cross the highway heading west and pass over a stile into a pasture. This is private land, so be sure to stay on the trail through this section. At the far side of the pasture, the trail crosses a set of railroad tracks via two stiles and then crosses some marshy terrain on planks and puncheons (a type of boardwalk planking constructed from split logs). After the wet area, the trail enters into the woods and passes over several small hills and then passes back through another marshy area via planks and puncheons. The small hills along this section of the path are referred to as kames, and they consist of large mounds of glacial till that were piled up during the most recent glacial period of the ice age.

After a mile, the A.T. reaches the Canal Road bicycle path, onto which it turns right, crosses the bridge over Wawayanda Creek, and then leaves the bike path to the left. Again it climbs over another kame through the trees, gaining and losing about 50 feet of elevation. At the end of the descent on the north side, the trail leaves the woods, crosses a small footbridge, and enters the swampland at the east end of the Pochuck Boardwalk.

Not unlike the wetlands at the Wallkill River National Wildlife Refuge west of here, the wetlands along Wawayanda Creek are filled with cattails, rushes, and reeds and provide excellent habitat for a variety of waterfowl and riparian species of wildlife. The character of the two wetlands is a little different though. This area is noticeably hemmed in by forest, and the creek is a much more significant feature. Enjoy the walk along the boardwalk as it curves through the wetlands. After 0.3 mile, you'll cross the suspension bridge, about 100 feet across, and then continue along the boardwalk. Soon the path makes a long bend to the east and crosses a particularly pretty and wide section of the Wawayanda Creek. At a hillside, the boardwalk ends briefly, and a dirt path turns sharply to the left and traverses the bottom of a small rise for a short distance. After rejoining it, the boardwalk works its way west, making some long graceful curves through the wild grasses.

At 2.5 miles, the boardwalk ends at CR 517 at the base of Pochuck Mountain.

Nearby Attractions

A few miles east of NJ 94, visit Wawayanda State Park, home to Wawayanda Lake, which has picnic areas and a swimming beach and on which boating and fishing are permitted. The park also has many miles of hiking trails and an Appalachian Trail shelter.

Directions

From Warwick, New York, an officially designated Appalachian Trail Community, follow NY 94 south to the New Jersey state line, where the road becomes NJ 94. Continue south another 1.9 miles. Pass Heaven Hill Farm on the right. The parking area is on the left (east) just beyond CR 515 (Prices Switch Road) on the right.

Wawayanda Mountain

THE REMARKABLE VIEW OF THE GREAT VALLEY LOOKING SOUTH FROM WAWAYANDA MOUNTAIN

GPS TRAILHEAD COORDINATES: N41° 13.161' W74° 27.303'

DISTANCE & CONFIGURATION: 3.0-mile out-and-back

HIKING TIME: 2 hours

HIGHLIGHTS: Nice mountain hike with excellent view of Wawayanda Creek environs from viewpoint

ELEVATION: 434' at trailhead; 1,295' at viewpoint

ACCESS: Open 24/7; no fees or permits required

MAPS: Appalachian Trail Conservancy *New York–New Jersey, Maps 3–4: New York 17A to Delaware Water Gap, Pennsylvania;* USGS *Wawayanda*

FACILITIES: None

CONTACT: Wawayanda State Park, 973-853-4462, tinyurl.com/wawayandasp

COMMENTS: The ascent of Wawayanda Mountain is quite rugged and involves walking over and around many large boulders.

Overview

Another deservedly popular New Jersey hike, the ascent of Waway-anda Mountain begins at the same parking area as the Pochuck Boardwalk hike. Though this out-and-back trip is not very long, it packs a punch. The trail climbs almost 900 feet. But the view from up on high is worth the effort, as is the passage of the trail itself as it meanders through a field of huge boulders.

Route Details

Follow the Appalachian Trail (A.T.) northbound (to the east) up a small rise out of the parking lot on NJ 94. Atop the rise, you'll pass a sign with some A.T. information. For the first 0.5 mile, the trail climbs fairly gently through some open terrain with low bushes and scattered trees before entering the woods. After entering the woods, you'll follow the trail directly east to the foot of Wawayanda Moun-tain, at which point it bends to the south and begins to traverse up the rocky hillside. The geology of the mountain consists of crystalline rock slabs that date back over a billion years.

Wawayanda is such an unusual name that I did try to find its origins. I assumed that it, like Pochuck, came from the language of the Lenni-Lenape. I discovered an interesting paper on its origin dating back to 1933 that indeed attributes its etymology to the Lenape lan-guage, though its meaning remains uncertain. One source cited in the paper explained it as meaning "egg-shaped," while another translated it as "way of the wild goose." Yet another source referred to in the paper also suggested that it comes from a mispronunciation of the phrase "way over yonder." You can take your pick, though personally the "way of the wild goose" flies best with me.

Up until about 0.7 mile, the hiking is never especially steep. But it gets increasingly rocky with each passing step. As the trail bends back to the east, the grade gets a fair bit steeper. For the next 10 min-utes or so, you'll be picking your way among the boulders up to a set of switchbacks. After the switchbacks, you'll pass a short section that

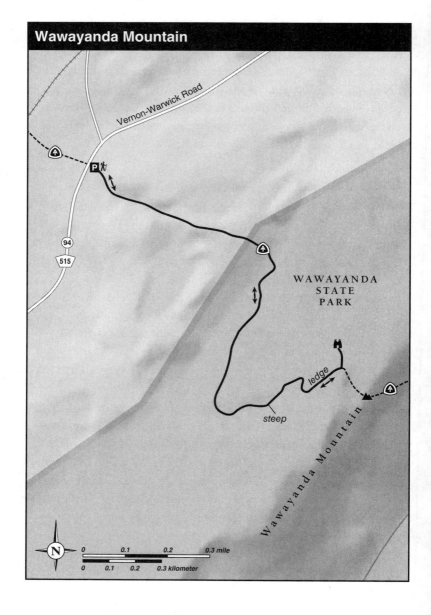

Wawayanda Mountain

Vernon-Warwick Road

P

94
515

WAWAYANDA
STATE
PARK

ledge

steep

Wawayanda Mountain

N

| 0 | 0.1 | 0.2 | 0.3 mile |
| 0 | 0.1 | 0.2 | 0.3 kilometer |

is quite steep and then traverse a broad ledge across a cliff face. The setting is quite dramatic, which is made even more so by the leathery rock tripe lichen that covers the rock in this area.

After the ledge, a little steep hiking through some stone steps takes you to a level area below the top of Wawayanda Mountain. Here you will find a very large cairn and a wooden sign nailed to a tree engraved with the words THE VIEW. A blue-blazed trail heads directly north from this spot to a large ledge on the west flank of the mountain, and at this location you will find "the view." It is impressive indeed. From atop the rock outcrop, you can scan the landscape of the Great Valley to the west and south. Mountain Creek ski area will be to your left. The Pochuck Boardwalk and Wawayanda Creek lie below you, and over the first significant rise, Pochuck Mountain, lies the Wallkill River Basin. It is extraordinary scenery, worthy of a photograph and some time spent soaking it up.

Just for kicks, and because I invariably wonder what's around the next corner, before heading down I decided to follow the A.T. to the top of Wawayanda Mountain to see what I would find. If you do so, you will see that there is indeed a top to Wawayanda Mountain, though any view is obstructed by trees. And that explains why most people finish the hike at the view below the summit. Use caution descending the trail back to the car, especially if it is wet.

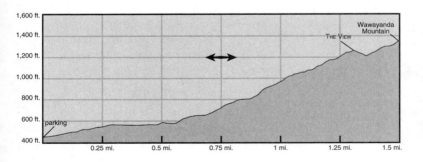

Nearby Attractions

A few miles east of NJ 94, visit Wawayanda State Park, home to Wawayanda Lake, which has picnic areas and a swimming beach and on which boating and fishing are permitted. The park also has many miles of hiking trails and an Appalachian Trail shelter.

Directions

From Warwick, New York, an officially designated Appalachian Trail Community, follow NY 94 south to the New Jersey state line, where the road becomes NJ 94. Continue south another 1.9 miles. Pass Heaven Hill Farm on the right. The parking area is on the left (east) just beyond County Road 515 (Prices Switch Road) on the right.

THE WAY THE BRANCHES GROW ON THIS PINE TREE IS EVIDENCE OF HOW
HARD THE WIND CAN BLOW UP THE SIDE OF WAWAYANDA MOUNTAIN.

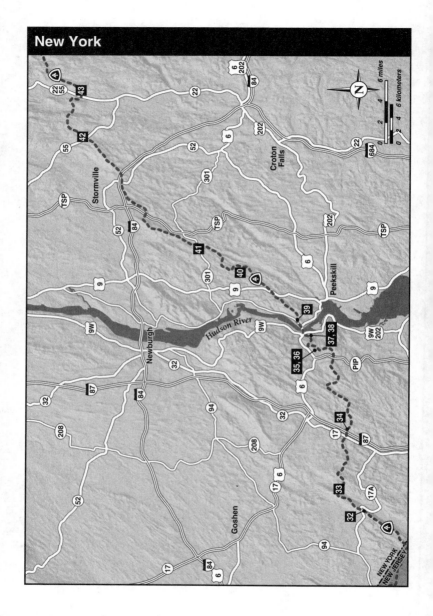

New York

THE NORTH-FACING ADIRONDACK CHAIR OF A PAIR ON THE SWAMP RIVER BOARDWALK *(See Hike 43, page 262.)*

32 **EASTERN PINNACLES AND CAT ROCKS** p. 204

33 **MOMBASHA HIGH POINT** p. 209

34 **ISLAND POND AND FINGERBOARD MOUNTAIN** p. 214

35 **SILVER MINE LAKE** p. 220

36 **WEST MOUNTAIN LOOP** p. 226

37 **BEAR MOUNTAIN LOOP** p. 231

38 **BEAR MOUNTAIN ZOO AND BRIDGE** p. 237

39 **ANTHONYS NOSE** p. 242

40 **CANOPUS HILL** p. 247

41 **SHENANDOAH MOUNTAIN** p. 252

42 **NUCLEAR LAKE** p. 257

43 **GREAT SWAMP AND DOVER OAK** p. 262

32 # Eastern Pinnacles
and Cat Rocks

THE VIEW TO THE NORTH FROM THE TOP OF CAT ROCKS

GPS TRAILHEAD COORDINATES: N41° 14.656' W74° 17.224'

DISTANCE & CONFIGURATION: 4.6-mile out-and-back

HIKING TIME: 2–3 hours

HIGHLIGHTS: Eastern Pinnacles, Cat Rocks, Wildcat Shelter

ELEVATION: 1,186' at parking area on summit of NY 17A; 1,285' on ridge before descending to Eastern Pinnacles

ACCESS: Open 24/7; no fees or permits required

MAPS: Appalachian Trail Conservancy *New York–New Jersey, Maps 1 & 2: Connecticut State Line to New York 17A;* USGS *Greenwood Lake* and *Warwick*

FACILITIES: Privy at the Wildcat Shelter

CONTACT: New York–New Jersey Trail Conference, 201-512-9348, nynjtc.org

COMMENTS: Getting to the A.T. for this hike can be a little confusing. The trail used to cross NY 17A at the crest of Bellvale Mountain (called Mount Peter at this point on some maps), where there is a large parking area with an A.T. sign on the south side of the highway. Now, however, the trail has been rerouted and crosses the highway 0.25 mile to the east of the crest of the hill. There is also parking where the trail crosses, though the lot is small. This hike description will begin from the upper lot. Resist the temptation to walk the shoulder of the road from the upper lot down to the trail—the highway is heavily traveled.

Overview

Though this hike generally follows the ridge of Bellvale Mountain, you'll never get the feeling of being on a ridge. Both the Eastern Pinnacles and Cat Rocks lie on the east side of the ridgecrest and somewhat below. After passing the two outcrops, the hike continues through a lovely forest filled with mountain laurel to the Wildcat Shelter.

Route Details

Beginning from the parking area on the crest of the ridge, where the Appalachian Trail (A.T.) used to cross the highway, follow a blue-blazed access trail from the A.T. sign heading south across Continental Road and into the woods. Traverse the hillside, descending somewhat for about 0.25 mile, to where the access trail meets the A.T. Turn left onto the A.T. and follow it northbound 0.3 mile back out to the highway at a lower parking lot. NY 17A is heavily traveled and makes a bend up and over the hill from the north, so use great care when crossing.

Once you have crossed the highway, walk into the woods a short distance to a junction with a blue-blazed trail that heads left. Follow the A.T. to the right. For the sake of clarification, that blue-blazed path parallels NY 17A uphill to a hawk-viewing platform on top of the ridge, approximately 0.3 mile from the junction.

The A.T. stays to the east side of the ridge and follows an old forest road for some distance. The hiking is level and pleasant, and the trail passes through a pretty hardwood forest with some small hemlocks here and there. The geology along this section of trail is rather interesting, especially if you have been hiking farther south or north on it. Here you begin to encounter outcrops of rust-colored conglomerate, not unlike what you might come across to the west along the Tuscarora Trail in central Pennsylvania. According to V. Collins Chew in his book *Underfoot: A Geologic Guide to the Appalachian Trail,* much of Bellvale Mountain consists of this rock, which has been polished smooth by the action of glaciers and displays occasional crystals of quartz.

Eastern Pinnacles and Cat Rocks

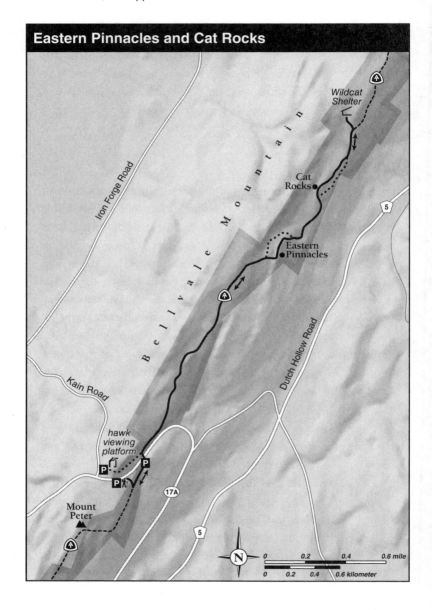

Around 1.1 miles, the A.T. leaves the old forest road and drops about 100 feet in elevation into a rhododendron- and hemlock-filled hollow at a large rock outcrop, known as the Eastern Pinnacles. More folded slabs than actual towers as the name implies, this outcrop too is formed by the same rust-colored conglomerate, and here it has significant dikes of quartz running through it. Before the trail takes to the rocks, a blue-blazed path heads north. That is the easy way around the Eastern Pinnacles. Crossing the outcrop without a pack is not especially difficult, though it does involve a bit of scrambling and requires you to use your hands to pass by a couple of sections.

The outcrop extends 100 yards, and then the trail drops down into the woods. The forest is quite pretty along the trail here, with many mountain laurels forming the understory of the forest. Not far beyond the end of the pinnacles, you'll cross over a stream via a couple of slippery logs, and less than 0.25 mile beyond that, you'll reach Cat Rocks, which also has a blue-blazed bypass trail around it on the east side. Formed by the same interesting rock as the Eastern Pinnacles, Cat Rocks is distinctly blockier in character and quite a bit taller. The western side of the outcrop drops off a good 80 feet or so to a confusion of broken and ragged boulders. The top of Cat Rocks rewards hikers with an excellent view of the surrounding area to the east and north as well as back to the Eastern Pinnacles, which are

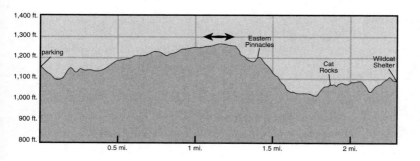

situated somewhat higher along the ridge. It is also a very comfortable place to lie down and have a snooze, if you are so inclined.

You can hang out on Cat Rocks, call it a day, and hike back to the car. Or you can extend the hike a little more by walking out to the Wildcat Shelter, which is worth the effort. From Cat Rocks, follow the A.T. off the north side and down into a small saddle, which has a cold, clear creek running through it before the creek spills off the hillside to the east. After crossing the creek, the trail climbs, passing some dense mountain laurel. Continue along the A.T. about 75 yards to the blue-blazed side trail to the Wildcat Shelter on the left. The trail is identified by a white sign with black lettering. You may have noticed some old blue blazes back near the creek. Those mark the old path to the shelter, and it is quite overgrown. The shelter is located about 150 yards or so from the A.T. around the back (west) side of a small hill. It sits above a broad hollow in an open forest of mountain laurel and oak. A bear box and second fire ring are both situated a couple of hundred feet from the shelter, where there is space to set up several tents. From the shelter, the distance back to the car is 2.3 miles.

Nearby Attractions

Just west of the crest of Bellvale Mountain on NY 17A, almost directly across from the upper parking lot at the corner of Kain Road and NY 17A, you'll find the Bellvale Farms Creamery (845-988-1818; bellvalefarms.com). It has an excellent homemade ice cream shop open April–October.

Directions

From downtown Warwick, New York, follow NY 94 south 0.5 mile to NY 17A. Turn left and follow NY 17A east 4.3 miles to the crest of Bellvale Mountain. The parking lot is on the right (south) side of the road at the summit between NY 17A and Continental Road. Additional parking may be available 0.25 mile farther east on the right where the A.T. crosses the highway.

33

Mombasha High Point

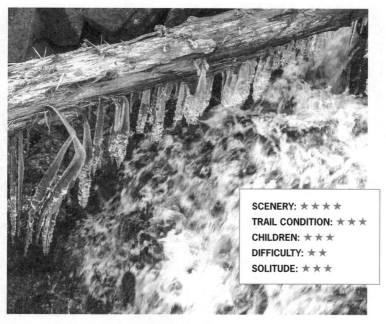

ICE FORMATION ON THE CREEK ABOVE FITZGERALD FALLS

GPS TRAILHEAD COORDINATES: N41° 16.428' W74° 15.248'

DISTANCE & CONFIGURATION: 4.6-mile out-and-back

HIKING TIME: 2.5 hours

HIGHLIGHTS: Fitzgerald Falls, Mombasha High Point

ELEVATION: 773' at trailhead; 1,265' at Mombasha High Point

ACCESS: Open 24/7; no fees or permits required

MAPS: Appalachian Trail Conservancy *New York–New Jersey, Maps 1 & 2: Connecticut State Line to New York 17A;* USGS *Monroe, Warwick*

FACILITIES: None

CONTACT: Sterling Forest State Park, 845-351-5907, nysparks.com/parks/74

COMMENTS: Parking at the trailhead is limited, and Fitzgerald Falls is a popular destination.

Mombasha High Point

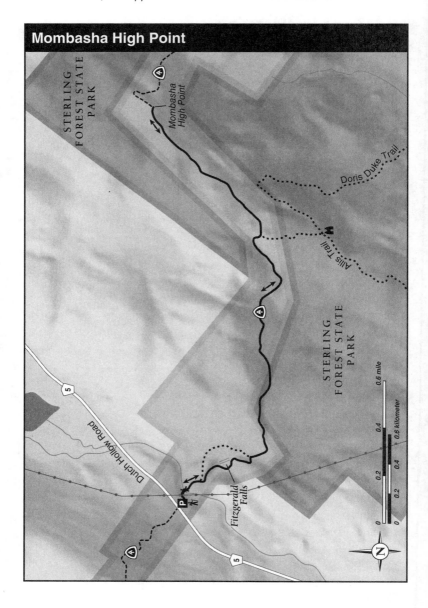

STERLING FOREST STATE PARK

Mombasha High Point

Doris Duke Trail

Allis Trail

STERLING FOREST STATE PARK

Dutch Hollow Road

Fitzgerald Falls

0.6 mile

0.4

0.6 kilometer

0.2

0.4

0.2

0

0

N

Overview

This lovely hike follows the Appalachian Trail (A.T.) first to Fitzgerald Falls and then into a high hollow below a ridge. Once on the ridge, the trail passes the junction with the Allis Trail, and a short distance beyond that it reaches the Mombasha High Point.

Route Details

From the trailhead, follow the A.T. northbound as it descends east and then curves north under the power lines. It crosses a creek via a footbridge and then climbs a short hillside and goes into the woods, heading in a more southeasterly direction. Soon you'll reach the bottom of the very pretty Fitzgerald Falls, which cascades off the hillside about 50 feet or so and into a large pool at the base (0.3 mile). Cross the creek below the falls via rocks. The A.T. turns left and ascends the hillside next to the falls via a set of stone steps.

Once above the falls, the A.T. passes a second smaller set of falls and crosses back over the creek to the north side. Just beyond, a blue-blazed trail leaves the A.T. to the left and traverses the hillside above the creek, offering a bypass around the falls. Stay to the right on the A.T., which now climbs the hillside to the south. Soon the trail crosses an old forest road and turns to the east. It continues climbing

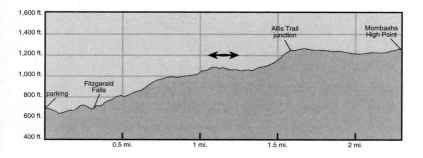

FITZGERALD FALLS AND THE STONE STEPS ALONG THE APPALACHIAN TRAIL THAT BYPASSES THEM

into a high hollow through a pretty hardwood forest that is crisscrossed in places with stone walls that remain from old settlements in the hollow. The trail surface becomes a little rocky and muddy in places, and then climbs fairly steeply to a ridge. Once on the ridge, the A.T. meets the northern terminus of the Allis Trail, which connects the A.T. with the Sterling Ridge Trail 4.1 miles to the south. Collectively, the Appalachian, Allis, and Sterling Ridge Trails comprise the Highlands Trail within Sterling Forest State Park. A Highlands Trail marker is on a post at the junction with the Allis Trail.

The Allis Trail heads to the south along the ridge, while the A.T. follows the ridge to the north. Stay left on the A.T. and follow it along the ridge through Gambel oaks for another 0.7 mile to the Mombasha High Point (2.3 miles). The high point is identified by an A.T. symbol on the polished rocks and by the fact that the trail descends from here. Though the view is not completely unobstructed, it is still pretty darn nice. The large Monroe Reservoir lies just below the high point to the east, and Buchanan Mountain (1,141 feet) sits just southeast of that.

If you have done the Eastern Pinnacles and Cat Rocks hike (see page 204) just south of this hike along the A.T., you may notice that the geology on top of Mombasha High Point is completely different than what is found just a couple of miles south on Bellvale Mountain. Whereas that ridge consisted of red conglomerate dating back about 400 million to 385 million years, now you are sitting on the billion-year-old metamorphic rock that makes up the geology of the Hudson Highlands. The change stems from the fact that Lakes Road lies on a fault line, and the ridge on the west side of it has folded down as the older rock uplifted east of it, exposing the great vertical slabs of sedimentary rock that make up Bellvale Mountain and Mount Peter.

On the descent, be sure to watch for the point where the blue-blazed falls bypass trail leaves the Appalachian Trail. To stay on the A.T., you have to make a left turn, and it would be easy to march right past it. The steps alongside the falls are rather steep, which might make the bypass appealing to some.

Nearby Attractions

The main recreation area at Sterling Forest State Park is nearby, and it has a lake, hiking trails, picnic areas, and plenty of other activities. It can be reached by following NY 17A east from Greenwood Lake about 4.5 miles to County Road 84 (Long Meadow Road). Turn right and follow that 3.7 miles to the park entrance.

Directions

From NY 17A in the town of Greenwood Lake, New York, follow Lakes Road (CR 5) north 3.6 miles. The parking area for this hike is located on the east side of Lakes Road, right by a power line crossing. A sign for Chester Township is located next to the parking area. Parking is very limited for this hike, with room for only three cars at the trailhead on the east side of the road. There is room for an additional three cars on the west side of the road, and there's room for a few more north of the power lines, also on the west side of the road.

34

Island Pond and Fingerboard Mountain

SCENERY: ★ ★ ★ ★ ★	
TRAIL CONDITION: ★ ★ ★ ★ ★	
CHILDREN: ★ ★ ★	
DIFFICULTY: ★ ★ ★	
SOLITUDE: ★ ★ ★ ★	

THE FINGERBOARD MOUNTAIN SHELTER IS A CHARMING OLD STRUCTURE BUILT OF LOCAL STONE.

GPS TRAILHEAD COORDINATES: N41° 15.879' W74° 9.258'

DISTANCE & CONFIGURATION: 9.8-mile balloon

HIKING TIME: 6–7 hours

HIGHLIGHTS: Island Pond, the Lemon Squeeze, Fingerboard Mountain

ELEVATION: 579' at trailhead; 1,341' at Fingerboard Mountain

ACCESS: Daily, sunrise–sunset; no fees or permits required

MAPS: Appalachian Trail Conservancy *New York–New Jersey, Maps 1 & 2: Connecticut State Line to New York 17A;* USGS *Monroe* and *Popolopen Lake;* New York–New Jersey Trail Conference *Harriman–Bear Mountain Northern: Trail Map 119*

FACILITIES: Privy at Fingerboard Mountain Shelter

CONTACT: Harriman State Park, 845-947-2444, nysparks.com/parks/145; New York–New Jersey Trail Conference, 201-512-9348, nynjtc.org

COMMENTS: This is one of the most beautiful hikes I have ever done. It is hard to believe that it lies only about an hour's drive from New York City. Overnight camping is limited to thru-hikers at designated areas. Pets are permitted in the park on leash only.

Overview

This long and varied hike through Harriman State Park passes through some beautiful terrain west of the Hudson River. It begins by following the Appalachian Trail (A.T.) past Island Pond and over the beautiful and distinctive glacially carved ridges of Harriman State Park. After 2.5 miles, the hike picks up the New York Long Path and uses that to make a loop around and over Fingerboard Mountain.

Route Details

Begin this hike from what is referred to on A.T. maps as the Elk Pen parking area. Follow the trail northbound 0.2 mile through an old field to a forest road, the Arden-Surebridge Trail. Turn right and follow the road for a short distance, then turn left at an A.T. sign with mileages listed for many destinations. The A.T. climbs fairly steadily from that point, gaining about 400 feet of elevation in 0.7 mile. At times, the path takes on the appearance of a creek bed, and following it instead of some random run-off does require a bit of attention.

At around 0.9 mile, the trail passes over a ridge and descends to an old carriage road at Island Pond (1.2 miles). The pond—surrounded by rock outcrops, hemlock trees, and mountain laurel—is about as pretty a place as you might imagine. Follow the A.T. along the northeast side of Island Pond to Island Pond Road, a gravel road in good condition that provides access to the pond. A tenth of a mile beyond Island Pond Road, the trail crosses the Island Pond outlet by a footbridge at an old mill site. From the crossing, the trail again follows the path of an old carriage road along the hillside north of the lake. Around 1.7 miles, it leaves the carriage road, climbs a rise, and passes through a notch in the rocks.

Once through the notch, you'll be facing a huge outcrop with a crack in the middle of it, into which the A.T. proceeds. This is the infamous Lemon Squeeze. Follow the A.T. into the crack, and at the back of it turn left. Squeeze through the narrow slot for about 30 feet. You have to climb out of the slot at its back end, and then the white blazes

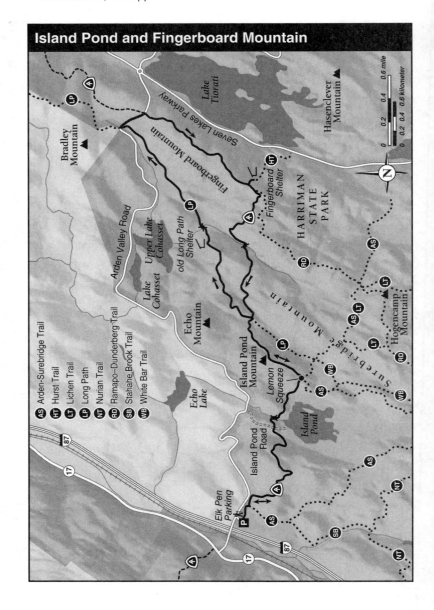

Island Pond and Fingerboard Mountain

Lake Tiorati

Hasenclever Mountain

Seven Lakes Parkway

Bradley Mountain

Fingerboard Mountain

Fingerboard Shelter

HARRIMAN STATE PARK

Upper Lake Cohasset

old Long Path Shelter

Arden Valley Road

Lake Cohasset

Echo Mountain

Surebridge Mountain

Hogencamp Mountain

Island Pond Mountain

Lemon Squeeze

Echo Lake

Island Pond

Island Pond Road

AS Arden-Surebridge Trail
HT Hurst Trail
LT Lichen Trail
LP Long Path
NT Nurian Trail
RD Ramapo–Dunderberg Trail
SB Stahahe Brook Trail
WB White Bar Trail

Elk Pen Parking

0   0.2   0.4   0.6 mile
0   0.2   0.4   0.6 kilometer

point the way up a dubious section of steep cliff. If it looks difficult, that's because it is (and it is even worse coming back). Thankfully, a blue-blazed side trail, identified by a sign reading THE EASY WAY, bypasses the steep section to the left.

Beyond the steep section, the trail emerges from the rocks onto a lightly forested ridge that was formed by the action of glaciers over the landscape. The setting is spectacular and the hiking easy and pleasant as the trail passes alternately through grassy sections and over stretches of bedrock. The trail proceeds north and climbs gently to a high point (Island Pond Mountain at 1,306 feet). Then it descends about 0.3 mile into a hollow filled with hemlocks, where it crosses paths with the aqua-blazed Long Path (2.5 miles). This begins the loop section of the hike.

Turn left onto the Long Path and follow it north 2.1 miles out to Arden Valley Road. The trail stays low for a while, then passes through some rolling terrain, and then gains another glacially carved ridge similar in character to Island Pond Mountain. The descent from the ridge to the northeast follows outcrops of gneiss before dropping to an old shelter (3.6 miles). Located on the side of a hill, the shelter is in a beautiful setting with open woods and grasslands all around it. The trail bends to the south at the shelter and then back east and enters a wetlands area. Cross over Surebridge Brook and

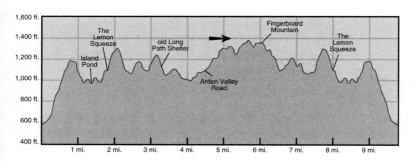

THE APPALACHIAN TRAIL CROSSES THE OUTFLOW FROM ISLAND POND OVER A WELL-CONSTRUCTED BRIDGE.

continue walking along rolling terrain through the forest for another mile out to the Arden Valley Road (4.7 miles). Turn right and follow the shoulder of Arden Valley Road east and uphill 0.25 mile to the crest of the hill where the A.T. crosses. Turn right and follow it southbound past a couple of water tanks, one of which is quite old.

From the tanks, the A.T. climbs gently to and along the shoulder of Fingerboard Mountain. The terrain is similar to the high terrain you've passed earlier in the hike, except it is more open with long stretches of exposed bedrock. The setting is truly remarkable. The A.T. meets the side trail to the Fingerboard Mountain Shelter at 1.2 miles from the Arden Valley Road. A side trip to the shelter is worth the effort. I can't imagine a more beautiful place to spend the night. The old stone shelter faces east and provides an excellent view across the surrounding countryside.

Return to the A.T. and continue southbound. From the shelter trail, the A.T. shares the path with the Ramapo–Dunderberg Trail (marked by white blazes with a red dot on them), and in a short distance, the two trails split. A short walk to the left along the Ramapo–Dunderberg Trail leads to the top of Fingerboard Mountain. From the fork in the trails, follow the A.T. down from the ridge and into the forest again. The trail descends consistently for 0.7 mile back to an old forest road that it follows south for a short distance. The A.T. leaves the road and crosses Surebridge Brook about 0.5 mile upstream from the earlier crossing via the Long Path (6.9 miles). From the crossing, another 0.7 mile of hiking along rolling terrain leads back to the beginning of the loop, where the A.T. crosses the Long Path (7.6 miles). From this point, continue southbound along the A.T., retracing the route past the Lemon Squeeze and Island Pond back to Elk Pen.

Nearby Attractions

There is not much near the Elk Pen lot. If you follow NY 17 north about 3 miles to Harriman, you'll find plenty of shops and restaurants for provisions.

Directions

From Suffern, New York, follow NY 17 north 12.3 miles to Arden Valley Road. Turn right onto Arden Valley Road. Pass over I-87 and turn right into the Elk Pen parking lot (about 0.3 mile).

35

Silver Mine Lake

SCENERY: ★ ★ ★
TRAIL CONDITION: ★ ★ ★ ★ ★
CHILDREN: ★ *(see comments below)*
DIFFICULTY: ★ ★ ★ ★ ★
SOLITUDE: ★ ★

SILVER MINE LAKE IS LOCATED ABOUT A MILE DOWNHILL FROM THE WILLIAM BRIEN SHELTER.

GPS TRAILHEAD COORDINATES: N41° 18.249' W74° 0.959'

DISTANCE & CONFIGURATION: 12.0-mile balloon

HIKING TIME: 7–8 hours

HIGHLIGHTS: Excellent views from West Mountain and Black Mountain, Silver Mine Lake

ELEVATION: 623' at trailhead; 1,235' on West Mountain; 600' near Palisades Parkway crossing; 1,185' on Black Mountain; 655' at outlet of Silver Mine Lake

ACCESS: Daily, sunrise–sunset; no fees or permits required

MAPS: Appalachian Trail Conservancy *New York–New Jersey, Maps 1 & 2: Connecticut State Line to New York 17A;* USGS *Popolopen Lake;* New York–New Jersey Trail Conference *Harriman–Bear Mountain Northern: Trail Map 119*

FACILITIES: None

CONTACT: Bear Mountain State Park, 845-786-2701, nysparks.com/parks/13; Harriman State Park, 845-947-2444, nysparks.com/parks/145; New York–New Jersey Trail Conference, 201-512-9348, nynjtc.org

COMMENTS: This is a difficult hike because of all the ascents and descents. The first mile from the parking area to the ridge of West Mountain is suitable for young children.

Overview

Though long and challenging, this balloon hike is worth the effort for the exceptional views it offers as well as the beautiful country it traverses in the eastern part of Harriman State Park. Additionally, you get to walk across the Palisades Parkway, which is something most people would never imagine doing.

Route Details

From the parking area on Seven Lakes Drive, follow Trail 1777 to the south 0.25 mile to where it joins the Appalachian Trail (A.T.), which is marked with signs indicating north- and southbound. You'll follow the A.T. for most of this hike, with the exception of the loop around Silver Mine Lake. It is worth noting that the stretch of the trail traversed in this hike is part of the first section of the A.T., constructed in 1923 between the Bear Mountain Bridge and Arden, New York, to the west.

From the junction with Trail 1777, turn right and follow the A.T. southbound along an old forest roadbed a short distance until it crosses the Fawn Trail, marked by white plastic blazes with a red letter *F* in the middle. At this point, the Fawn Trail follows the roadbed, and the A.T. becomes a footpath winding its way over old moraines to the south up to the West Mountain ridge. The ascent is pleasant enough, not too steep, and upon attaining the ridge (0.9 mile), you'll reach the first of several excellent vistas, this one to the west. Along the ridge, the A.T. shares the path with the blue-blazed Timp–Torne Trail, which traverses the entire ridge of West Mountain, for about 0.75 mile. Just beyond a small saddle when the path is on the west side of the ridge below its crest, the Timp–Torne Trail departs to the left and continues out to the West Mountain Shelter. A side trip to the shelter is certainly worth the effort; it offers a superb view of the Hudson River Valley to the south.

After the trails split, the A.T. descends to the west, at first quite steeply and then very pleasantly. The soft dirt path switchbacks

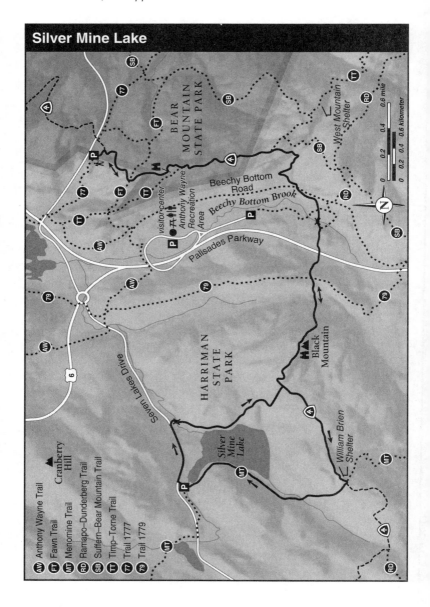

Silver Mine Lake

BEAR MOUNTAIN STATE PARK

West Mountain Shelter

Beechy Bottom Road

Beechy Bottom Brook

visitor center

Anthony Wayne Recreation Area

Palisades Parkway

HARRIMAN STATE PARK

Black Mountain

William Brien Shelter

Seven Lakes Drive

Cranberry Hill

Silver Mine Lake

AW Anthony Wayne Trail
FT Fawn Trail
MT Menomine Trail
RD Ramapo–Dunderberg Trail
SB Suffern–Bear Mountain Trail
TT Timp–Torne Trail
77 Trail 1777
79 Trail 1779

through a forest of tall hardwoods down to the bottom of the valley (2.2 miles). Make your way through the valley, passing several signed trails, the most prominent of which is a ski and bike path that takes you to parking for the Anthony Wayne Recreation Area, accessible from the Palisades Parkway at Exit 17, in 10 minutes. Continue along the A.T., crossing Beechy Bottom Brook via a footbridge. A short distance farther, the trail meets the Palisades Parkway, which you will have to cross.

Thanks to a forested median, you'll get a break after crossing the northbound lanes and before crossing the southbound lanes. The speed limit on the parkway is 55 miles per hour, and traffic can be quite heavy, so the crossing can be a little nerve-racking. Be very careful. After crossing the southbound lanes, be sure to note the sign along the highway. New York City is only 35 miles south of the trail.

After the parkway, ascend a short but steep hill to a ridge and cross an unnamed path that runs north and south along its top. Not far beyond the path, the A.T. ascends Black Mountain. The ascent isn't especially long, only 0.25 mile or so, but it is fairly steep, especially just below the crest. The top of Black Mountain is covered with low stands of oak, but it affords some extraordinary views in all directions. The body of water just northwest of Black Mountain is Silver Mine Lake. Black Mountain is a good place to assess your stamina

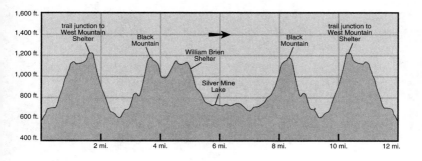

and desire to continue on and make the loop around the lake. Round-trip from this point consists of about 5.5 miles of rolling terrain and includes climbing Black Mountain. Consider that you have already walked 3.8 miles, and the return trip from this point also includes climbing West Mountain. Even if you decide that Black Mountain is far enough, be sure to follow the A.T. southbound a little farther across the ridge and downhill a short distance to the amazing slab of gneiss that faces west. It is a great place for a nice, long break.

If you decide to continue, follow the A.T. downhill through a forest of tall hardwoods to an old carriage road running north and south (4.2 miles). That is the return path from the lake, located 0.5 mile or so

THE WILLIAM BRIEN SHELTER IN HARRIMAN STATE PARK IS POPULAR WITH WEEKEND HIKERS ON THE TRAIL.

to the north. Stay on the A.T. southbound across an especially beautiful ridge for almost a mile to the William Brien Shelter. The final descent to the shelter is short and quite steep. At the shelter, the A.T. joins an old forest road marked with yellow blazes. Here you'll leave the A.T. and follow the yellow blazes along the forest road northbound and downhill through a forest of huge trees to Silver Mine Lake, about 0.6 mile distant. Continue following the road along the west shore of the lake and out to the large Silver Mine Lake parking area.

Walk out of the parking area onto Seven Lakes Drive, turn right, and follow the shoulder to the east 0.5 mile to a little stone house on the right side of the road. The carriage road crosses Seven Lakes Drive here, and onto it you will turn right. Once on the carriage road, cross the creek below the dam via a lovely old bridge dating back to when the carriage road was still in use. Follow the road uphill 0.8 mile back to the Appalachian Trail. Turn left (northbound) on the A.T. and follow it back to your car, 4.2 miles distant.

Nearby Attractions

Bear Mountain State Park is 2.5 miles east along Seven Lakes Drive from the A.T. parking area.

Directions

From Peekskill, New York, follow US 202 west 0.7 mile, and turn left onto US 202/US 6/US 9 and cross the Jans Peeck Bridge. Exit the roundabout at the third exit for US 202/US 6. Continue 4.0 miles to the Bear Mountain Bridge. Cross the bridge and enter the roundabout. Exit the roundabout at the second exit, following the signs for US 6 West. Follow US 6 2.3 miles to Exit 19 for Perkins Memorial Drive and Bear Mountain State Park. Follow Seven Lakes Drive south toward Perkins Memorial Drive and Bear Mountain State Park 0.5 mile. The parking lot for the A.T. is on the right about 0.1 mile before the A.T. crosses Seven Lakes Drive.

West Mountain Loop

SCENERY: ★ ★ ★ ★ ★
TRAIL CONDITION: ★ ★
CHILDREN: ★ *or* ★ ★ ★ ★
(see comments below)
DIFFICULTY: ★ ★ ★ ★ ★
SOLITUDE: ★ ★ *or* ★ ★ ★ ★ ★ ★
(see comments below)

THE VIEW SOUTH ALONG THE HUDSON RIVER FROM THE SHELTER ON WEST MOUNTAIN IS PRETTY HARD TO BEAT.

GPS TRAILHEAD COORDINATES: N41° 18.249' W74° 0.959'

DISTANCE & CONFIGURATION: 5.2-mile balloon

HIKING TIME: 3–4 hours

HIGHLIGHTS: West Mountain ridge and West Mountain Shelter, excellent views, remote environs of Suffern–Bear Mountain Trail

ELEVATION: 623' at trailhead; 1,262' on West Mountain

ACCESS: Daily, 8 a.m.–sunset; no fees or permits required

MAPS: Appalachian Trail Conservancy *New York–New Jersey, Maps 1 & 2: Connecticut State Line to New York 17A;* USGS *Popolopen Lake;* New York–New Jersey Trail Conference *Harriman–Bear Mountain Northern: Trail Map 119*

FACILITIES: None

CONTACT: Bear Mountain State Park, 845-786-2701, nysparks.com/parks/13

COMMENTS: The 2.25 miles from the parking area to the West Mountain Shelter is suitable for hiking with children. The return via the yellow-blazed trail can be quite steep and rocky in places and passes through a relatively remote section of the park.

Overview

The hike along the crest of West Mountain out to the West Mountain Shelter is quite popular for several reasons: The ascent of West Mountain along the Appalachian Trail (A.T.) is not especially steep or difficult, the walk along the ridge passes many excellent vantage points with views in all directions, and the West Mountain Shelter makes a great destination and place for a picnic. From there, you can trace your route back to the car or make a loop using the Suffern–Bear Mountain Trail. The latter option is quite challenging.

Route Details

From the parking area on Seven Lakes Drive, follow Trail 1777 to the south 0.25 mile to where it joins the A.T., which is marked with signs indicating north and south. Turn right and follow the A.T. southbound along an old forest roadbed for a short distance until it crosses the Fawn Trail, marked by white plastic blazes with the red letter F in the middle. At this point, the Fawn Trail follows the roadbed and the A.T. becomes a footpath, winding its way over old moraines to the south up to the West Mountain ridge. The ascent is pleasant enough, not too steep, and upon attaining the ridge (0.9 mile), you'll reach the first of several excellent vistas, this one to the west. Along the ridge, the A.T. shares the path with the blue-blazed Timp–Torne Trail, which traverses the entire ridge of West Mountain for about 0.75 mile. Just beyond a small saddle when the path is on the west side of the ridge below its crest, the Timp–Torne Trail departs to the left and continues out to the West Mountain Shelter (1.75 miles). A signpost is located at the junction with a sign that explains that the trails are maintained by the NY–NJ Trail Conference. Stay to the left and follow the Timp–Torne Trail south.

The ridge of West Mountain becomes wide and lightly forested through this next section, and the trail passes by some large outcrops of exfoliated gneiss along the way. At 2.1 miles, the yellow-blazed Suffern–Bear Mountain (S–BM) Trail joins the Timp–Torne

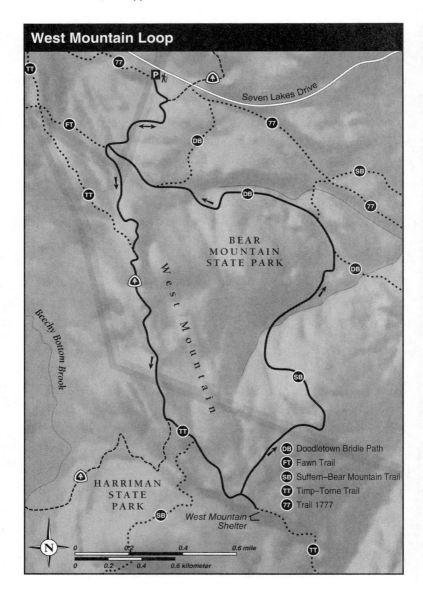

West Mountain Loop

Seven Lakes Drive

BEAR
MOUNTAIN
STATE PARK

W e s t   M o u n t a i n

Beechy Bottom Brook

HARRIMAN
STATE
PARK

West Mountain
Shelter

DB Doodletown Bridle Path
FT Fawn Trail
SB Suffern–Bear Mountain Trail
TT Timp–Torne Trail
77 Trail 1777

N

| 0 | 0.2 | 0.4 | 0.6 mile |
| 0 | 0.2 | 0.4 | 0.6 kilometer |

Trail and then shortly thereafter leaves it, heading northwest. Continue following the blue blazes to the right out to the shelter situated on a rock outcrop on the south shoulder of West Mountain. The West Mountain Shelter is truly one of the great shelters of the Appalachian Trail. Constructed of stone and timbers, it provides its guests with an excellent view of the Hudson River to the south and the Manhattan skyline. It has room for about six people to sleep inside, but there are plenty of places to pitch a tent nearby. Due to its proximity to Bear Mountain, the shelter is heavily used.

From the shelter, follow the Timp–Torne Trail back to the S–BM Trail. Turn right onto the S–BM Trail and follow it northwest along the ridge for a short distance before it begins to descend. The descent of West Mountain will take some time. The S–BM Trail is quite rocky and at times incredibly steep, so be sure to exercise great caution. From the crest of West Mountain, the trail descends about 0.25 mile into a hollow, which it then climbs out of over a knoll and then continues its descent into the steep-sided, but pleasantly named, drainage of the Doodlekill brook. The location is quite lovely and quite secluded, unusual for Bear Mountain State Park, but the trail is still steep and rocky. At around 3.3 miles, the trail crosses the creek and becomes considerably less steep and before too long less rocky. At 3.7 miles, it joins the old Doodletown Bridal Path that once provided access to the Doodletown Mine, located

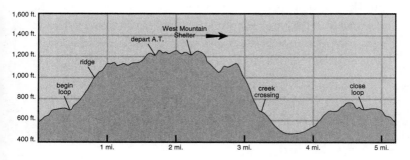

at about 700 feet of elevation on the east flank of West Mountain. Turn left onto the path, following yellow blazes northwest.

After another 0.1 mile or so, the S–BM Trail leaves the bridal path to the right across a swampy area and up a rise. Continue straight along the path, now blazed by white dots with a red *F* on them. The blazes indicate that the bridal path in this area is called the Fawn Trail. The path climbs gently to the east, following a creek up to a ridge and a T intersection with another section of the bridal path. Turn left, staying on the Fawn Trail. Soon the path comes to a saddle, and the Fawn Trail stays low, while a forest road veers off to the left. Continue straight along the Fawn Trail through a notch in the rocks amid a very beautiful forest of hardwoods and mountain laurel. At 4.7 miles, the Fawn Trail crosses the Appalachian Trail. Be sure to turn right onto the A.T. here, following it northbound almost 0.5 mile to Trail 1777, onto which you will turn left and follow it back to the parking area.

Nearby Attractions

Bear Mountain State Park is 2.5 miles east along Seven Lakes Drive from the A.T. parking area.

Directions

From Peekskill, New York, follow US 202 west 0.7 mile, and turn left onto US 202/US 6/US 9 and cross the Jans Peeck Bridge. Exit the roundabout at the third exit for US 202/US 6. Continue 4.0 miles to the Bear Mountain Bridge. Cross the bridge and enter the roundabout. Exit the roundabout at the second exit, following the signs for US 6 West. Follow US 6 2.3 miles to Exit 19 for Perkins Memorial Drive and Bear Mountain State Park. Follow Seven Lakes Drive south toward Perkins Memorial Drive and Bear Mountain State Park 0.5 mile. The parking lot for the A.T. is on the right about 0.1 mile before the A.T. crosses Seven Lakes Drive.

Bear Mountain Loop

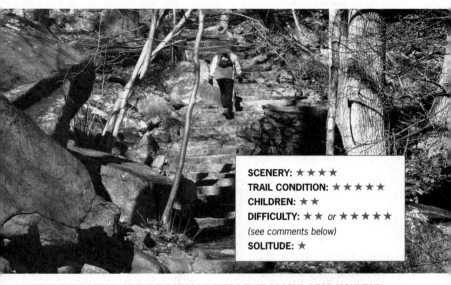

SCENERY: ★ ★ ★ ★
TRAIL CONDITION: ★ ★ ★ ★ ★
CHILDREN: ★ ★
DIFFICULTY: ★ ★ or ★ ★ ★ ★ ★
(see comments below)
SOLITUDE: ★

NEAR THE BOTTOM OF THE IMPRESSIVE STEPS THAT ASCEND BEAR MOUNTAIN FROM HESSIAN LAKE

GPS TRAILHEAD COORDINATES: N41° 18.754' W73° 59.323'

DISTANCE & CONFIGURATION: 4.4-mile loop

HIKING TIME: 3 hours

HIGHLIGHTS: Bear Mountain Lookout, amazing stone steps along the A.T., Mammoth Slabs on descent

ELEVATION: 161' at parking lot; 1,316' at Bear Mountain summit

ACCESS: Daily, 8 a.m.–sunset; $10/day parking fee

MAPS: Appalachian Trail Conservancy *New York–New Jersey, Maps 1 & 2: Connecticut State Line to New York 17A;* USGS *Peekskill* and *Popolopen Lake;* New York–New Jersey Trail Conference *Harriman–Bear Mountain Northern: Trail Map 119*

FACILITIES: Restrooms, picnic area, vending machines, and restaurants in Bear Mountain State Park

CONTACT: Bear Mountain State Park, 845-786-2701, nysparks.com/parks/13

COMMENTS: Though the ascent of Bear Mountain via the A.T. is straightforward and never especially steep, the Mammoth Slabs on the descent route are quite steep, require good shoes, and may be impassable in the rain. Use extra caution, and return via the A.T. if you have any reservations. The A.T. is wheelchair accessible for about 0.25 mile at the summit of Bear Mountain, from the Perkins Memorial Tower to the trailhead for the Major Welch Trail.

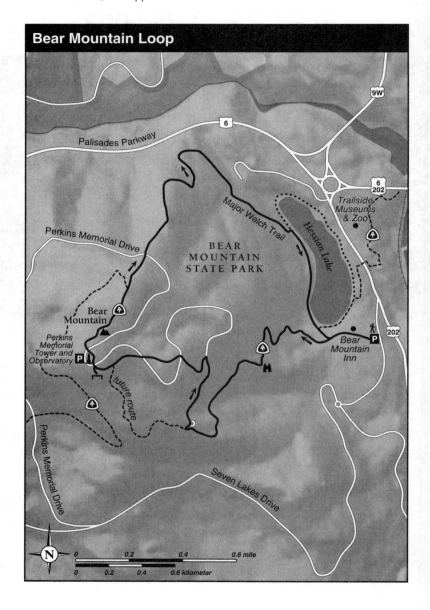

Bear Mountain Loop

9W

6

Palisades Parkway

6
202

Perkins Memorial Drive

Major Welch Trail

Trailside Museums & Zoo

Hessian Lake

BEAR
MOUNTAIN
STATE PARK

Bear
Mountain

*Perkins
Memorial
Tower and
Observatory*

P

future route

Bear
Mountain
Inn

P

202

Perkins Memorial Drive

Seven Lakes Drive

N

| 0 | 0.2 | 0.4 | 0.6 mile |

| 0 | 0.2 | 0.4 | 0.6 kilometer |

Overview

This exciting loop hike follows the Appalachian Trail (A.T.) from Hessian Lake at the bottom of the east face of Bear Mountain to its summit and returns down the huge exfoliation slabs along the Major Welch Trail on the northeast face of the mountain. You'll have excellent views of the Hudson River, the Hudson Highlands, and Harriman State Park from many places along the route.

Route Details

Begin hiking from parking lot 1 at Bear Mountain State Park, next to Bear Mountain Inn. Head straight to the southeast corner of Hessian Lake and follow the paved path along the south end of the lake. This path is the A.T., though you won't see any blazes until the path meets the woods at the southwest corner of the lake. Here a carriage road departs to the right, staying at the level of the lake—the end of the loop. Follow the A.T., which remains paved for a short distance farther, as it now ascends the southeast flank of Bear Mountain. From the paved section of trail, the terrain above appears quite steep and the hiking more difficult than it actually is. In fact, beyond the end of the pavement (about 0.25 mile), the A.T. has recently been

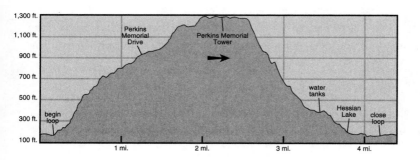

THE PERKINS MEMORIAL TOWER ON THE SUMMIT OF BEAR MOUNTAIN IS OPEN TO VISITORS APRIL 1–NOVEMBER 30, WEATHER PERMITTING.

renovated, and it easily ascends the rocky treed hillside via stone steps, switchbacks, and a log bridge.

At 0.7 mile, the trail reaches a level area on the edge of Bear Mountain that offers an excellent view of the Hudson River to the south. From this point, the A.T. heads east into a drainage and soon afterward crosses a creek with a small waterfall just uphill from the trail. After the creek, the trail continues in a southerly direction, climbing gently along a very pleasant cinder path to a beautiful stand of pine trees and a rock outcrop on the shoulder of Bear Mountain— a great place to take a break and enjoy the view to the west (1.2 miles).

Beyond the shoulder, follow the trail to the north and in another 0.25 mile join a dirt road heading left that starts at a paved cul-de-sac on the right, the end of Perkins Memorial Drive, named for George W. Perkins, the first president of the Palisades Interstate Park Commission. The road is open to vehicles April–late November. At the time of this writing, the New York–New Jersey Trail Conference was working on rerouting the A.T. in this area to continue directly west across the dirt road and up the ridge. The anticipated completion date of that project is fall 2017. Until that project is completed, follow the A.T. to the right, through the cul-de-sac, and along the pavement. At 1.5 miles, the trail departs the road to the left, zigzags up the open hillside, and soon crosses Perkins Memorial Drive again. From that crossing, another 0.3 mile takes you to huge slabs adorned with wooden benches and coin-operated viewing scopes that allow you to look out over Harriman State Park to the west and to the Manhattan skyline about 40 miles to the south. A couple of hundred feet farther along the trail to the east is the prominent Perkins Memorial Tower. The tower and its observatory were constructed as a joint effort by the New York State Temporary Emergency Relief, the Works Progress Administration, and the Civilian Conservation Corps during the 1930s. The view from the observatory encompasses four states.

After you've had a nice rest on top of Bear Mountain, it's time to find the Major Welch Trail and the route down, in and of itself a somewhat perplexing task. Follow the A.T. past the observatory on its south side. When you reach a parking lot, you'll see a blue-blazed shortcut to the A.T. southbound departing the lot to the left. Don't go that way. Continue along the main trail about 0.25 mile; this section of trail is wheelchair accessible. In the area of a huge slab of metamorphic gneiss on the left, the Major Welch Trail—identified by round, white plastic disks with a red circle in the center of them nailed to trees—leaves the A.T. to the right and descends steeply to the northeast. Named for Major William A. Welch, who served as chief landscape engineer of Bear Mountain State Park beginning in 1914 and as the first chairman of the Appalachian Trail Conference, the descent trail follows precipitous exfoliated slabs of gneiss and is not a good place for inexperienced hikers. Nor is it a good place for people in flip-flops, sandals, high heels, bare feet, or anything short of a good pair of walking shoes. A sign at the top of the trail says as much. In the rain, the route would certainly demand great care.

Follow the white and red blazes downhill for a short distance, and cross Perkins Memorial Drive. Now the fun begins. As soon as you cross the road, you'll find yourself looking down outcrops of long metamorphic slabs with the occasional white-and-red blaze painted on them. Work your way down the slabs to their end. The trail makes a couple of switchbacks through the woods, then traverses the rocky east slope of Bear Mountain heading south. When the trail reaches a dirt access road for a couple of water tanks, turn right. Follow the road uphill 75 yards until the trail departs near the water tanks. Another 0.3 mile takes you to the carriage road along Hessian Lake, leaving the difficulties behind. Turn right (south) on the carriage road and follow it back to the junction with the A.T. at the southwest corner of the lake, and past the inn to your car.

Nearby Attractions

Visit the zoo along the trail in Bear Mountain State Park, or take a paddleboat ride on Hessian Lake, or fly a kite, or ride the merry-go-round in the park. There is plenty to do.

Directions

From Peekskill, New York, follow US 202 west 0.7 mile, and turn left onto US 202/US 6/US 9 and cross the Jans Peeck Bridge. Exit the roundabout at the third exit for US 202/US 6. Continue 4.0 miles to the Bear Mountain Bridge. Cross the bridge and enter the roundabout. Take the third roundabout exit southbound, following the signs for US 202 West/US 9W South. Head south 0.5 mile, and turn right onto Seven Lakes Drive. Use the parking for the Bear Mountain Inn, on the right in 0.1 mile.

38 Bear Mountain Zoo and Bridge

SCENERY: ★ ★ ★
TRAIL CONDITION: ★ ★ ★ ★ ★
CHILDREN: ★ ★ ★ ★ ★
DIFFICULTY: ★
SOLITUDE: ★

STATUE OF WALT WHITMAN ALONG THE APPALACHIAN TRAIL NEAR THE ENTRANCE TO THE TRAILSIDE MUSEUMS & ZOO

GPS TRAILHEAD COORDINATES: N41° 18.734' W73° 59.339'

DISTANCE & CONFIGURATION: 3.0-mile out-and-back

HIKING TIME: 2 hours

HIGHLIGHTS: Trailside Museums & Zoo, lowest point on A.T., nice views of the Hudson River

ELEVATION: 189' at trailhead; 120' at the black bear exhibit in the zoo, the lowest point on the Appalachian Trail

ACCESS: Zoo: Daily, 10 a.m.–4:30 p.m. (closed Thanksgiving and December 25); Bear Mountain State Park parking, $10; suggested donation for zoo, $1

MAPS: Appalachian Trail Conservancy *New York–New Jersey, Maps 1 & 2: Connecticut State Line to New York 17A;* USGS *Peekskill;* New York–New Jersey Trail Conference *Harriman–Bear Mountain Northern: Trail Map 119*

FACILITIES: Restrooms, picnic area, vending machines, and restaurants in Bear Mountain State Park

CONTACT: Bear Mountain State Park, 845-786-2701, nysparks.com/parks/13

COMMENTS: If you don't return across the bridge before the zoo closes at 4:30 p.m., you'll need to follow the bypass trail around the zoo east of US 9W/US 202 to get back to the A.T. The bypass is rather overgrown, so try to time your hike to walk back through the zoo.

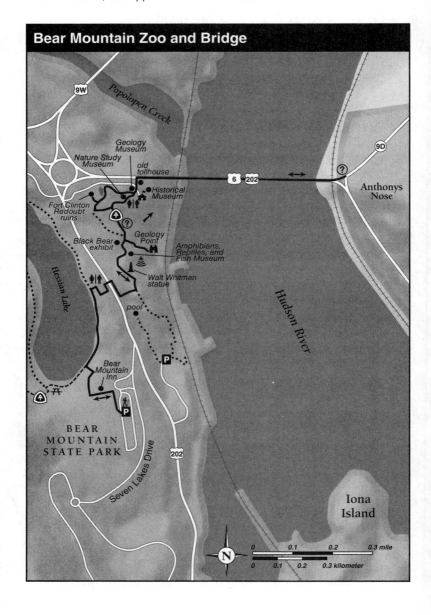

Bear Mountain Zoo and Bridge

Overview

A great hike with the kids, this trek begins near the inn at Bear Mountain State Park, follows the Appalachian Trail (A.T.) on the paved path along Hessian Lake, and then goes underneath NY 202 into and through the Trailside Museums & Zoo—the only zoo the A.T. runs through—out to the bridge over the Hudson River.

Route Details

From parking lot 1, follow the path next to the Bear Mountain Inn toward Hessian Lake, and turn right past the inn. You can take any one of several parallel paths along the east side of the lake; they all lead to the same area. Whichever you choose, keep your eyes open for signs pointing to the zoo about midway along the lake. Turn right (east) on the A.T., and follow signs to the zoo past a set of restrooms. Just beyond the restrooms, the path comes to the road, makes a sharp left turn, and descends via a ramp to a paved passage beneath the road.

Follow the path under the road and into the zoo. White trail blazes mark the path of the A.T. through the zoo, and it passes by most of the major exhibits and all four of the zoo's museums. The first major attraction you'll come to is a statue of Walt Whitman. It was given to the Palisades Interstate Park Commission in 1940 by Averell Harriman, whose mother, Mary Williamson Harriman, gave

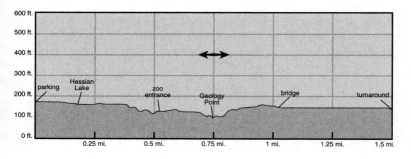

10,000 acres of land and $1 million to the state of New York for the creation and development of Bear Mountain and Harriman State Parks in 1910. Alongside the statue are engraved several lines from Whitman's famous poem "Song of the Open Road" that seem appropriate to the experience of the A.T. hiker:

> *Afoot and light-hearted I take to the open road*
> *Healthy, free, the world before me,*
> *The long brown path before me leading wherever I choose.*

Beyond the statue, the trail passes by the Amphibians, Reptiles, and Fish Museum on the right, and just beyond that, it reaches the popular black bear exhibit on the left. One would think that Bear Mountain was named for the black bears that are common to the area. That may or may not be the case. Several signs along the trail offer possible explanations, one being that the mountain was named Bare Mountain because its steep eastern face is largely free of trees. Another explains that romantic 19th-century settlers thought the mountain looked like a reclining bear. Whatever the origin of the name, the bear exhibit in the park offers an excellent opportunity to get a good look at these impressive animals. And at 120 feet in elevation, the site of the exhibit is the geographic low point of the trail. Just beyond the bear exhibit, a side path called the Geology Trail departs to the right and descends a short distance to Geology Point, an overlook with an excellent view of Anthonys Nose on the east side of the river (see page 242).

Beyond the Geology Trail, the main path through the zoo forks. The A.T. follows the right fork. The left fork, which soon rejoins the A.T., passes by the ruins of the Fort Clinton West Redoubt. Common around the time of the Revolutionary War, a redoubt was a military fortification that stood at a strategic point, often to defend a bridge or a ford. As part of the Fort Clinton complex, this redoubt was constructed to defend the advance of British ships up the Hudson River.

After passing the redoubt, the path rejoins the A.T. in the area of the park's remaining three museums: the Nature Study Museum, the Geology Museum, and the Historical Museum. From the museums, the A.T. exits the zoo at a service gate that also serves as handicap access to the zoo. Once outside, the A.T. turns right and crosses the Hudson River via the Bear Mountain Bridge. The old tollhouse sits beside the trail on the west edge of the bridge.

Though the bridge sees a fair amount of auto traffic, pedestrian walkways traverse both its north and south sides. When it was constructed in 1924, it had the longest main suspension span in the world and was the first vehicular crossing of the river between New York City and Albany. It was constructed for several reasons, one of which was the popularity of Bear Mountain State Park. After the park opened in 1916, the ferries in use along the river were no longer able to serve the volume of people and cars wanting to visit the region west of the river.

Once you have crossed the bridge, you have walked 1.5 miles from the parking lot. From here, you can retrace your steps back to the park and enjoy some of its many activities.

Nearby Attractions

During the summer, you can rent paddleboats and tool around Hessian Lake. Or you can visit the merry-go-round at the south side of the large field by the parking area. Or you can have a picnic. The park offers no shortage of things to do.

Directions

From Peekskill, New York, follow US 202 west 0.7 mile, and turn left onto US 202/US 6/US 9 and cross the Jans Peeck Bridge. Exit the roundabout at the third exit for US 202/US 6. Continue 4.0 miles to the Bear Mountain Bridge. Cross the bridge and enter the roundabout. Take the third roundabout exit southbound, following the signs for US 202 West/US 9W South. Head south 0.5 mile, and turn right onto Seven Lakes Drive. Use the parking for the Bear Mountain Inn, on the right in 0.1 mile.

SCENERY: ★ ★ ★ ★
TRAIL CONDITION: ★ ★ ★ ★
CHILDREN: ★ ★ ★ ★
DIFFICULTY: ★ ★
SOLITUDE: ★ ★

THE VIEW WEST FROM THE SUMMIT OF ANTHONYS NOSE OVER THE HUDSON RIVER TO BEAR MOUNTAIN

GPS TRAILHEAD COORDINATES: N41° 19.361' W73° 58.546'

DISTANCE & CONFIGURATION: 2.4-mile out-and-back

HIKING TIME: 2 hours

HIGHLIGHTS: Excellent views of the Hudson River Valley from Anthonys Nose

ELEVATION: 277' at trailhead; 918' at Anthonys Nose

ACCESS: Daily, sunrise–sunset; no fees or permits required

MAPS: Appalachian Trail Conservancy *New York–New Jersey, Maps 1 & 2: Connecticut State Line to New York 17A;* USGS *Peekskill;* New York–New Jersey Trail Conference *Harriman–Bear Mountain Northern: Trail Map 119*

FACILITIES: None

CONTACT: Hudson Highlands State Park Preserve, 845-225-7207, nysparks.com/parks/9

COMMENTS: Parking for this hike is alongside NY 9D, which is a busy road. Use extra caution around cars. It can be very busy on weekends.

Overview

As part of a day trip from New York City, this short hike will provide one of the best views that can be had of the Hudson River and the surrounding countryside.

Route Details

Located at the eastern edge of the Bear Mountain Bridge over the Hudson River, Anthonys Nose is the large promontory that defines the horizon looking east from Bear Mountain State Park. This deservedly popular hike, suitable for families and kids with a bit of stamina, offers views of the Hudson River Valley to both the north and south that are rivaled by few locations in the region. Getting to the top takes a bit of effort, especially for the first 0.5 mile, but the views attained there are worth every step. The spoils of your efforts, though, come at a price: on weekends in particular, the hike can be very busy. If you can get out during the week, you're bound to have quite a bit more privacy. I last did this hike on a Friday in February. The temperature was in the mid-40s, the sky was crisp and clear, and I had the place to myself. The next day, it was mobbed.

After crossing the Bear Mountain Bridge, the Appalachian Trail (A.T.) follows NY 9D north about 0.25 mile, and then leaves the road to the east and begins the ascent of Anthonys Nose at the Westchester and Putnam County line. A large sign identifies the trailhead along the road. Most people park for this hike along the shoulder of NY 9D in the area of the trailhead or along the shoulder on both sides of the road south of the trailhead. I found the roadside parking rather unsettling, as NY 9D is a busy thoroughfare, and cars typically move along at a good clip. Exercise extreme caution if you choose to park there. The alternative is to park at the Bear Mountain State Park parking lot, which will cost $10 for the day on weekends. In effect, doing so involves combining the previous hike in this book, the Bear Mountain Zoo and Bridge, with this hike, which tacks on an additional 3 miles.

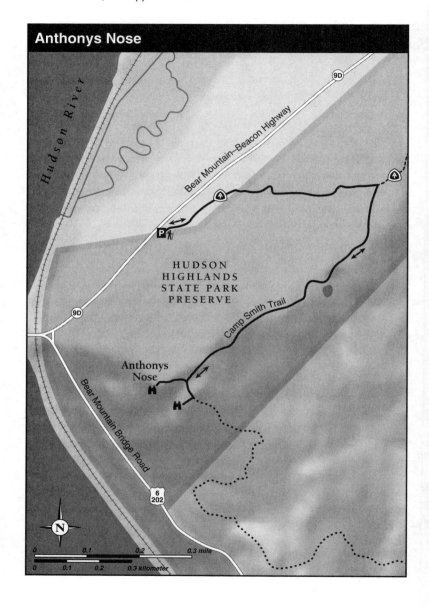

Anthonys Nose

Hudson River

9D

Bear Mountain–Beacon Highway

P

HUDSON
HIGHLANDS
STATE PARK
PRESERVE

9D

Camp Smith Trail

Anthonys
Nose

Bear Mountain Bridge Road

6
202

N

0   0.1   0.2   0.3 mile

0   0.1   0.2   0.3 kilometer

Departing the road, the A.T. ascends rather steeply through the woods along a rocky hillside. The trail crosses a few small creeks and, at 0.25 mile, reaches a large boulder and then a couple of switchbacks. Shortly after the switchbacks, you'll find a flat area that serves as a good place to catch your breath before the final grunt up to the ridge. At 0.5 mile, the trail joins an old dirt road on the ridge, and the steep climb comes to an end. At the road, the A.T. follows the road to the left (north), and the hike out to Anthonys Nose follows the road and blue blazes to the right (south). The road surface can be a little rocky at times, but the hiking is considerably less strenuous along its surface than it was for the beginning of the hike.

Follow the road another 0.5 mile, passing a small pond on the east side of the trail and climbing gently for the entire distance. At 0.9 mile, the trail forks and the road continues straight south and begins to descend. Anthonys Nose proper follows the trail to the right, which emerges from the woods after a short distance and ends atop some exposed slabs. An American flag marks the end of the hike.

From these slabs, the view across the river to Bear Mountain is quite remarkable; you'll get an excellent sense of just how prominent a piece of rock it really is. To the south, the Hudson River tapers off to the horizon like a glistening silver thread, and to the north the landscape is dominated by Storm King Mountain, the subject of many

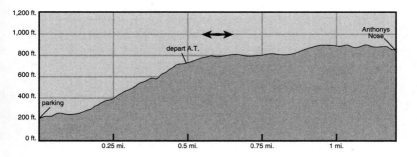

paintings by the Hudson River School during the 19th century, most notably in Samuel Colman's *Storm King on the Hudson* (1866).

After soaking up the view on the west edge of Anthonys Nose, have a walk over to the slabs on the east side of the ridge via the other fork in the aforementioned trail. Though the view to the east is not quite as dramatic as it is to the west, it is still quite grand and expansive. After you've had your fill of long horizons, follow the path back to the car.

Nearby Attractions

Bear Mountain State Park just across the bridge has lodging and activities that are suitable for the entire family. Don't neglect to visit the trailside zoo at the park.

Directions

From Peekskill, New York, follow US 202 west 0.7 mile, and turn left onto US 202/US 6/US 9 and cross the Jans Peeck Bridge. Exit the roundabout at the third exit for US 202/US 6. Continue 4.0 miles to the Bear Mountain Bridge. Stay to the right on NY 9D North instead of crossing the bridge. The trailhead is 0.25 mile ahead on the right. Most people park along the shoulder of NY 9D.

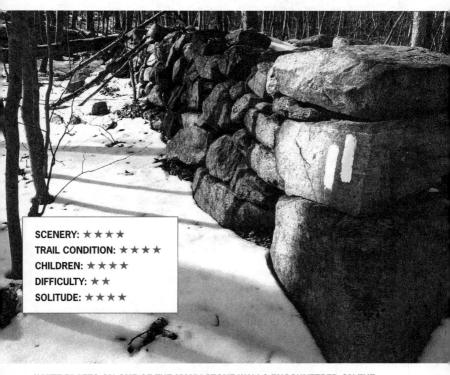

SCENERY: ★ ★ ★ ★
TRAIL CONDITION: ★ ★ ★ ★
CHILDREN: ★ ★ ★ ★
DIFFICULTY: ★ ★
SOLITUDE: ★ ★ ★ ★

WHITE BLAZES ON ONE OF THE MANY STONE WALLS ENCOUNTERED ON THE WAY TO CANOPUS HILL

GPS TRAILHEAD COORDINATES: N41° 23.966' W73° 52.557'

DISTANCE & CONFIGURATION: 3.6-mile out-and-back

HIKING TIME: 2.5 hours

HIGHLIGHTS: Canopus Hill, many old stone walls in forest

ELEVATION: 628' at trailhead; 858' at Canopus Hill

ACCESS: Daily, sunrise–sunset; no fees or permits required

MAPS: Appalachian Trail Conservancy *New York–New Jersey, Maps 1 & 2: Connecticut State Line to New York 17A;* USGS *Oscawana Lake* and *West Point*

FACILITIES: None

CONTACT: Hudson Highlands State Park Preserve, 845-225-7207, nysparks.com/parks/9

COMMENTS: Parking for this hike is very limited.

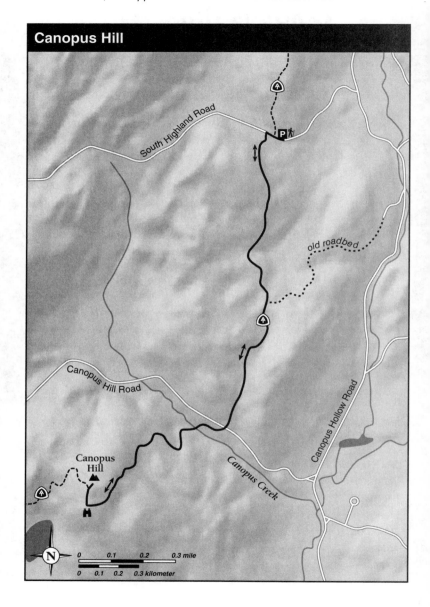

Canopus Hill

Overview

This pleasant hike follows the Appalachian Trail (A.T.) through hollows and drainages crisscrossed by old stone walls, the remnants of a settlement dating back to the 1700s. It concludes with an ascent of Canopus Hill, where you can get the northernmost view of the New York skyline from the Appalachian Trail.

Route Details

Canopus Hill would seem, by virtue of its rather humble elevation of only around 830 feet, to be hardly worth the effort of exploring. Yet even though the views from the top of Canopus Hill are partly obstructed by trees, on a clear day you can still get a view of the New York skyline—the last one heading north on the Appalachian Trail. Aside from the potential for a view, the draw of this trek is really the hike itself, which is extremely pleasant. It is a nice trip if you're hiking with younger kids who have a bit of hiking experience. With the exception of the last steep little bit to the top of Canopus Hill, the path follows easy rolling terrain. And considering how busy the Appalachian Trail can be in the nearby Clarence Fahnestock Memorial State Park, this is a hike that generally affords some solitude. Interestingly, the trail passes through a wonderful forest crisscrossed by old stone

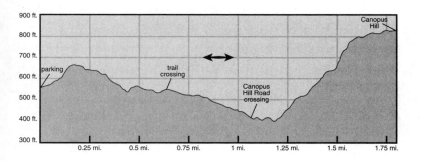

walls, which brought to mind Robert Frost's poem "Mending Wall" as we passed through it on a sunny Saturday morning in January.

The hike begins at the A.T. crossing on South Highland Road. Probably one reason that this hike sees relatively little traffic is because parking is quite limited. There is room for only three, maybe four, cars along the shoulder of this winding, narrow road. Please don't block any of the forest roads. From the car, pick up the A.T. and follow it southbound. Initially, the trail traverses a hillside, climbing gently for about 0.4 mile and into a hollow where you will encounter the first of the stone walls and an old roadbed passing through the area.

From that hollow, for the next 0.6 mile, the A.T. passes through a valley tracked by an amazing number of walls. Though none are more than 3 or 4 feet tall, many of them are several feet thick; one wall near Canopus Hill Road is quite complex, with what appears to be several different rooms or stalls constructed in it. My hiking buddy, Jackson, who spends more time in New England these days than I do, explained that they were often constructed to create pens for farm animals or enclosures for gardens. That explanation has been confirmed by further reading about the trail in this area. Many years have probably passed since the last of the farms were abandoned or sold because some of the hardwoods in the forest are quite large.

At 1.0 mile, the drainage you are walking through opens up into the Canopus Creek drainage. Here the A.T. crosses Canopus Hill Road (no parking available) and works its way along the shallow valley to the bank of Canopus Creek. After crossing the creek, you'll begin the climb to Canopus Hill. The climb starts off gently, and when the hill steepens, the trail makes a switchback to the right (northwest). After traversing the hillside for a short distance, the trail bends to the southwest at an old skid path. Be sure to watch for the white blazes. Beyond the skid path, the trail climbs more steeply and directly to the top of Canopus Hill, which it gains from the south side. Just after it levels out, the trail makes a sharp right turn and follows the ridge of Canopus Hill for 75 yards. You'll find a good place to sit, with views to the south and west, to the left of the trail where it makes the right

AN UNUSUAL VINE WINDS ITS WAY UP A TREE.

turn. Or you can follow it across the ridge to the point where it begins to descend. Another nice place to take a break is the actual top of Canopus Hill, 100 feet to the right of the trail among some trees. This makes a good turnaround point to return to your car.

Nearby Attractions

Located 8 miles away on the Hudson River along NY 9D, Cold Spring, New York, is a quaint town with many shops and restaurants where you can grab a bite to eat and take in some of the beautiful architecture of the many historical buildings.

Directions

From I-84 and US 9 south of Fishkill, New York, follow US 9 south to NY 301 (7.0 miles). Turn left onto NY 301 and follow it east 2.7 miles. Turn right onto Dennytown Road and drive 2.6 miles to South Highland Road. Turn right and follow South Highland Road 0.3 mile to where the Appalachian Trail crosses. Parking is limited to three or four cars along the shoulder of this narrow, winding road.

41 # Shenandoah Mountain

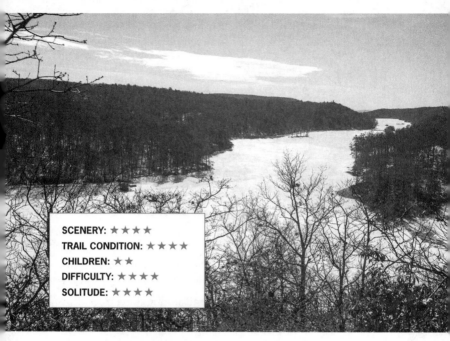

CANOPUS LAKE EXTENDS TO THE SOUTH FROM THE FIRST OVERLOOK EN ROUTE TO SHENANDOAH MOUNTAIN.

GPS TRAILHEAD COORDINATES: N41° 27.157' W73° 50.270'

DISTANCE & CONFIGURATION: 8.8-mile out-and-back

HIKING TIME: 5 hours

HIGHLIGHTS: Excellent views of Canopus Lake, Shenandoah Mountain

ELEVATION: 989' at trailhead; 1,282' at Shenandoah Mountain

ACCESS: Daily, sunrise–sunset; no fees or permits required

MAPS: Appalachian Trail Conservancy (A.T.C.) *New York–New Jersey, Maps 1 & 2: Connecticut State Line to New York 17A;* USGS *Hopewell Junction* and *Oscawana Lake*

FACILITIES: Seasonal restrooms at beach at north end of Canopus Lake

CONTACT: Clarence Fahnestock Memorial State Park, 845-225-7207, nysparks.com /parks/133

COMMENTS: It is worth noting that in order to fit the terrain on the printed sheet, the A.T.C. map is oriented with the grid north at about two o'clock on the map. This can cause a bit of confusion with respect to orientation if you are not cognizant of the fact.

Overview

This lovely out-and-back hike follows the Appalachian Trail (A.T.) above the west shore of Canopus Lake. After passing the lake, the trail ascends glacially carved ridges to the summit of Shenandoah Mountain (1,282 feet).

Route Details

Pick up the Appalachian Trail northbound at the trailhead on NY 301 at the south end of Canopus Lake in Clarence Fahnestock Memorial State Park. The trail initially heads directly west from the road toward a large rock outcrop that it passes to the left (south) side via some stone steps in the hillside. Once beyond the outcrop, the trail bends around to the north. It climbs some more stone steps, and near the top of those, a trail departs to the left, identified by one of the region's many colored trail markers reading TRAIL MARKER TACONIC REGION (this one blue). During the winter season, the network of trails in the park is used for snowshoeing and collectively forms Fahnestock Winter Park (information is available at 845-225-3998 or nysparks.com/parks/147/details.aspx).

Beyond the junction, the A.T. continues northbound about 300 feet above the west bank of Canopus Lake, along the hillside, following a wide, rocky ledge below the main ridgeline. After the initial climb from the road to the top of the rock outcrops, the trail stays at between 1,000 and 1,200 feet of elevation for the first 2 miles of the hike. Though it sports no dramatic variation in elevation, the hiking is fairly rugged. You'll have to pass through some rock outcrops and up and down some short, steep sections of trail. It is beautiful country, however, with some excellent views of the lake and surrounding terrain.

At just about 2 miles, another blue-blazed side trail descends from the A.T. to the northeast and the north end of Canopus Lake. Stay on the A.T., and shortly thereafter, it makes a switchback and traverses through a cliff up to an overlook about 1,100 feet in

Shenandoah Mountain

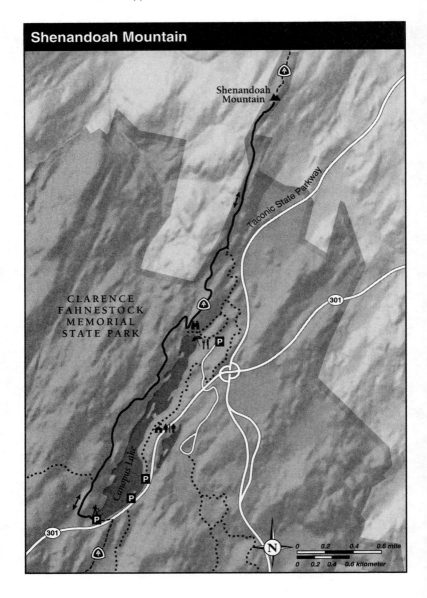

Shenandoah
Mountain

Taconic State Parkway

301

CLARENCE
FAHNESTOCK
MEMORIAL
STATE PARK

Canopus Lake

301

N

| 0 | 0.2 | 0.4 | 0.6 mile |
| 0 | 0.2 | 0.4 | 0.6 kilometer |

elevation. According to the park's winter maps, this section of the
A.T. doubles as one of the most difficult snowshoe trails. It would,
indeed, be rather intimidating on snowshoes. The overlook provides
the first completely unobstructed view of the entirety of Canopus
Lake and the surrounding countryside to the south and east. It is a
wonderful location, worthy of an out-and-back trip itself. It is also
worth noting that the schist and quartzite rocks that form this overlook date back more than a billion years.

From the overlook, continue following the A.T. northbound.
Sections of the remaining 2.2 miles to Shenandoah Mountain are
more exposed than the first 2 miles. The distribution of trees is
sparser, and their trunks are more stunted. The going can get a bit
treacherous heading north from the overlook during winter, especially in icy conditions. After 0.75 mile, the trail descends from the
ridgecrest proper into a hollow, where it meets with another side trail
on the right. This trail heads back over to the main parking area for the
lake. We explored it on the return trip, and it eventually took us back
to the A.T. at the junction just south of the overlook by heading to the
north end of the lake and following the path along the west shore. My
sense is that the trail would get rather mucky during the spring, as it
passes through some wetlands by the edge of the lake.

After that side trail, the A.T. continues another mile or so
through some dense mountain laurel and hardwoods before emerging

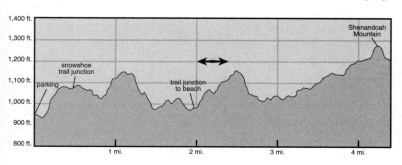

back onto the ridge around 3.8 miles. Soon afterward, you'll come to the top of Shenandoah Mountain. At 1,282 feet, the summit is a long, open outcrop of metamorphic rock that has been worn smooth by the action of glaciers during past periods of glaciation. It is quite exposed to the wind and elements. The view from the top spans all directions. To the east runs a valley that is occupied by the Taconic State Parkway. To the west is the Hudson River Valley. Canopus Lake to the south looks a long distance off. Soak it up. Enjoy the situation. And then follow the A.T. back to the car.

Nearby Attractions

If you like Mexican food, you must visit the Maya Café & Cantina 6.3 miles north on US 9 (845-896-4042; mayacafecantina.com). The *pocchuc* is excellent. It is located on US 9, on the southeast corner at the first traffic light south of I-84. It gets very busy.

Directions

From I-84 and US 9 south of Fishkill, New York, follow US 9 south to NY 301 (7.0 miles). Turn left onto NY 301 and follow it east 4.7 miles to where the A.T. crosses the road at the south end of Canopus Lake. Park on the left or the right.

Nuclear Lake

SCENERY: ★ ★ ★ ★
TRAIL CONDITION: ★ ★ ★
CHILDREN: ★ ★ ★
DIFFICULTY: ★ ★ ★
SOLITUDE: ★ ★ ★ ★

A FROZEN NUCLEAR LAKE FROM THE NORTH

GPS TRAILHEAD COORDINATES: N41° 35.387' W73° 39.545'

DISTANCE & CONFIGURATION: 4.3-mile balloon

HIKING TIME: 3 hours

HIGHLIGHTS: Beekman Uplands, Nuclear Lake area

ELEVATION: 755' at trailhead; 910' at Beekman Uplands; 671' at swamplands before final ascent back to parking area

ACCESS: Open 24/7; no fees or permits required

MAPS: Appalachian Trail Conservancy *New York–New Jersey, Maps 1 & 2: Connecticut State Line to New York 17A*; USGS *Poughquag*

FACILITIES: None

CONTACT: New York–New Jersey Trail Conference, 201-512-9348, nynjtc.org

COMMENTS: The blue blazes on sections of the Beekman Uplands Trail are somewhat faint and a little hard to follow, creating some route-finding challenges on this hike. The USGS map comes in as a handy addition to the official Appalachian Trail Conservancy map.

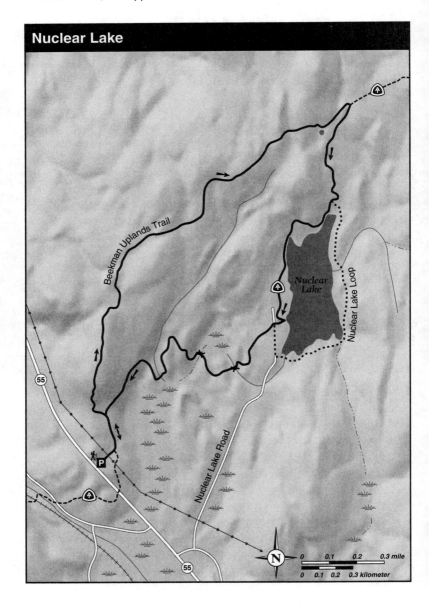

Nuclear Lake

Beekman Uplands Trail

Nuclear Lake

Nuclear Lake Loop

Nuclear Lake Road

55

55

N

0   0.1   0.2   0.3 mile

0   0.1   0.2   0.3 kilometer

Overview

This hike uses the infrequently traveled Beekman Uplands Trail in conjunction with the Appalachian Trail (A.T.) to create a loop hike that provides a nice alternative to the standard loop that most people make around Nuclear Lake.

Route Details

Nuclear Lake is so named because the area around the lake was purchased in 1955 by an outfit called Nuclear Development Associates and used as a nuclear research facility. The Federal Atomic Energy Commission sponsored work there until 1972, when there was a bit of an accident. An explosion in one of the laboratories shattered some windows, which spread an undetermined amount of plutonium around the area. Cleanup efforts costing millions of dollars ensued, and the place was declared safe in 1975.

Follow the blue-blazed access trail northeast out of the parking lot about 30 yards to a sign with information about the Nuclear Lake Loop. Note the abundance of information about Lyme disease in this area, and prepare accordingly. The access trail continues past the sign under a set of power lines and meets the A.T. just beyond them. Turn left, heading northbound on the Appalachian Trail. After just a

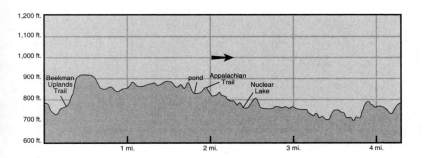

short distance, 0.3 mile from the parking lot, you'll see the junction with the blue-blazed Beekman Uplands Trail and the beginning of the loop. Turn left (east) onto the Beekman Uplands Trail, and follow it as it meanders among boulders, gaining about 150 feet before topping out in a beautiful, dense forest of mountain laurel. The hiking on this initial section of trail is quite reminiscent of Sunset Rocks in Pennsylvania (see page 71).

For the next 1.5 miles, the trail weaves in and out of hollows, around swampy areas, through forest filled with grand hardwoods and hemlocks, and between wild bedrock slabs covered in mountain laurel. This is truly a remarkable, if little visited, stretch of trail. At 1.8 miles, you'll reach an area that might present some route-finding difficulties. The trail descends and appears to bend toward the southeast (right), when in fact it continues east and northeast, directly toward the west edge of a small pond. Blue blazes mark the correct path, but they are old and a little difficult to keep track of. Continue to the edge of the pond, and pass by it on the north side. Follow the hollow and the creek that feeds the pond to the north and up over a rise. The track is much clearer after crossing the creek and the blue blazes more prominent. On the east side of the rise, you'll reach the A.T., onto which you will turn right, heading southbound.

In 0.4 mile (2.4 miles total), the A.T. joins the north end of the yellow-blazed Nuclear Lake Loop, which provides a variation to this hike. It follows the east side of Nuclear Lake southward over dramatic rock outcrops to the lake's outflow for about 1 mile. At the outflow, it crosses the creek and gains the old Nuclear Lake Road, onto which it turns right (north) and follows that a couple hundred yards back to the A.T., onto which you will turn left. If you follow the east side of the lake, it is imperative that you turn right onto the old Nuclear Lake Road after crossing the creek. Following it to the south will leave you with a long walk along the shoulder of NY 55 back to the car.

For this hike, continue along the west side of the lake. The A.T. is easy enough to follow, and about 0.5 mile beyond the loop trail, you'll reach the end of the old road and shortly thereafter an old boat launch

A FROSTED BIT OF LAST YEAR'S GROWTH ALONG THE TRAIL NEAR NUCLEAR LAKE

at the lake. The lake access is a great spot for a break and to take in the scenery. From the launch, continue south along the road an additional 75 yards. The A.T. leaves the road to the right and begins the mile-long, meandering trek back out to NY 55. This remaining stretch of the hike begins by ascending and descending several small ridges and crossing a couple of creeks between each via footbridges located at 0.3 and 0.5 mile from Nuclear Lake. After the second bridge, the trail crosses a rise and passes by open swampland to the south. From the swamp, the trail climbs 0.3 mile to the head of the Beekman Uplands Trail and shortly thereafter to the blue-blazed trail to the parking lot. The power lines serve as a good point of reference to begin watching for the access trail, which one could conceivably walk past.

Nearby Attractions

Pawling, New York, an officially designated Appalachian Trail Community about 4 miles to the south near the intersection of NY 55 and NY 22, is your nearest place for victuals and other supplies.

Directions

From Pawling, New York, follow NY 55 west 4.5 miles. The A.T. parking lot is on the right (east) side of the road directly across from the Taghkanic Woodworking shop. The lot has space for seven or eight cars.

43 # Great Swamp and Dover Oak

SCENERY: ★ ★ ★ ★
TRAIL CONDITION: ★ ★ ★ ★ ★
CHILDREN: ★ ★ ★
DIFFICULTY: ★ ★
SOLITUDE: ★ ★ ★

THE MAGNIFICENT DOVER OAK—REPORTEDLY THE LARGEST TREE ALONG THE APPALACHIAN TRAIL

GPS TRAILHEAD COORDINATES: N41° 35.697' W73° 35.178'

DISTANCE & CONFIGURATION: 5.4-mile out-and-back

HIKING TIME: 3 hours

HIGHLIGHTS: A.T. Metro-North Railroad stop, the Great Swamp, beaver lodges, very pretty high meadows, the Dover Oak

ELEVATION: 451' at trailhead; 773' at the first high meadow

ACCESS: Open 24/7; no fees or permits required

MAPS: Appalachian Trail Conservancy *New York–New Jersey, Maps 1 & 2: Connecticut State Line to New York 17A;* USGS *Pawling*

FACILITIES: None

CONTACT: New York–New Jersey Trail Conference, 201-512-9348, nynjtc.org

COMMENTS: The trail skirts private property when crossing the ridge, so be sure to stay along the path.

Overview

Beginning at the Appalachian Trail (A.T.) stop on the Harlem line of the Metro-North Railroad, this hike follows the trail across New York's Great Swamp, over a ridge through high meadows, and ends at the magnificent Dover Oak.

Route Details

This final hike in the mid-Atlantic section is just full of interesting features! To begin, hikers from Manhattan will love the fact that you can actually take the train from Grand Central Station directly to the trailhead for this hike—at least on weekends. The Metro-North Railroad's Harlem Line stops at the A.T. along NY 22 outside of Pawling, New York, an officially designated Appalachian Trail Community. It is the only trailhead on the entire Appalachian Trail serviced by rail. And it is the beginning of quite a pleasant hike to boot.

For hikers planning to drive to the trailhead, park in one of the two lots along NY 22 about 200 yards north of the trailhead, and walk the shoulder over to the railway platform and station sign for the Appalachian Trail. After crossing the tracks, continue southbound on the trail directly into the Great Swamp. There is no need to worry about getting your feet wet, as the Swamp River Boardwalk, constructed in 2012, begins a couple of hundred feet beyond the tracks and wends its way all throughout the swampland. At 0.3 mile in length, this boardwalk is considerably shorter than the Pochuck Boardwalk (see page 191), but the landscape is equally beautiful. According to information posted along the trail by Harlem Valley, an officially designated Appalachian Trail Community, the Great Swamp extends 20 miles, making it New York's third-largest freshwater wetlands. You can canoe and kayak on sections of it, and doing so offers excellent opportunities to observe many of the migratory waterfowl that utilize the wetlands habitat, as well as the many other types of wildlife you might encounter in a wetlands environment.

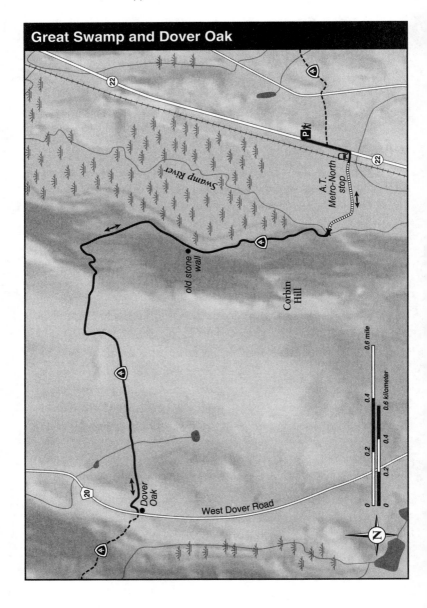

Great Swamp and Dover Oak

For the length of the walkway, the track passes through cattails and rushes and past several beaver lodges, the largest of which is located just left of the trail at the bridge over the Swamp River proper. Along the way, you'll pass a couple of Adirondack chairs (the southernmost one is engraved with Georgia and the northernmost with Maine), a couple of benches, and plenty of opportunities to see birds and reptiles that inhabit the swamp.

After passing the boardwalk, the trail turns to the north and enters a lovely forest of tall hemlock, oak, birch, and maple trees. About 0.25 mile beyond the end of the boardwalk, an old roadbed joins the trail from the right in the area of a couple of enormous hemlock trees and an old stone wall. The ground is flat here, with plenty of room to sit and enjoy the forest and swamp scenery. The trail continues along the edge of the swamp with no real elevation gain for another 0.25 mile or so, and then, at about 1 mile from the railroad crossing, just beyond a second stone wall and some car-size boulders, it begins a steady, though not very steep, ascent of the hillside to the west. As it approaches the top of the hillside, the terrain gets considerably steeper, but the path switches back, so the grade is never unpleasant. At 1.5 miles, the trail reaches the top of the hill and follows the southern edge of a broad, high meadow. The path along the meadow is flat and smooth, and the view along the valley to the north, with West Mountain on the left, is quite picturesque.

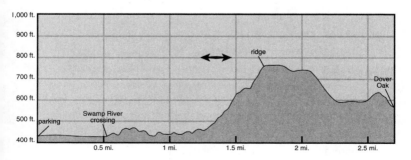

After 5 minutes of walking, the path takes a sharp turn to the south, passing through some shrubbery between fields. Soon afterward, it curves back to the west and descends to a second broad meadow. Follow the path along the edge of the meadow over a second, considerably less impressive, boardwalk (it's just a couple of planks for 100 yards), over a small rise with a house and a gazebo to the north, and then downhill to West Dover Road (County Road 20), where you will find the awesome Dover Oak. Named for the road beside which it stands, this arboreal specimen is supposedly the largest white oak in New York and the largest tree along the Appalachian Trail. It measures approximately 20 feet in circumference, stands over 100 feet tall, and is estimated to be more than 150 years old. At the Dover Oak, be sure to get your photographs, and take a break. Then retrace your steps back to the car.

Nearby Attractions

Native Landscapes Inc. (845-855-7050; nativelandscaping.net), which is located on NY 22 between the parking lots and the trailhead, is an A.T. through station. It provides services for thru-hikers, such as supplying outdoor showers, holding packages, and allowing cell phone charging on the front porch. It has a small supply of snacks and drinks for sale and an outside area to sit and eat. It provides a great service to the Appalachian Trail community, as well as landscaping services to the Pawling community. So stop in before or after your hike and grab a snack.

Directions

From NY 22 and Coulter Avenue in Pawling, New York, follow NY 22 north 2 miles. Ample parking is available just beyond Native Landscapes, Inc. on both the east and west sides of the road, about 100 yards beyond the southbound Appalachian Trail.

CATTAILS IN THE SWAMP

MOUNTAIN CREEK RUNS ALONGSIDE THE APPALACHIAN TRAIL FOR PART OF THE HIKE TO POLE STEEPLE. *(See Hike 10, page 78.)*

Appendix A:
Contact Information

Here is the contact information for the parks, state forests, and public lands used by the Appalachian Trail hikes included in this book.

MARYLAND

Gathland State Park
301-791-4767
tinyurl.com/gathlandsp

Pen Mar County Park
240-313-2700
washco-md.net/parks_facilities
/p-PenMarPark.shtm

South Mountain State Park
301-791-4767
tinyurl.com/southmtnsp

Washington Monument State Park
301-791-4767
tinyurl.com/mdwashington

NEW JERSEY

High Point State Park
973-875-4800
tinyurl.com/njhighpointsp

Stokes State Forest
973-948-3820
tinyurl.com/stokessf

Wallkill River National Wildlife Refuge
973-702-7266
fws.gov/refuge/wallkill_river

Wawayanda State Park
973-853-4462
tinyurl.com/wawayandasp

Worthington State Forest
908-841-9575
www.state.nj.us/dep/parksandforests
/parks/worthington.html

NEW YORK

Bear Mountain State Park
845-786-2701
nysparks.com/parks/13

**Clarence Fahnestock Memorial
State Park**
845-225-7207
nysparks.com/parks/133

Harriman State Park
845-947-2444
nysparks.com/parks/145

Hudson Highlands State Park Preserve
845-225-7207
nysparks.com/parks/9

Sterling Forest State Park
845-351-5907
nysparks.com/parks/74

PENNSYLVANIA

Caledonia State Park
717-352-2161
dcnr.state.pa.us/stateparks/findapark
/caledonia

(continued on page 270)

PENNSYLVANIA

(continued from page 269)

**Delaware Water Gap National
Recreation Area**
570-426-2452
nps.gov/dewa

**Michaux State Forest
Michaux District Office**
717-352-2211
tinyurl.com/michauxsf

Pennsylvania Game Commission
717-787-4250
tinyurl.com/pagamelands

Pine Grove Furnace State Park
717-486-7174
tinyurl.com/pinegrovefurnacesp

Swatara State Park
717-865-6470
tinyurl.com/swatarasp

WEST VIRGINIA

Harpers Ferry National Historical Park
304-535-6029
nps.gov/hafe

Appendix B:
Hiking Clubs and Organizations

Here is the contact information for primary hiking clubs and organizations in the mid-Atlantic region that maintain or administer sections of the trail.

DELAWARE
Wilmington Trail Club
302-307-4017
wilmingtontrailclub.org

MARYLAND
Potomac Appalachian Trail Club
North Chapter: Maryland/Pennsylvania
to Pine Grove Furnace
patcnorth.net

NEW JERSEY AND NEW YORK
New York–New Jersey Trail Conference
201-512-9348
nynjtc.org

PENNSYLVANIA
Appalachian Trail Conservancy
Mid-Atlantic Regional Office
717-258-5771
appalachiantrail.org

BATONA Hiking Club
batona.wildapricot.org

Blue Mountain Eagle Climbing Club
610-375-4375
tinyurl.com/bluemtneagleclub

Cumberland Valley Appalachian
Trail Club
cvatclub.org

Keystone Trails Association
717-766-9690
kta-hike.org

Susquehanna Appalachian Trail Club
satc-hike.org

York Hiking Club
yorkhikingclub.com

WEST VIRGINIA
Appalachian Trail Conservancy
Headquarters and Visitor Center
304-535-6331
appalachiantrail.org

Appalachian National Scenic Trail
304-535-6278
nps.gov/appa

Appendix C:
Appalachian Trail Communities

The Appalachian Trail Community program is an Appalachian Trail Conservancy initiative that seeks to develop mutually beneficial relationships with interested towns and counties along the Appalachian Trail to enhance their economies, further protect the trail, and engage a new generation of volunteers.

WEST VIRGINIA

Harpers Ferry/Bolivar

PENNSYLVANIA

Greater Waynesboro
Boiling Springs
Duncannon
Wind Gap
Delaware Water Gap

NEW YORK

Warwick
Harlem Valley (Dover and Pawling)

Index

A

Access (hike profiles), 10
animal hazards, 19–21
Annapolis Rock, MD, 27, 37, 48–52
Annapolis Springs, 51
Anthonys Nose, NY, 242–246
Anthony Wayne Recreation Area, NY, 223
Antoine Dutot Museum, PA, 162
Appalachian Trail (A.T.), introduction to, 1–4
Appalachian Trail Communities, 272
Appalachian Trail Conservancy, 1, 2, 85, 282–283
Appalachian Trail Conservancy regional office, PA, 87
Appalachian Trail Conservancy Visitor Center, 33
Appalachian Trail Museum, the, 70, 73, 76–77, 82

B

Bear Mountain, 4
Bear Mountain Loop, NY, 231–236
Bear Mountain State Park, NY, 225, 229, 230, 233, 236, 239, 241, 243, 246, 269
Bear Mountain Zoo and Bridge, NY, 4, 237–241, 243
Bear Rocks from PA 309, 152–157
bears, 19
Bear Spring Cabin, MD, 39, 41
Bellvale Farms Creamery, NY, 208
Bellvale Mountain, 205, 208, 213
birding, best hikes for, xi
Bistro, Harper's Ferry, MD, 33
black bears, 19
Black Mountain, 223–224
Black Rock, MD, 49, 51
Blondies, MD, 57
Blue Mountain, 2, 87, 89, 91, 135, 141, 153

Blue Mountain Outfitters, Marysville, PA, 92, 97
Blue Ridge, 1
Blue Ridge Physiographic Province, 1
Blue Rocks Family Campground, 149
Boiling Springs, PA, 1, 2, 85
boots, 15
Brown, John, 29
Buchanan Mountain, 212

C

Cabela's, Hamburg, PA, 151, 157
Caledonia State Park, PA, 64, 67, 70, 269
Camp Michaux ruins, PA, 75
Canopus Hill, NY, 247–251
Canopus Lake, NY, 253, 255
Carlisle Iron Works Furnace, PA, 85, 87
Catoctin Mountains, 41
Cat Rocks and Eastern Pinnacles, NY, 204–208
Catskill Mountains, 184
cell phones, 17, 24
Center Point Knob, PA, 83–87
Chew, V. Collins, 174, 205
children
    hike recommendations, 7
    star ratings, 7
Chimney Rocks, PA, 60–64
Chocolate World, Hershey, PA, 132
Civil War sites
    Crampton's Gap, MD, 42
    Harpers Ferry, WV, 29
    Weverton Cliffs, MD, 35
Clarence Fahnestock Memorial State Park, NY, 12, 249, 253, 269
Clark Creek, PA, 123
Clarks Ferry and Peters Mountain, PA, 109–114
Clarks Ferry Shelter, 105, 107, 112, 114
Clarks Ferry via Susquehanna Trail, PA, 104–108

C *(continued)*

clothing for hiking, 14–15
clubs, hiking, 271
Cold Spring and Rausch Gap, PA, 128–132
Cold Spring, NY, 251
Cold Spring, PA, 129, 139
Comments (hike profiles), 11
Contact (hike profiles), 11
contact information, 269–270
copperhead snakes, 20–21
coral snakes, 20–21
cottonmouths, 20–21
Council Rock, PA, 159
Cove Mountain, 89
Cove Mountain North, PA, 98–103
Cove Mountain Shelter, PA, 99
Cove Mountain South, PA, 93–97
Crampton's Gap, MD, 2, 39, 42
Culvers Fire Tower Overlook, NJ, 171–175
Cumberland Valley, 2

D

Dan's Restaurant and Tap House, Boonsboro, MD, 42
Darlington Shelter, PA, 91, 96
Delaware hiking club, 271
Delaware River, 159, 167
Delaware Water Gap, 2, 159, 162
Delaware Water Gap National Recreation Area, PA, 170, 270
difficulty, star ratings, 7
Distance & Configuration (hike profiles), 9
Dover Oak and Great Swamp, NY, 203
Doyle Hotel, Duncannon, PA, 103, 108, 114
drinking water, 13–14, 16
Dunnfield Creek Natural Area, NJ, 167
Dutch Shoe Rock, NJ, 177

E

Eastern Pinnacles and Cat Rocks, NY, 204–208

Elevation (hike profiles), 10
elevation profiles, 6
Elk Pen lot, NY, 219
etiquette, trail, 23–24

F

Facilities (hike profiles), 11
Fingerboard Mountain and Island Pond, NY, 214–219
first aid kits, 16
Fitzgerald Falls, NY, 211
footwear, 15
Fort Clinton West Redoubt, NY, 240
Frederick, MD, 49
Frost, Robert, 250
Fuller Lake, PA, 79
Furnace Creek, PA, 147, 151

G

Gapland Lodge, MD, 42
Gathland State Park, MD, 39, 42, 269
gear, essential, 15–16
General, the, PA, 131–132, 138
geological formations, best hikes for, xi
GPS
    described, using, 5
    trailhead coordinates, 8–9
Great Appalachian Valley, 1
Great Swamp and Dover Oak, NY, 203, 262–266
Greenbrier State Park, 47, 51, 52
guidebook, how to use this, 5–8

H

Hamburg Reservoir, PA, 147
Happy's Diner, PA 895, 157
Harpers Ferry National Historical Park, 32, 33
Harpers Ferry, WV, 1–2, 28–33
Harriman, Averell, 239
Harriman, Mary Williamson, 239–240
Harriman State Park, NY, 4, 215, 221, 233, 235, 240, 269
Harrisburg, PA, 117

Hawk Rock, PA, 99, 101
hazards: animal, insect, and plant, 19–21
heat exhaustion (hyperthermia), 18
Hershey, PA, 132
Hessian Lake, NY, 233, 236, 239, 241
High Point State Park, NJ, 177, 180,
    181–185, 269
High Rock, MD, 53–57
High Rock Overlook, 56
Highlights (hike profiles), 10
hike profiles, 6–7
hikes. *See also specific hike*
    in Maryland, 26–57
    in New Jersey, 164–201
    in New York, 202–267
    in Pennsylvania, 58–163
    star ratings, 7–8
    in West Virginia, 26–57
hiking
    clothing, 14–15
    clubs, 271
    first aid kits, 16–17
    recommendations, xi–xii
    safety tips, 17–19
    tips on enjoying, 24–25
    trail etiquette, 23–24
    winter, 12
hiking boots, 15
Hiking Time (hike profiles), 9
Hinch, Stephen W., 5
history, best hikes for, xi
Horse-Shoe Trail, PA, 125
Hosack Run, PA, 65–70
Hudson Highlands, NY, 3, 184, 189, 213
Hudson Highlands State Park Reserve,
    NY, 269
Hudson River, 4, 233, 234, 240, 241,
    245, 251
hunting, 22
Hurricane Ivan, 2004, 139
hypothermia, hyperthermia, 18

I

insect hazards, 19–21
Island Pond and Fingerboard
    Mountain, NY, 214–219

J

Jackson, Gen. Thomas "Stonewall," 46
Jefferson, Thomas, 31
Jefferson Rock, WV, 31
John Brown Museum, WV, 32
John Brown's Fort, WV, 29, 32

K

kids, best hikes for, xii
Kittatinny Mountain, 3, 161, 167, 173,
    175, 184
Kittatinny Point Visitor Center, NJ,
    170
Knife Edge, PA, 155–156

L

Lake Marcia, NJ, 185
Lake Rutherford, NJ, 176–180
lakes, best hikes for, xii
Lambs Knoll and White Rocks, MD,
    38–42
latitude and longitude, 8–9
Laurel Lake, PA, 79
Lee, Robert E., 29
Lemon Squeeze, NY, 215
Lenape Lake, 159, 162
Lenni-Lenape tribe, 193, 197, 217
Liberty Loop Trail, Wallkill River
    National Wildlife Refuge, NJ,
    186–190
Long Pine Run Reservation, PA, 67
longitude and latitude, 8–9
Lyme disease, 21, 259

M

map legend, 5, inside back cover
maps. *See also specific hike*
    essential gear, 15
    Maryland, 26
    New York, 202
    overview, key, 5
    Pennsylvania, 58
    trail, 5–6
    West Virginia, 26
Maps (hike profiles), 10

M *(continued)*

Maryland, 58
  contact information, 269
  featured hikes, 27–57
  hiking clubs, 271
  map, 26
Maya Café & Cantina, NY, 256
meridians and parallels, 8–9
Michaux State Forest, PA, 73, 79, 270
Mombasha High Point, NY, 209–213
Monroe Reservoir, NY, 212
Monterey Pass Pub & Eatery, MD, 57
mosquitoes, 19–20
Mount Katahdin, 76–77, 82
Mount Minsi, PA, 158–162
Mount Peter, 213
Mount Tammany, 159, 161

N

National Park Service, 29
Native Landscapes Inc., NY, 266
natural scenery, best hikes for, xi
New Jersey
  contact information, 269
  featured hikes, 165–201
  map, 164
New Jersey fire towers, 174–175
New Jersey High Point, 2, 3, 25
New Jersey High Point Monument,
    180, 183
New York
  Appalachian Trail Communities,
    272
  contact information, 269
  featured hikes, 203–267
  map, 202
Nuclear Lake, NY, 257–261

O

Old Forge Picnic Area, PA, 61, 64
Outdoor Navigation with GPS (Hinch),
    5

P

PA 309 to Bear Rocks, 152–157
PA 325 to PA 443, 121–127

PA 443
  from PA 325, 121–127
  to Yellow Springs, 133–139
PA 850 to Tuscarora Trail, 88–92
parallels and meridians, 8–9
Pawling, NY, 261, 263, 266
Pen Mar County Park, MD, 55, 269
Penn's woods, 153
Pennsylvania
  Appalachian Trail Communities, 272
  contact information, 269–270
  featured hikes, 59–163
  hiking clubs, 271
  map, 58
Pennsylvania Game Commission, 270
Pennsylvania State Game Lands 211,
    119–120, 123
Perkins, George W., 234–235
Perkins Memorial Tower, NY, 235
Peters Mountain, 95, 101, 105, 107,
    111, 113, 117
Peters Mountain and Clarks Ferry, PA,
    109–114
Pine Grove Furnace State Park, PA, 70,
    73, 76, 79, 82, 270
Pine Knob Shelter, MD, 49
Pinnacle, and Pulpit Rock, PA,
    145–151
plant hazards, 19–21
Pochuck Boardwalk, NJ, 165, 191–195
Pochuck Mountain, 199, 200
Pocono Mountains, 184
poison ivy, oak, sumac, 20
Pole Steeple, PA, 59, 78–82
Potomac Grille, Harper's Ferry, MD, 33
Potomac River, 1, 31, 33, 35, 37
Pulpit Rock and the Pinnacle, PA,
    145–151
Pulpit Rock Astronomical Park, 149

Q

Quarry Gap, PA, 68

R

rain, weather, 12–13
ratings, star, 4, 7–8
rattlesnakes, 20–21

Rattling Run, PA, 125
Rausch Gap, PA, 125, 126, 128–132, 137, 139
recommendations, hiking, xi–xii
regulations, 22–23
Rhododendron Forest, PA, 125
Ridge and Valley Physiographic Province, 2, 187
Roadside America, PA, 144
Round Head and Shikellamy Overlook, PA, 140–144
Rutherford Shelter, 179

S

safety tips, 17–19
Salt Spring Trail, PA, 131
Sawmill Lake, NJ, 185
scenery, star ratings, 7
Second Mountain, 95, 127, 135, 136
Sharp Mountain, 126, 129, 137
Shenandoah Mountain, NY, 252–256
Shenandoah River, 31, 32
Shikellamy Overlook and Round Head, PA, 140–144
Showers, Lloyd, 141, 143
Showers Steps, PA, 141, 143
Silver Mine Lake, NY, 220–225
Ski Big Bear, NJ, 184
snakes, 20–21
snow, weather, 12–13
solitude
    best hikes for, xii
    hike recommendations, 7
South Mountain, 2, 37, 39, 46, 49, 55, 86
South Mountain State Park, MD, 37, 41, 269
Space Farms Zoo & Museum, Sussex, NJ, 175, 190
St. Anthony's Wilderness, PA, 137
star ratings, 4, 7–8
Stauch, Jim, 69
Steeny Kill Lake, 185
Stephen T. Mather Training Center for the National Park Service, 29
Sterling Forest State Park, NY, 213, 269
St. John's Episcopal Church, WV, 31

Stokes State Forest, MD, 269
Stone Tower, PA, 126
Stony Creek Inn, PA, 127
Stony Creek, PA, 127
Stony Mountain, 119, 123, 125
Stony Valley Rail-Trail, PA, 126, 129, 137
Storer College, WV, 29
Storm King Mountain, 245–246
St. Peter's Roman Catholic Church, WV, 31
streams, best hikes for, xii
Sturgis Jr., Cyrus C., 125
Sunfish Pond, NJ, 3, 166–170
Sunset Rocks and Toms Run, PA, 71–77
Susquehanna River, 2, 22, 97, 101, 105, 111, 114, 117, 119
Susquehanna Trail from Clarks Ferry, PA, 104–108
Swamp River Boardwalk, NY, 263
Swatara State Park, PA, 123, 139, 270

T

Table Rock, PA, 115–120, 159, 162
Tammany Mountain Overlook, NJ, 170
temperatures, weather, 11–13
ticks, 21
Toms Run and Sunset Rocks, PA, 71–77
Toms Run Shelter, 87
Townsend, George "Gath" Alfred, 39
trail condition, star ratings, 7
trail etiquette, 23–24
trail maps, 5–6
Tumbling Run, PA, 61, 64
Tuscarora Trail from PA 850, 88–92

U

Underfoot: A Geologic Guide to the Appalachian Trail (Chew), 174, 205
Underground Railroad, 39

V

Valley Forge National Historical Park, PA, 125

V *(continued)*

views, best hikes for, xii
Village Farmer and Bakery, PA, 162

W

Wallkill River, 187
Wallkill River Basin, 199
Wallkill River National Wildlife Refuge,
  NJ, 4, 184, 186–190, 194, 195,
  200, 269
War Correspondents Memorial Arch,
  MD, 39
Washington, George, 46
Washington Monument, MD, 43–47
Washington Monument State Park,
  MD, 46, 52, 269
water, drinking, 13–14, 16
waterfalls, best hikes for, xii
Wawayanda Creek, 193, 195
Wawayanda Lake, 195, 200
Wawayanda Mountain, NJ, 184, 194,
  196–201
Wawayanda State Park, NJ, 200, 269
Waynesboro Reservoir, PA, 61, 63
weather, 11–13
Welch, Major William A., 235
West Mountain, 221, 224

West Mountain Loop, NY, 226–230
West Mountain Shelter, NY, 227, 229
West Nile virus, 19
West Virginia, 58
  Appalachian Trail Communities, 272
  contact information, 270
  featured hikes, 27–57
  hiking clubs, 271
  map, 26
Weverton Cliffs, MD, 34–37
whistles, 18
White Rocks, 86
White Rocks and Lambs Knoll, MD,
  38–42
Whitman, Walt, 239, 240
Wildcat Shelter, NY, 208
wildlife, best hikes for, xi
William Brien Shelter, NY, 224
Windsor Furnace, PA, 148, 149
Windsor Furnace Shelter, PA, 149
winter hiking, 12
Worthington State Forest, NJ, 269

Y

Yellow Springs from PA 443, 133–139
Yellow Springs, PA, 125–126, 138

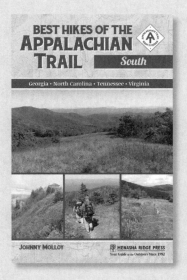

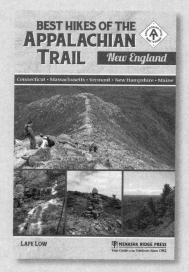

About the Author

photographed by Cynthia Kasales

MATT WILLEN is a writer, explorer, and photographer. He spends much of his time exploring little-known and remote places around the globe, most recently in areas above 50°N and below 50°S latitude. Matt is also the author of *60 Hikes Within 60 Miles: Harrisburg* and *Best Tent Camping: Pennsylvania* (both published by Menasha Ridge Press). He divides his time seasonally between Pennsylvania, where he can often be found trekking and skiing around the woods, and Nova Scotia, where he spends much of his time exploring the Atlantic coast by sea kayak. When he isn't out in the field, he enjoys playing his guitar and mandolin, taking photographs, reading and writing, and cooking interesting dishes. He has two teenage boys, whose company he enjoys most of all.

About the Appalachian Trail Conservancy

THE APPALACHIAN TRAIL (A.T.) is incredibly well-known around the world, not just among the diverse hiking and backpacking communities. Less well-known is what put it on the ground in the 1920s and '30s and manages it to this day: the staff and more than 6,000 volunteers under the umbrella of the Appalachian Trail Conservancy, founded in 1925 by 22 pioneers.

Yes, the A.T. has been a part of the national park system since 1968, but part of the deal with Congress was that this small, private, nonprofit organization would continue to do the bulk of the work and raise most of the money to pay for that work—rather than have taxpayers underwrite what would be a typical national park staff to care for 250,000 acres of public land. (The National Park Service does have a small A.T. office of fewer than a dozen employees working with us on major legal issues of environmental and historic preservation compliance and law enforcement.)

What does "take care of" mean? It means keeping the footpath of more than 2,189 miles open and safe for outdoor recreation of most nonmotorized types (including hunting for about half the area). It means maintaining in good condition overnight shelters and tent sites, absolutely necessary bridges, and other facilities.

It means monitoring the health of more than 550 rare, threatened, or endangered species that call the trail lands home (we don't yet have a count on the animals)—more than almost any other national park. It means preserving more cultural artifacts still in place than in any other park. (Remember, these ridgelines were the Colonial frontier before the seas and the West, and they were the site of Underground Railroad stops and then dozens of Civil War battles, as well as farms taken over by freed slaves.)

It means working cooperatively with the National Park Service, U.S. Forest Service, and 14 states that hold title to those lands for the public—altogether almost 100 agency partners. It means bringing into the fold for mutual benefit 85 counties' officials and the governments and businesses for almost three dozen places officially designated as an Appalachian Trail Community. It means watching for and combating threats to all from incompatible development.

It means providing the public with timely, comprehensive, and useful information about the A.T.'s wealth of natural beauty and how best to enjoy it—for example, through books such as this, in which we are proud to have a role.

We consider it our job to conserve, promote, and enhance the Appalachian National Scenic Trail every day. We do all that for less than $6.75 in private funds per day per mile (and about $2.75 more in targeted federal contracts).

You can support that effort by going to appalachiantrail.org to learn more and/or become a member. Old school (like us)? You can write to Appalachian Trail Conservancy, P.O. Box 807, Harpers Ferry, WV 25425, or call 304-535-6331.

Most of all, we hope that you enjoy in some way the People's Path. It *is* yours, after all.

DEAR CUSTOMERS AND FRIENDS,

SUPPORTING YOUR INTEREST IN OUTDOOR ADVENTURE, travel, and an active lifestyle is central to our operations, from the authors we choose to the locations we detail to the way we design our books. Menasha Ridge Press was incorporated in 1982 by a group of veteran outdoorsmen and professional outfitters. For many years now, we've specialized in creating books that benefit the outdoors enthusiast.

Almost immediately, Menasha Ridge Press earned a reputation for revolutionizing outdoors- and travel-guidebook publishing. For such activities as canoeing, kayaking, hiking, backpacking, and mountain biking, we established new standards of quality that transformed the whole genre, resulting in outdoor-recreation guides of great sophistication and solid content. Menasha Ridge Press continues to be outdoor publishing's greatest innovator.

The folks at Menasha Ridge Press are as at home on a whitewater river or mountain trail as they are editing a manuscript. The books we build for you are the best they can be, because we're responding to your needs. Plus, we use and depend on them ourselves.

We look forward to seeing you on the river or the trail. If you'd like to contact us directly, visit us at menasharidge.com. We thank you for your interest in our books and the natural world around us all.

SAFE TRAVELS,

Bob Sehlinger

BOB SEHLINGER
PUBLISHER